SPARTA AND PERSIA

CINCINNATI
CLASSICAL STUDIES

NEW SERIES

VOLUME I

LEIDEN
E. J. BRILL
1977

DAVID M. LEWIS

SPARTA AND PERSIA

Lectures delivered at the University of Cincinnati, Autumn 1976
in Memory of

DONALD W. BRADEEN

LEIDEN
E. J. BRILL
1977

Published with financial support of the Classics Fund of the University of Cincinnati established by Louise Taft Semple in memory of her father, Charles Phelps Taft.

ISBN 90 04 05427 8

PRINTED IN THE NETHERLANDS

CONTENTS

PREFACE

Some of the ideas in these lectures started to emerge in routine teaching in Oxford in the summer of 1975. I am grateful to the Department of Classics of the University of Cincinnati for giving me the opportunity to develop them by asking me to deliver lectures in memory of Donald Bradeen in the autumn of 1976 and for accepting the lectures for publication in *University of Cincinnati Classical Studies*. Its members not only listened patiently, but did much more to make my stay pleasant and easy. On the academic level, Professor G. M. Cohen saved me from some slips and one serious exhibition of ignorance.

The investigation has taken me into several fields where I am not at home. Individual pieces of help are acknowledged in their places, but I must single out Professor R. T. Hallock of the Oriental Institute of Chicago, not only for having opened whole new areas by his published work, but also for the patience and generosity with which he has answered my questions and told me of unpublished evidence. The errors which certainly remain in my dealings with Elamite texts will concern those problems on which I did not consult him. Mr. P. R. S. Moorey has also given me helpful advice.

The book owes a special debt to two Oxford colleagues. The frequency with which Geoffrey de Ste Croix is mentioned in these pages is a function of the fullness and clarity with which he has expounded Spartan policy-making; the plan of the work has meant that I have been more concerned with matters in which I cannot follow him completely than with, for example, his exemplary treatment of the Peloponnesian League. He read an earlier version of Chapter Five and his detailed criticisms have helped me greatly in refining my views, with which he should not be thought to agree.

There are some topics here which I have been discussing with Tony Andrewes for twenty years, and much of the book would hardly exist but for the stimulus of his forthcoming commentary on Thucydides VIII. He has read the whole in its first draft, to its great profit. It will be safe to assume that its errors and extravagances correspond pretty exactly to places where I have wilfully ignored his warnings.

Cincinnati
November 1976

D. M. L.

ABBREVIATIONS

Those approaching the book from the Greek side should have little trouble. I note only that references to Arrian (Arr.) are always to the *Anabasis*, that the Hellenica Oxyrhynchia (apart from the newest fragments, *Studia Papyrologica* 15, 1976, 55-76) are cited from Bartoletti's Teubner, and that Photius' epitome of Ktesias is cited by Henry's edition of 1947 (the marginal figures in Jacoby, *FGH* 688 FF 14-16).

BE	*The Babylonian Expedition of the University of Pennsylvania*, IX, 1898, X, 1904.
Beloch *GG*	Beloch, *Griechische Geschichte*, second edition 1912-27.
Busolt *GG*	Busolt, *Griechische Geschichte* III 2, 1904.
Cameron *PTT*	Cameron, *Persepolis Treasury Tablets* (Oriental Institute Publications LXV) 1948.
Cardascia *Archives*	Cardascia, *Les archives des Murašû*, 1951.
Cowley *AP*	Cowley, *Aramaic Papyri of the Fifth Century B.C.* 1923.
De Ste Croix *OPW*	De Ste Croix, *The Origins of the Peloponnesian War*, 1972.
Driver *AD*	Driver, *Aramaic Documents of the Fifth Century B.C.* abridged edition, 1957.
Eilers *IBKU*	Eilers, *Iranische Beamtennamen in der keilschriftlichen Überlieferung* I (all published) 1940.
Finley *Sparta*	in Vernant (ed.), *Problèmes de la guerre en Grèce ancienne*, 1968, 143-60, reprinted in Finley, *Use and Abuse of History*, 1975, 161-77. I cite by the former.
Hallock *Evidence*	Hallock, *The Evidence of the Persepolis Tablets*. (Middle East Centre, Cambridge, 1971, to appear in *The Cambridge History of Iran*, Vol. II.)
Hallock *PFT*	Hallock, *Persepolis Fortification Texts* (Oriental Institute Publications XCII) 1969.
HCT	Gomme, Andrewes, Dover, *A Historical Commentary on Thucydides* I-IV (1945-70).
Hüsing *Porusatis*	Hüsing, *Porušātìš und das achämenidische Lehenswesen* (Bausteine zur Geschichte, Völkerkunde und Mythenkunde, Erg. Heft 2) 1933.
JNES	*Journal of Near Eastern Studies*.
Kahrstedt	Kahrstedt, *Griechische Staatsrecht I: Sparta und seine Symmachie*, 1922.
Kent *OP*	Kent, *Old Persian, Grammar, Texts, Lexicon*, second edition, 1953.
Meyer *GdA*	Meyer, *Geschichte des Altertums* (ed. Stier), IV 1, 1939, IV 2, 1956.
ML	Meiggs and Lewis, *A Selection of Greek Historical Inscriptions*, 1969.
Olmstead *HPE*	Olmstead, *History of the Persian Empire*, 1948.
PF	A text published in Hallock *PFT*. (Some unpublished texts are cited as e.g. Fort. 3544 or V-2349, with the prefix letters referring to Hallock's categories.)
PT	A text published in Cameron *PTT* (Treasury texts with the prefix 1963 are published in *JNES* 24, 1965, 167-92.)

TMHC — *Texte und Materialen der Frau Professor Hilprecht Collection* II/III, 1933.

Tod II — Tod, *A Selection of Greek Historical Inscriptions* II, 1948.

UM — Clay, *Business Documents of Murashû sons of Nippur dated in the reign of Darius II* in University of Pennsylvania: The Museum, Babylonian Section, II/1, 1912.

Wade-Gery *Essays* — Wade-Gery, *Essays in Greek History*, 1958.

CHAPTER ONE

I begin these lectures with mixed feelings. It is both an honour and a pleasure to come to Cincinnati and to be associated with the Semple Fund, to enter into a succession which has done so much for our studies and which is connected for me with the name of many friends and colleagues. One of these friends is however very close to my mind today. When Don Bradeen died on April 11, 1973, he was engaged in a plan to bring me here earlier on another occasion, and, as I reread that animated correspondence, I still find it hard to believe in our heavy and premature loss and hard to think that I am now here to deliver lectures in his memory. Of his time here as a graduate student and his nearly twenty years as a distinguished member of this department, of his life as a husband and a father, it would be impertinent for me to attempt to speak. As a scholar, he had reached the height of his powers. There is none of his earlier papers which does not throw some permanent light on the subject under discussion, but it will not be denied that he only came to his full stature when he became involved in Attic epigraphy or, as I should prefer to say, when he took to topics where epigraphical material lay at the root. He never lost sight of the whole picture. His familiarity with the material was such that he could see the smallest technical observation, and he was very good at making them, and the smallest fragment of stone as parts, not merely of the whole practice of Athenian stonecutters, but of the whole pattern of Athenian society and history. He had detected in the scattered mass of the evidence for the Athenian public funeral patterns to which only details will be added; I can add as an illustration the fact that this year the unexpected evidence of a papyrus has produced some confirmation of one of his most complex arguments.[1] In his publication of the unpromising debris of the private funeral monuments from the Athenian Agora, there is implicit a deep understanding of the whole complex picture of many

---

[1] The new fragment of the Hellenica Oxyrhynchia (*Studia Papyrologica* 15, 1976, 55-76) has an Athenian Pasion as a subordinate commander of Thrasyllos at the Battle of Ephesos in 409 (Col. I 7). Since Bradeen showed good ground (*Hesperia* 33, 1964, 50-55) for believing that a large casualty list showing a Pasiphon as ἄρχων τοῦ ναυτικοῦ belonged to 409, it is tempting to emend the Πασίωνος of the papyrus to Πασιφῶντος.

centuries of development. Of the work he was doing on Athenian
letterforms, only enough survives to show the contribution he was
making to restore sense and order to a tiresome and difficult field.
As a collaborator in work still not published, he was a model,
punctual, accurate, comprehensive and clear. As a friend and a
working companion, he was incomparable. In the fall of 1970 we
had six weeks together in Princeton. From early in the morning
until far into the night, we discussed each other's problems, punc-
tured each other's bubbles, developed each other's better ideas. It
is not an experience I shall forget, and, although the topics I shall
be treating in these lectures will seldom cross the path of his
published work, I am confident that he would have laid an unerring
finger on their weaknesses and have been able to see ways of
developing the argument.

In the winter of 425/4 Aristeides, an Athenian general com-
manding on a tribute-collecting expedition, arrested at Eion at
the mouth of the Strymon a Persian, Artaphernes,[2] going by land
from the King of Persia to Sparta. We do not know how he had got
across the Hellespont, and, although we may think that his chances
of getting through to Sparta might have been reasonable once he
had reached, say, Thessaly, we are not told how he proposed to
bypass the still quite substantial Athenian presence in the Thrace-
ward area. He was brought to Athens, and the Athenians had his
letters translated from what Thucydides calls Assyrian writing.
Almost certainly, however, he was carrying an Aramaic document [3]

---

[2] This is this man's only appearance. Artaphernes, Darius' brother, was
given the satrapy of Sardis after the Scythian Expedition (Hdt. V 25.1)
and held it at least until 492 (Hdt. VI 42.2); we find him authorising a
journey to Persepolis in this capacity in November-December 495 (*PF*
1404, cf. *PF* 1455, undatable). His son of the same name is general on the
Marathon campaign in 490 and commands Lydian and Mysian troops in
480 (Hdt. VII 74.2). There is an unplaceable fourth-century satrap of the
name visited by Aristippos (D.L. II 79). The name Irdapirna under which
Artaphernes appears in Elamite is also borne by an 'elite-guide' who takes
a large party from Susa to Persepolis in 495/4 (*PF* 1421; the 'fast messenger'
of *PF* 2052 is presumably the same man); in view of the evidence that
Darius III started life as a royal messenger, Plut. *Alex*. 18.4, it would be
socially possible for him to be Artaphernes II in his youth. We should at
least bear in mind the possibility that our Artaphernes is of royal stock and
descended from a family of experience in western matters.

[3] So, rightly, Olmstead *HPE* 354, Momigliano, *Alien Wisdom* 9. There are
no merits in attempting with Gomme HCT III 498 to save Thucydides'
credit by assuming that the text was in Old Persian in the Assyrian cuneiform script. The alternative of Old Persian in Old Persian syllabary is also

on parchment or papyrus. As our understanding of Persia improves, it steadily becomes clearer that Persian is a language for speech, which secretaries reproduce in their own language, by this time generally Aramaic.[4] There was much else in the letters, but the gist was that he did not know what the Spartans wanted: many ambassadors had come, but none of them said the same thing; if they wanted to say something clear, they should send men with the Persian to him. Later on the Athenians sent Artaphernes on a trireme to Ephesos with ambassadors. At Ephesos they learnt that the King Artaxerxes son of Xerxes was dead (for he died at that time) and went home.[5]

I shall eventually be contemplating the background to this episode and its sequels, but I propose to devote the first part of these lectures to looking at fifth-century Persia and Sparta and considering the way in which their foreign policies were formed. My justification is slightly different in the two cases. For Persia, it lies in an enormous accession of new evidence about Persian administration which, although it seldom bears directly on the points which principally concern us, nevertheless sometimes suggests new approaches. For Sparta, there is next to no new evidence, but there has been a good deal of recent discussion and I think it may be useful to try to bring some of the threads together.

The best introduction to the new Persian evidence may be by way

---

unattractive. Gershevitch, among others, has recently argued (ap. Hallock *Evidence* 4-9) that that syllabary was used only for texts put up by the King himself, was invented for that purpose in the reign of Darius and could not have been read by more than a few people even then. Cameron, *JNES* 32, 1973, 51-54, used the evidence of monoglot seals in Old Persian to show that Gershevitch was exaggerating. They do not imply any widespread ability to read Old Persian, since the types could be recognised. What does bother me is a worry about the Old Persian seals of private individuals, Kent *OP*, Sa-Se. Sc and Sd are Sassanian or forgeries and Sb problematic. But Sa (Wiseman, *Cylinder Seals of Western Asia* 103) looks western and Se (Speleers, *Catalogue des Intailles des Musées Royales du Cinquantenaire* (1917) 217-8 no. 47) decidedly provincial, in the judgement of John Boardman, who looked at them for me. They are evidence of non-royal use of Old Persian in the provinces, but will not go far to prove that any one at Athens could read Old Persian or that it was used for letters. About Aramaic there is no difficulty, and Thucydides is simply using Ἀσσύρια γράμματα for any kind of oriental script.

[4] On this, the views of Gershevitch, loc. cit. seem unassailable. They further make it unnecessary to believe that Artaphernes could read the letters himself; he will have travelled with an interpreter.

[5] Thuc. IV 50.

of considering Artaphernes' journey to the Hellespont. No doubt
he had travelled from Susa along the Royal Road described in
Herodotus V 52-54, with its one hundred and eleven royal staging-
posts with excellent rest-houses. We can now make some fairly
good guesses about some aspects of his journey. As long as we took
our view of Persia from Herodotus and Xenophon, we could preserve
a fairly idealised picture of a feudal aristocracy. There seemed to
be relatively little evidence of the bureaucratic economies of earlier
empires of the Near East. I find even in a book published this year
the sentence "The Achaemenid kings ... had not developed any
elaborate bureaucratic or military system to support their power"[6]
but recent discoveries have changed the picture substantially. We
have always had a few texts of the Persian period from Babylonia
suggesting that there, in continuity from the Assyrian and Babylonian periods, there was a fairly detailed system of ration allowances
for those who worked for the state.[7] I suspect that, insofar as
people thought about it at all, there may have been an impression that this was a pure survival in a heavily bureaucratised
part of the empire. There is indeed the evidence of Herakleides
of Kyme[8] for the way in which official salaries were normally
paid in food in the empire, but that gives very little idea of the
detail of the administration.[9] The publication of the Persepolis
Fortification Tablets by Professor Hallock has shown that the
whole system went much further und that, even in Persia itself,
virtually everyone, even the highest, was on a regular ration-scale
or, since for some of them the amounts go far beyond what anyone

---

[6] Brunt, *Arrian* I (Loeb) lxiv.

[7] The best text I know both for the practice and for continuity is Ebeling,
Neubabylonische Briefe aus Uruk C 45, which I quote in Ebeling's translation:
Bevor ich komme, werde ich das Ohr meines Herrn wegen der Kost öffnen.
Die Tafeln Nergalšarrusurs und Nabunaids möge der Herr ansehen, wie
die Gesamtmenge an Gerste und Mehl dem Lande Akkad gewährt ist und
was du mir vor Kyros für die Leute von Laheri gegeben hast, dement-
sprechend möge der Herr die Gesamtmenge herstellen.
For a discussion of Persian ration-distributors in Babylonia, the evidence
then available from Egypt and the possible relevance of ποτίβαζις in Deinon
FGH 690 F 4, which now seems to have been very much on the right lines,
see Eilers *IBKU* 59-81.

[8] *FGH* 689 F 2; cf. Meyer *GdA* IV² 1.84-5.

[9] The impression which it leaves that subordinates were fed *out of* the
allocations made to the great is almost certainly false. At Persepolis Parnaka
gets a daily ration beyond the capacity of one man to consume, but an
unpublished text shows him receiving both this 'salary' and a normal
ration for 300 underlings (Hallock *PFT* p. 23).

could possibly consume himself, a salary. It is in this context that the grants made to Themistocles belong,[10] and the discovery puts a new light on some old evidence. Plutarch[11] knows a story that the younger Cyrus revolted because he was not satisfied with what he got for his daily dinner and thinks it a very silly story. If, however, round 500 B.C., we find that the chief official of Persis, of royal blood, has a daily salary of two sheep, 90 quarts of wine and 180 quarts of flour [12] and, although we do not have the full details, Gobryas father of Mardonios was apparently on a scale 11% higher,[13] we can see that the system was certainly capable of producing a fair amount of irritation and hurt pride even at the highest levels.

Most relevant to us at this point are the travel-tablets, sent in to the central records of Persis by officials who had issued rations to travellers who carried the proper authority and who acknowledged their receipt. This is a fairly typical one: "11 BAR of flour Abbatema received. For his own rations daily he receives 7 BAR. 20 men receive each 2 QA (i.e. 1/35 of Abbatema's ration). He carried a sealed document of the king. They went forth from India. They went to Susa. Second month, 23rd year. Išbaramištima is his elite-guide. The seal of Išbaramištima was applied to this tablet." Abbatema is evidently a distinguished foreigner.[14] This is a text of 499 and in Elamite, but the system continued. Our

---

[10] Thuc. I 138.5. I return to these grants later.

[11] *Art.* 4.1-3. As it happens, other younger brothers of kings have been known to behave in this way. In 1465 Charles Duke of Berry complained to Louis XI that his pension and the Duchy of Berry were too meagre for his dignity. The King made some concessions and promised more, but Charles still joined the League of the Public Weal. See H. Stein, *Charles de France* (1919) 56, P. M. Kendall, *Louis XI* (Cardinal Books edition) 172.

[12] *PF* 654-669.

[13] *PF* 688 (Hallock *Evidence* 12-13).

[14] *PF* 1318. Abbatema is on his way from India to Susa in the first and second months of Darius' 23rd year (April-May 499) under the guidance of Išbaramištima (*PF* 785, 1317-8, 1558). In the second and third months he is apparently at rest, and Miramana secures rations for his 19 horses and 15 mules at his *Kiti* (Hallock suggests 'stable', which does not suit *PF* 1344) (*PF* 1785, 1704). In the third month he is going from Susa to India, again under the guidance of Išbaramištima (*PF* 1556, with Išbaramištima's seal, though he is not named). The episode is obscure. Abbatema's name is not Indic (Prof. Burrow and Dr. Gombrich *per epist.*); Gershevitch (*Studia Classica et Orientalia Antonino Pagliaro Oblata*, 1969, II 180) suggests an OP *Apa-daiva- "He who turns away from the daivas" (?). I do not see why his journey is not authorised from his point of origin.

only example of such a sealed document authorising rations is
nearly a hundred years later and in Aramaic. It is not quite parallel
since it is issued by the satrap of Egypt to his own officers for the
provision of food from his own estates, but it gives a good idea of
what Artaphernes would be carrying:

From 'Aršam to Marduk the officer who is at ...., Nabû-
dalâni the officer who is at La'ir, Zātōhī the officer who is [at]
'Arzûḥin, 'Upastabar the officer who is at Arbel, Ḥalṣu (?) and
Māt-âl-Ubaš (?), Bagafarna the officer who is at Sa'lam, Frāda-
farna and Gavazāna (?) the officers who are at Damascus.

And now:—behold! one named Neḥtiḥûr, [my] officer, is going
to Egypt.

Do you give [him] (as) provisions from my estate in your
provinces every day two measures of white meal, three measures
of inferior (?) meal, two measures of wine or beer, and one sheep,
and for his servants, 10 men, one measure of meal daily for each,
(and) hay according to (the number of) his horses; and give
provisions for two Cilicians (and) one craftsman, all three my
servants who are going with him to Egypt, for each and every
man daily one measure of meal; give them these provisions, each
officer of you in turn, in accordance with (the stages of) his
journey from province to province until he reaches Egypt; and,
if he is more than one day in (any) one place, do not thereafter
assign them more provisions for those days.

Bagasrava is cognizant of this order: Rāšt is the clerk.[15]

I doubt whether Artaphernes would actually have suffered the
indignity of this practical injunction to haste.[16]

At the risk of wandering from my general theme, I give a further
example of the kind of historical illumination the tablets provide.
We find people moving around in large ethnic groups, for example,
547 Egyptian workers going from Susa to Tamukkan, a place on
the Persian Gulf from which people do not seem to come back.[17] We
also find settled ethnic groups. You will recall the Paeonians of
Thrace transported to Asia in Herodotus V, whom we find later

---

[15] Driver *AD* VI.

[16] Note the mystery of the Treasurer convoying silver who stopped in one
place for 16 days (Hallock *PFT* p. 43).

[17] *PF* 1557.

living in Phrygia in a place and village by themselves.[18] Here, much further east, we still find Thracians, Skudrians, from the empire's newest province, around in some quantity. We are not often told what they are doing. Some are not surprisingly described as horsemen,[19] some more surprisingly as grain-handlers.[20] The most interesting fact about them is the demographic pattern of the settled groups. The largest[21] has 250 men, 15 boys, 3 boys, 220 women, 25 girls, 7 girls. That this is a whole population trans-planted or a settlement deliberately contrived to maintain itself as a breeding group is clear, and the existence of a policy in these matters is confirmed by a group of three Skudrian settlements in villages evidently very near each other, since their supplies come from the same source.[22] Village 1: 9 men, 1 boy, 9 women. Village 2: 16 men, 1 boy, 16 women, 1 girl. Village 3: 30 men, 2 boys, 34 women. One wonders uneasily what had become of the other 4 men in village 3, but this does seem to be evidence that the empire went in literally for transplanting populations rather than allowing rootless slave-teams. Concern for breeding reappears in a series of payments to mothers who have recently given birth.[23] They get extra rations, 10 quarts of wine or beer or 20 quarts of flour if they have borne a boy, half as much for a girl. Bureaucracy is up to a point beneficent.

That is perhaps a sufficient taste of bureaucracy for the moment, and it is no part of my topic to discuss either the workings of the Persepolis Treasury or the elaborate supply-administration re-vealed by the Fortification Tablets. They have been excellently treated by Professor Hinz[24] and we are not much helped in discuss-ing policy-making by the knowledge that supply was organised under a *Hofintendant* and his deputy and divided into five *Ab-teilungen* for corn, animals, wine and beer, fruit, and poultry. The main interest for us lies in the information about secretarial staff, which seems to me to extend our knowledge of what a satrap and, by implication, the King may have at his disposal.

The principal person in the Fortification Tablets is Parnaka or

---

[18] Hdt. V 15.3, 98.1.
[19] *PF* 1957.10.
[20] *PF* 1823.
[21] *PF* 1010.
[22] *PF* 851-853.
[23] Hallock *PFT* pp. 37-8.
[24] *Zeitschrift für Assyriologie* 61, 1971, 279-301.

Pharnakes son of Arsam or Arsames, uncle of Darius,[25] but unknown
to Greek sources, except as the father of the Artabazos who commanded the Parthians and Chorasmians in 480.[26] He bears no title
and Hallock wisely does not give him one, referring to him as the
chief economic official and denying a rigid hierarchy: "no doubt the
exact nature of the position that Pharnaces occupied depended to
a considerable extent on his own ability and influence".[27] Hinz has
given him the title of *Hofmarschall*, Court-marshal[28] and assumes
that his responsibilities are those of a member of the central
government. I find this difficult to accept. If Hinz is right, we
would expect to find Parnaka constantly with the King and in fact
Hinz says as much.[29] However, we find four tablets, two dated,
two not, where Parnaka and the King appear to be physically
separated,[30] and the published evidence might suggest that Parnaka
was normally at home in Persepolis. The best evidence comes from
the travel-tablets, from observing the direction of journeys authorised by Parnaka, and these certainly show one period of fifteen
months when Parnaka appears to be continually in or based on
Persepolis,[31] including months when the King would normally be

---

[25] For his placing in the royal family, I am satisfied with the demonstration by Hallock *Evidence* 11-14. I do not understand Hinz's conviction that
he is a Mede (*Altiranische Funde und Forschungen*, 1969, 63 ff.; *Orientalia* 39,
1970, 425; *Zeitschrift für Assyriologie* 61, 1971, 302) and suspect that it is
conditioned by a desire to find him in the Median figure before Darius on the
Persepolis Treasury relief. If his name has a Median form, the same can also
be said for the Persians Vištāspa, Aspacanā and Vidafarnā (Kent *OP* 8 n. 1).
[26] Hdt. VII 66.2, VIII 126-129. The identification removes him from the
scanty list of 'commoners' in positions of command on Xerxes' expedition
(cf. Burn, *Persia and the Greeks* 324).
[27] *Evidence* 11, 13.
[28] See the references in n. 25.
[29] *Zeitschrift für Assyriologie* 61, 1971, 311.
[30] *PF* 1394, 1535 (9th month, 23rd year), 1560, 1787 (1st month, 22nd year).
[31] From the 9th month of the 22nd year to the 12th month of the 23rd
year he is frequently named as authorising journeys starting in Persepolis
or finishing in Susa (22/9 *PF* 1374-1375; 23/1 *PF* 1360, 1511; 23/4 *PF* 1293;
23/7 *PF* 1296; 23/9 *PF* 1381, 1535, 1782; 23/10 *PF* 1509; 23/11 *PF* 1446;
23/12 *PF* 1432). The only published text which seemed to break this pattern
was a journey to Persepolis authorised in 23/1 (*PF* 1478), but Professor
Hallock has pointed out to me that I had missed the evidence of *PF* 665
that he was in Hatarikkaš in 23/2. He also adds three unpublished texts of
this period: Q-2214 (22/11) where a journey from Parnaka to Ziššawiš,
normally in Persepolis, passes Kurdusum; Q-1329 (23/8) authorising a
journey to Persepolis; Q-1516 (23/10) authorising a journey from Hunar
to Persepolis which passes Parmadan. There is therefore some evidence for
peregrination in this period. I have sometimes wondered whether authorisa-

expected to be in Susa or Babylon.[32] But there now seems to be evidence for an earlier long stay at Susa,[33] and I think I must repress my original inclination to think of him as in effect satrap of Persis, a designation which, in view of the special position of Persis in the empire, might not have been appropriate in any case.[34]

Whatever the truth about his position, I do not think he should be quite as closely connected with the court as Hinz wants, but this does not invalidate the detail of what Hinz has to say about the staff of his chancellery, his secretariat.[35] At a minimum, he has a nuclear group of Babylonian scribes writers on parchment, i.e. who are writing Aramaic, which in early summer 501 consists of 5 men, 2 boys of varying ages, 8 women, 3 girls and 8 servants; his principal subordinate Ziššawiš has at the same time 3 men and 3 servants. After some fluctuation we find in January 496 13 men, 2 boys, 6 women, 2 girls and 8 servants; the groups may have been combined.[36] There will certainly have been Elamite scribes as well.[37]

---

tions might not cover a round trip, but the tempting case of PF 1522, where Bakabana, who almost always authorises parties from Susa (Hallock *Evidence* 13), may appear to be authorising a journey to Susa, disappears, Hallock tells me, on rereading. It is clear that points of origin of the travellers do not always indicate where the authorisation was issued; cf. PF 1552 (23/-) where Parnaka authorises a journey from India to Susa.

[32] Cf. Hallock *PFT* p. 41 and add the passages quoted by Meyer *GdA* IV² 1, 25 n. 2, which relate to a time when Persepolis was seldom used.

[33] The published texts are confusing: 21/- PF 1308 (Susa-Persepolis); 22/1 PF 1370 (Susa-Matezziš), 1371 (Parnaka-Matezziš), but 1787 (to the King at Susa); 22/- PF 1409 (Susa-Maknan). Hallock tells me that five unpublished texts put Parnaka in Susa in 21/-, 21/12, 21/12 (?), 22/1, 22/2.

[34] Hdt. III 97.1. I know of no satrap of Persis before the reign of Darius III (Arr. III 18.2) nor any discussion of the point later than P. Krumbholz, *De discriptione regni Achaemenidarum* (Progr. Eisenach 1890-91) 5. That Herodotus III 71.3 makes Hystaspes satrap of Persis in 522 (III 70.3) has long been proved by the Behistun Inscription (II 93-4) to be an error for Parthia.

[35] *Zeitschrift für Assyriologie* 61, 1971, 308-11.

[36] I am assuming continuity between the groups in PF 1947.23-26, 29-30 (21/1-3), 1807 (23/9), 1810 (23/12), 1828 (25/10-11). I do not know whether the individual of PF 1808 (24/7) and the travelling group of six of PF 1561 (undated) belong to this category. The wine-scale of PF 1561 is three times as high as that in PF 1808, which seems to be the normal wine scale of the category (PF 1807), but they may have been expected to be thirstier when travelling.

[37] The only possible Elamite-writing scribes who receive rations are the Persian 'boys' copying texts at Pittanan who are under the ration-department (PF 871; 23/1). Notice that 16 of these 29 are on a monthly corn-scale of $4\frac{1}{2}$ BAR, 50% more than the normal parchment-writer and only attained by the odd one on detachment (PF 1947.17, 21).

In between Parnaka and Ziššawiš on one hand and the scribes on
the other come persons whom I would suggest we call their aides.
We learn of these from texts containing or referring to letters. The
high Persian official himself speaks rather than writes, so that
the form of a Persian letter is: "Tell so-and-so; Parnaka spoke as
follows ..." The higher an official the more likely it is that the
letter will end with a subscript. The precise interpretation is complicated, but there is now no doubt that these subscripts name,
besides the scribe, persons who are involved in formulating for the
scribe the will of the high official.[38] Over a period of seven years,

----

[38] Hallock *PFT* pp. 51-2, Hinz, *Zeitschrift für Assyriologie* 61, 1971,
310-1. The difficulties which remain concern the interpretation of the
phrases which stand after 'X wrote the text': "pattikamaš Y lišta" (henceforth P) and "dumme Z (in the ablative) dušta" (henceforth D), translated
by Hallock "The message Y delivered. The *dumme* he received from Z."
The word *dumme* has not yet been interpreted. Some points do not yet
seem to have been made. (1) There may be a divergence between the practice
of different scribes as to what they thought it necessary to record. Of the
seventeen occasions in Fortification and Treasury texts where both phrases
appear together, all but one have the scribe Hintamukka (Hinpirukka in
transcriptions of Treasury texts). In letters even he omits one phrase five
times (*PF* 1816, 2069, 1825 (where I suspect scribal error), *PT* 1, 3) and he
never thinks both phrases necessary in receipts (*PF* 672-673, 675-678).
(2) Formula P comes in later than formula D. It does not appear until
Darius 18/9 (*PF* 1792) and before that date two people who otherwise
nearly invariably use it appear with formula D (Maraza in *PF* 1789 (18/2),
Kamezza in *PF* 1812 (17/10)). It also disappears early, only appearing in
Treasury texts of Darius 32 (*PT* 2, as revised in *JNES* 24, 1965, 187, and
PT 9, both with Hintamukka as scribe). 3) Near the beginning of formula
P, *PF* 1790 (which refers to the 18th and 19th years) has an aberrant formula
"Maraza knew about this". Since formula D also appears in this subscript,
it would appear that this aberrant formula is functionally equivalent to
formula P, and this casts some doubt on the view of Hallock and Hinz that
formula P simply indicates the person who did the drafting. Clearly, drafting
and 'knowing about this' are not easily separable. 4) After the disappearance
of formula P, one text, PT 19 (Xerxes 4/7-8), names two persons in formula
D. This again suggests some fluidity. 5) Hinz rightly draws attention to the
fact that there are Persian letters in Aramaic which have similar subscripts.
Six documents in Driver *AD* (IV, VI-X) have subscripts which name,
besides the scribe, a man (always with a Persian name) who *ydᶜ ṭᶜmᵓ znh*
'knows about this order'. (Cf. Cowley AP 26.23 Anani the scribe is the
bᶜl ṭᶜm, 'author of the order'; Nabuᶜakab wrote it.) I would tentatively
suggest going a stage further and finding an actual linguistic link between
Elamite *dumme* (written *du-um-me* or *du-me*) and Aramaic *ṭᶜm*; Driver
p. 48 suggests for the latter a connexion with Acc. *ṭêmu* 'order, report'.
I have considered a further possibility, that the Chronicler has extracted
the *bᶜl ṭᶜm* and the *sfr* of Ezra IV 8-9, 17 from a similar subscript and put
them at the head of their letter, but the inhabitants of Samaria may well

Parnaka has the services of seven such individuals, though he need not have more than four at any one time [39] and one of these certainly has nothing to do with the chancellery; he is Parnaka's personal steward.[40] Over a period of nine years, Zissawis has eight subordinates.[41] The total is thirteen, since there is some interchange between the staffs.[42] We can see some traces of promotion.[43]

---

have retained Assyrian institutions; for *be-el ṭēmi* as the name of an office, see e.g. Kinnier Wilson, *The Nimrud Wine Lists*, 73-4.

It should further be noticed that formula D is never used in connexion with Parnaka's personal affairs, either in relation to his own rations or those of his boys (see n. 40 on Mannunda), though it is sometimes used in connexion with Zissawis's rations (*PF* 670-1, 675-6, 678; contrast *PF* 672 (formula P), 674 and 677 (no intermediary named). But this may be connected with the status of the intermediary, rather than the nature of the business.

Hinz and Hallock hold that, when formula P and formula D both appear, they have the same subject, i.e. that it is the subject of formula P who receives the *dumme* and not the scribe. I am by no means sure about this, and on the large majority of occasions the scribe must be the recipient of the *dumme*. It can make little practical difference.

[39] I give a summary account of their length of service with the formula normally appropriate to them. Nanitin (D) from 17/3 to 21/7. Mannunda (P) from 18/10 to 23/8 (see note 40). Maraza (P) from 18/2 to 21/6. Puzina (D) 19/2 (*PF* 2025 is his only appearance, but he belongs to Parnaka's staff, as we see from the appearance of Maraza and Parnaka's seal). Ribaya (D) in 21/5-6. Pilidan (D) in 22/3. Lakip (D) in 23/7. Yaūna (D) from 23/9 to 24/7.

[40] Mannunda appears (with formula P only) in letters authorising payments for Parnaka's boys and in receipts for Parnaka's 'rations' (*PF* 654-662, 665-669). When we observe that all but one of his receipts for grain and flour which do not mention Parnaka do mention Persepolis (*PF* 5, 33, 95-96, 326, 835-840), we may suspect that they also have some direct connexion with Parnaka. Mizirma (*PF* 95-96, 840) and Umardada (*PF* 326, 835-839) are sometimes associated with him in these texts; if this is their only function, Hallock may not have been right to assume that all stores referred to in his E texts are royal.

[41] Nanitin (D) in 16/7. Ribaya (D) in 18/8-9 and 25/10-11. Ripiš (D) in 19/10-11. Abbalaya (D) in 22/9-12. Hitibel (D) from 22/12 to 24/1-3. Kamezza (P) from 22/12 to 25/10-11 (full-time; see note 43). Nutanuyya (P) and Bariktimiš (D) in 25/8.

[42] Nanitin works for Zissawis before he works for Parnaka. Ribaya has a short spell with Parnaka between his widely-separated appearances for Zissawis. Note that Nutanuyya goes on to work for Appišmanda (*PT* 2, 9, cf. 1963:19) and Hitibel for Rumatenda (*PT* 3; possibly in *PT* 3a and 1963:5).

[43] Kamezza is basically a scribe from 17/3 to 19/7 (*PF* 661, 1788-9), though he does appear with formula D during the period (*PF* 1812 of 17/10), before going to Zissawis's personal staff. Maraza goes from Parnaka's staff to be wine-supplier (from 22/1-6 to 24/5-7) and from 24/3-6 to 24/13 he

Of these thirteen aides [44] only one bears an unequivocally Iranian name, though five more names are capable of being analysed as Iranian.[45] One is pretty certainly Elamite.[46] There is one probable and one possible Babylonian.[47] Three have so far defeated the linguists.[48] The thirteenth is called Yaūna, and from December 499 to September 498 he is Parnaka's only visible aide.

This name is a valuable asset to our enquiry. Although Hallock himself has offered no opinion, no one else seems to have doubted that Yaūna is a Greek, known by his ethnic instead of his strange and no doubt unpronounceable name, just as the Greeks habitually called slaves Skythes or Kar.[49] There are others of the name in the Persepolis tablets. It is just conceivable that our man appears, three or four years before he came into Parnaka's service, as a grain-handler in an out-station.[50] In January or February 481 we find another one holding the same position with the high official Artatakma as our Yaūna does with Parnaka;[51] in view of the gap of more than sixteen years there is no reason to suppose that they are the same.

If Greeks were not attested directly in this capacity, we would still be able to infer their presence. The bulk of these ration tablets are in Elamite. There are some, as yet unpublished, in Aramaic, despite the unsuitability of clay tablets for writing it. There are two oddities. One is in Phrygian,[52] one is in Greek.[53] The Greek tablet says οἶνος δύο (ι) μάρις Τέβητ. μάρις is a wine-measure, previously not known in Greek before Aristotle. Τέβητ is a month-name, curiously a Babylonian one, not one of the Persian or Elamite names

---

is assigning workers and giving instructions of his own. (The assistant fruit-handler of *PF* 1979-80, 1990, 2080 is a different person; I do not quite know what to make of *PF* 1945.4-5, 1946.79-80, 2001.)

[44] What follows is entirely dependent on Mayrhofer, *Onomastica Persepolitana* (1973).

[45] Maraza; Ribaya, Puzina, Abbalaya, Kamezza, Nutanuyya.

[46] Nanitin.

[47] Hitibel, Pilidan. Should we not add Bariktimiš?

[48] Bariktimiš, Ripiš, Lakip (though four of the other five Persepolis names ending in -p are claimed as Elamite by Mayrhofer).

[49] Cameron *PTT* pp. 119-20; Beneveniste, *Titres et noms propres en Iranien ancien*, 96; Gershevitch, *Studi. . . . Pagliaro* II 246; Mayrhofer s.v.

[50] *PF* 1942.27 (19/7), 1965.29 (20/-).

[51] *PT* 21.

[52] Friedrich, *Kadmos* 4, 1965, 154-6; Cameron, *JNES* 32, 1973, 52-3, has found an Old Persian month name on it.

[53] *PFT* p. 2.

otherwise used in the tablets. Hallock finds the document curiously curtailed, and I must say that I at first wondered whether it was an aide-memoire for Yaūna on his way to tell a scribe what Parnaka wanted to say. But it turns out that it has two seal-impressions.[54] This removes the problem of intelligibility, since the seals will have done the job of indicating who issued the wine and to whom, and it proves that the tablet did actually form the record of a transaction. Somewhere out on the administrative circuit there was someone to whom it came most naturally to write in Greek and who, moreover, knew that there was someone at the administrative centre who would know what it meant.[55]

We already knew that in the reign of Darius I there was a Greek doctor at the Persian court,[56] the first of a longish sequence,[57] as well as a person of the status of Histiaios of Miletos, whatever precise Persian status may lie behind the Greek view that he was summoned to Susa to be Darius' table-companion and adviser.[58] Lower down the social scale, Greek craftsmen at Persepolis and Susa are known to us by direct reference[59] as well as by their work[60] and their graffiti,[61] and there are Greeks engaged in the transport of their building materials.[62] The new texts seem to go lower still, down to a group of twenty-three women irrigationworkers.[63] It now appears that, as far east as Persis and as early as this reign, Greeks could make themselves useful in the regular administration

[54] I am greatly indebted to Hallock for sending me a photograph and drawing of this tablet.

[55] The writing is unsurprising Ionic of about 500, save for one feature. The sigma of οἶνος is unexceptionably four-bar, the sigma of μάρις is unmistakably lunate, taking the history of that form back a couple of hundred years. Since at this point we are at the most curving end of the tablet, it is not surprising that the scribe found the job of inscribing a four-bar sigma on a curve rather difficult.

[56] Demokedes of Kroton (Hdt. III 125.1, 129-137). Cf. Sandison, The first recorded case of inflammatory mastitis, *Medical History* 3, 1959, 317-22.

[57] Apollonides of Kos (Artaxerxes I, Ktesias 42), Ktesias of Knidos (Artaxerxes II), Polykritos of Mende (Artaxerxes II, Plut. *Art.* 21.3).

[58] Hdt. V 24.4.

[59] Kent *OP* DSf line 48; *PT* 15.6.

[60] A difficult subject, but see e.g. Gullini, *Parola del Passato* 142-4, 1972, 13-39.

[61] Pugliese Carratelli, *East and West* 16, 1966, 31-2.

[62] Kent *OP* DSf lines 30-35. Cf. Mazzarino in *La Persia e il mondo Greco-Romano* (Accademia dei Lincei 1966) 75-83 for an inflated theory, rightly doubted by Momigliano, *Alien Wisdom* 126.

[63] *PF* 1224. We do not know what the 16 or 17 Ionians at Radkan of *PF* 2072 were doing in early 504.

to high Persian officials, after they had picked up a little Persian. (Since our Yaūnas only dictate, they will not need to know Elamite as well.)

There are of course possible implications for intellectual history. Professor West [64] has argued for Iranian origins for some Greek philosophy. The point can be endlessly discussed, particularly in the existing uncertainty about the state of Zoroastrianism in the late sixth century,[65] and I certainly do not intend to join the argument. However, I cannot resist pointing out that one of the messages transmitted by Yaūna for Parnaka was an instruction to issue flour to Limepirda the Magus.[66] Of course, Yaūna need not have met him or understood him if he did.

If we find Greeks in a secretarial capacity as early as this and as far east as this, there should be no reason to doubt their availability to the King and to other satraps, particularly in the west, in all relevant periods. The line between a secretary or aide and an exiled Greek maintained at the court of the King or of a satrap for his possible usefulness will not be an easy one to draw. For the period which will eventually concern us most, I draw attention to Kalligeitos of Megara and Timagoras of Kyzikos, exiles resident with Pharnabazos, satrap of Hellespontine Phrygia,[67] and the Carian Gaulites, described as δίγλωσσος, on the staff of Tissaphernes, satrap of Sardis.[68] Thucydides is presumably thinking of his two languages as Greek and Persian; doubtless he spoke his native Carian as well. Later we find Tissaphernes with a Greek military expert.[69] It is to people of this kind that we have to look when we are considering the availability to the Persians of knowledge of Greek institutions and psychology, and they should certainly be thought of when we come to the detailed working out of diplomatic documents. It would be mistaken, I think, to look for any Persian or Aramaic original for, say, the three treaties of Thucydides VIII outside verbal instructions given by Tissaphernes to his Greek sub-

[64] *Early Greek Philosophy and the Orient* (1971).

[65] Cf. e.g. Momigliano, *Alien Wisdom* 126-9.

[66] *PF* 1798.

[67] Thuc. VIII 6.1.

[68] Thuc. VIII 85.2. If the exiled Samian of the same name in the service of the younger Cyrus (X. *Anab.* I 7.5) is the same man, some one has gone wrong. Pigres, Cyrus' official interpreter (ibid., I 2.17, 5.7, 8.12) sounds like another Carian.

[69] Phalinos of Zakynthos (X. *Anab.* II 1.7 ff, Plut. *Art.* 14.5, D.S. XIV 25.1).

ordinates. They are composed and negotiated in a fully Greek terminology by people who know their way about Greek diplomatic usage perfectly well.

I turn now to the court of the King himself to see what kind of advice he may get and what kind of influences there may be on his policies. I begin with questions about how far and when his immediate staff may have developed a fixed and institutionalised structure. The literature on the subject is quite large, but it is unbelievably irresponsible. No one doubts that some strands of Persian official practice descended from the Achaemenids to the Parthians and the Sassanids and even beyond, but this is no justification for the constant projection of later evidence back even to the earliest periods. Sometimes, the warrant of contemporary evidence is claimed for Achaemenid practice, but this contemporary evidence turns out to involve presuppositions about the Book of Esther or the sources of Plutarch which no biblical scholar or Greek historiographer would dream of holding.[70] Some articles quoted as standard by Iranists turn out to make a regular practice of quoting their own interpretation of Greek texts rather than what the texts say.[71] My favourite example of the last involves a slightly different point, the one fact everybody knows about the Medes and Persians, the immutability of their laws. Every few years someone says that this is illustrated by a passage of Diodorus.[72] What the passage actually says is that Darius III put Charidemos to death and was afterwards sorry, but his royal power was not capable of undoing what had been done.[73]

[70] I am thinking of Benveniste, *Titres et noms propres en Iranien ancien* 52-3, who is arguing for a recognisable Achaemenid concept of 'second in the Kingdom'. His 'contemporary' evidence involves using Esther (V 8) and First Esdras (III 7 with no echo in Ezra). He goes on with the Plutarchan version of Xerxes' accession (*Mor.* 173c, 488e; *Them.* 14.3-4 is the end of the story). This version cannot be taken further back than Pompeius Trogus (Justin II 10) and provides Xerxes with a full brother unknown to Herodotus and Ktesias. I would only class one of Benveniste's texts as contemporary (Nep. *Con.* 3.2; Deinon ?) and it proves nothing by itself.

[71] Junge, *Klio* 33, 1940, 13-38 is the principal offender here, although he can be used with caution. It may be desirable to say that König, *Die Persika des Ktesias von Knidos* (1972) should not be used at all; I shall cite him occasionally for amusement only.

[72] My latest respectable example is H. H. Rowley, *Men of God* (1963) 238 n. 3.

[73] D.S. XVII 30.4-6. I have not taken this idea further back than Brissonius, *De regio Persarum principatu libri tres* (editio altera, Commelin of Heidelberg, 1595) 88 (it should be said that this remarkable book has not as

The texts and monuments of Darius and Xerxes provide us with two titles and a number of distinguishable officers. The two titles, *arštibara* (spear-bearer) and *vaçabara* (bow-bearer) are held under Darius by high personages, Gobryas[74] and Aspathines[75], of whom at least the second is found exercising administrative functions. Unfortunately, these titles do not as yet appear later.[76] When we turn to unlabelled monuments, the field for speculation becomes wider. A particularly prominent figure, appearing on three Persepolis reliefs,[77] is a Mede carrying a staff. Hinz[78] has called him the Court-marshal and has correctly linked him both with the other staff-carrying persons round the court on the Persepolis reliefs and with those persons called message-carriers (ἀγγελιηφόροι) by Herodotus.[79] Such persons are described by Xenophon as staff-carriers (σκηπτοῦχοι), not only at the mythical court of Cyrus the Great,[80] but also with the younger Cyrus who has, on royal model, his most faithful of his σκηπτοῦχοι.[81] Another distinguishable person in close attendance on the King clearly has some functions in relation to his personal comfort.[82] Bearded under Darius, he appears to be an eunuch in the time of Xerxes.

When we turn to the Greek literary evidence, the position is more

yet been fully replaced). The error was exposed by Wesseling ad loc. in 1745. A fair statement of our present evidence on the point in Bickerman, *Four Strange Books of the Bible*, 192-3; the origins of signing as opposed to sealing need investigation.

[74] See *Reallexicon der Assyriologie* s.v. Gubarru and *PF* 688.

[75] See Cameron *PTT* p. 103, Hallock *PFT* p. 670 s.v. Aš-ba-za-na.

[76] I cannot make up my mind about the status of the 'bow-bearer' of *PF* 1256 (? cf. 346) and the 'battle-axe-bearer' of *PF* 1560, but neither of them look very important.

[77] Schmidt, *Persepolis* I 164-5.

[78] *Altiranische Funde und Forschungen* 63 ff.

[79] III 34.1 (their chief Prexaspes), 77.2 (eunuchs), 118.2, all cited by Junge, op. cit. (n. 71), as εἰσαγγελεῖς, a short-circuiting perhaps justified by ἐσαγγεῖλαι in 118.2 and ἐσαγγελέος in 84.2. Cf. I 120.2 at the Median court.

[80] X. *Cyr.* VIII 4.2 Γαδάτας δὲ τῶν σκηπτούχων ἦρχεν αὐτῷ, καὶ ἦ ἐκεῖνος διεκόσμησεν ἡ πᾶσα ἔνδον δίαιτα καθειστήκει. Junge, op. cit., 30 n. 4, seems to show that it is in this passage that Hinz's belief (see note 28) that the high economic official Parnaka and the *Hofmarschall* are identical originates, but I see nothing here beyond the immediate management of the royal table-arrangements. Cf. ibid., VIII 1.38, 3.15 (VII 3.15 is problematical). VIII 3.19 is a particularly good passage associating σκηπτοῦχοι with message-carrying, this time in war.

[81] X. *Anab.* I 6.11, 8.28. I suppose him to be a eunuch from the emphasis given in the latter passage to the lavishness of the honours given him.

[82] Cf. Eilers *IBKU* 81-106 on *vistarbara*, Junge, op. cit., 16, 19-21. Is he the κατακοιμίστης of D.S. XI 69.1?

complex. It has long been agreed[83] that we should identify two words, ἀζαβαρίτης, which appears in Ktesias 46 as an evidently high officer in 424 B.C., and ἀζαραπατεῖς which appears in the plural in Hesychius who glosses it οἱ εἰσαγγελεῖς παρὰ Πέρσαις[84] and further identify it with an Old Persian word *hazarapatiš*, leader of a thousand, chiliarch, which does not appear itself in Old Persian texts, but is necessarily inferred from later appearances.[85] It is not in dispute that a special office known to the Greeks as χιλίαρχος was eventually a very high Achaemenid office indeed and passed from the Persian kingdom into Hellenistic monarchies.[86] The normal place to look for the origins of a particularly important chiliarch[87] has been the particularly distinguished royal bodyguard of one thousand within the Ten Thousand Immortals,[88] but this is to overlook the probably superior claims of the Persian cavalry-group of one thousand, described as 'best and most noble' by Herodotus,[89] given the title of Kinsmen and said to be chosen for courage and loyalty in Diodorus.[90] By the end of the Achaemenid empire it seems to be their commander who is *the* chiliarch,[91] and that seems to be the model followed by Alexander.[92]

The office of chiliarch as Grand Vizier has been taken back at

---

[83] Marquart, *Philologus* 55, 1896, 227-34 (cf. Justi, *ZDMG* 50, 1896, 659-64).

[84] The singular could as well be ἀζαραπατεὺς as ἀζαραπάτης. I deduce that the plural appeared in some Greek text. We cannot tell whether this text referred to many simultaneous holders of the office or, generically, to a series of them.

[85] See, besides Junge, op. cit., Benveniste, *Bull. soc. ling. Paris* 58, 1963, 41-57, *Titres et noms propres* 67-71.

[86] The key passage is D.S. XVIII 48.4-5, where it is presumably Hierony-mos who offers this comment on Antipater's promotion of his son Cassander to the chiliarchy.

[87] So, e.g., Meyer *GdA* IV² 1 31, Junge, op. cit. 32.

[88] Hdt. VII 41.2. Herakleides of Kyme *FGH* 689 F 1 ap. Ath. 514 B distinguishes these more clearly from the rest of the Immortals. Herodotus gives them gold pomegranates on their spears, Herakleides gives them gold apples, and apples are standard in the fourth century (cf. Klearchos F 49 Wehrli, Arr. III 11.5, D.S. XVII 59.3); apples in Herodotus are reserved for those closest to Xerxes.

[89] Hdt. VII 41.1.

[90] D.S. XVII 59.2. Arr. III 11.5 has the Kinsmen without specifying their number. Some on detachment at the Granicus, D.S. XVII 20.2.

[91] Cf. Arr. III 21.1 with 23.4.

[92] It can only be the weight of authority which makes Berve, *Alexander-reich* 112, think that Alexander was innovating in combining the 'viziership' with the cavalry command. I have found my preferred view only in Welles' note to D.S. XVII 59.2 (Loeb).

least as far as Darius I, but the evidence should not be stretched so far, nor should we see a Grand Vizier every time a chiliarch is mentioned.[93] It is however quite likely that by the 420s there could be a permanent official of great power. The Ktesias passage I have mentioned clearly attaches some importance to the fact that the usurper Secundianos appoints Menostanes his ἀζαβαρίτης and we know that Menostanes was the son of a satrap of Babylonia, had large estates there himself and was of royal blood.[94] As far as the officer known to the Greeks as the chiliarch is concerned, it is unfortunate that, before the last years of the empire, his appearances are more or less confined to passages where an application by a visiting Greek to see the King comes through him and he raises the question of whether the visitor is prepared to do *proskynesis* to the King.[95] Some evidence suggests that the persons named in these anec-

---

[93] Junge is the principal offender and also goes to considerable trouble to identify him with the *Hofmarschall* of the Persepolis reliefs; if we have to find a guard-commander there, I prefer Hinz's candidate (*Altiranische Funde und Forschungen* 78 with pl. 33). Many of the early references to chiliarchs need be no more than 'commanders of a thousand' appearing frequently in the same context as myriarchs; so under Darius Orontopatas (Pherekydes *FGH* 3 F 174) and, for what he is worth, Rhanosbates (Polyaen. VII 12) who has evaded the collectors, under Xerxes Dadakes (Aesch. *Pers.* 304) and Bowman, *Aramaic Ritual Texts from Peresepolis*, passim, if the Aramaic is rightly interpreted. For the first chiliarch with court-functions, Artabanos in Phainias ap. Plut. *Them.* 27.2, see note 96; even supposing Phainias' information were authentic, there is another chiliarch in the story (ibid., 29.1).

[94] Ktesias 38 (his father Artarios satrap of Babylon and brother of Artaxerxes), 45-6, 48, 51. Menostanes is the better form. He appears as Manuštanu son of Artarīme, a *mâr-bîti* of the King, i.e. a member of the royal house, in four Nippur tablets of the 40th and 41st years of Artaxerxes (references in Cardascia *Archives* 105 n. 10). This is by far the most impressive evidence we have for Ktesias' reliability for events near his own day; cf. Hüsing *Porysatis* 50-2.

[95] Hdt. VII 136 stands at the head of the sequence without involving a chiliarch. For the rest there is a useful discussion by Wehrli, *Die Schule des Aristoteles* IX 36. The main passages in chronological order of the alleged occurrences are these: Plut. *Them.* 27 (=Phainias F 26 Wehrli). Themistocles applies to the chilarch Artabanos. Nep. *Con.* 3.2-3 (=Deinon? cf. 5.4) Conon first *ex more Persarum ad chiliarchum, qui secundum gradum imperii tenebat, Tithrausten accessit seque ostendit cum rege colloqui velle. Nemo enim sine hoc admittitur* (The purpose of Conon's visit is probably unhistorical). Aelian, *V.H.* I 21 (a fuller version of Plut. *Art.* 22.8). Ismenias (Pelopidas is not mentioned in Aelian) deals with ὁ χιλίαρχος ὁ καὶ τὰς ἀγγελίας ἐσκομίζων τῷ βασιλεῖ καὶ τοὺς δεομένους ἐσάγων. The chiliarch is again Tithraustes, thirty years after the previous passage.

These passages and the Hesychius paraphrase of ἀζαραπατεῖς have naturally led to a disposition to identify chiliarch and εἰσαγγελεύς. But a) I suspect

dotes are of considerable influence, but it is not without difficulty.[96]

Various other court-officials are intermittently visible. The King's Eye, familiar to Greeks from the time of Aeschylus,[97] turns up once

---

the anecdotes of borrowing detail from each other, b) the εἰσαγγελεὺς of D.S. XVI 47.3 is probably not chiliarch and is only the most faithful friend of the King (Artaxerxes III) after Bagoas, c) Alexander's εἰσαγγελεὺς, who belongs to his phase as Great King, is quite distinct from his chiliarch (Berve, *Alexanderreich* 20). Meyer *GdA* IV² 1 38 rightly distinguishes the posts, without comment.

[96] The obvious identification for Themistocles' Artabanos is the murderer of Xerxes (D.S. XI 69, Justin III 1, Ktesias 29-30; Arist. *Pol.* 1311 b 34 ff. has a mysterious variant version), δυνάμενος πλεῖστον παρὰ τῷ βασιλεῖ Ξέρξη καὶ τῶν δορυφόρων ἀφηγούμενος (Diodorus), *praefectus eius* (Justin). Ktesias, who gives him no title, projects his influence back to Xerxes' accession (20), confusing him with Xerxes' uncle. Our Artabanos does not appear in Herodotus nor does his father Artasyras (Ktesias 20; cf. Nic. Dam. *FGH* 90 F 66 § 45 for an earlier Artasyras). Since Ktesias 19 synchronises Artasyras' death with that of Darius, he is not the Irdašura of *PT* 68, 75 (Xerxes' 20th year). The Irdabanuš who is satrap of Bactria in 500/499 (*PF* 1287, 1555) is conceivably to be associated with the Artapanos who is satrap of Bactria in 465 (Ktesias 31). That the Bactrian contingent of 480 is commanded by Xerxes' full brother Hystaspes (Hdt. VII 64.2) is not an objection, but it may be relevant to the conflict of evidence about Bactria in 465; D.S. XI 69.2 gives it to Hystaspes *son* of Xerxes.
We must accept a powerful guard-commander of the name in 465, but this does not prove much for the authenticity of Phainias' story. It is unclear whether Phainias thought that Themistocles came to Xerxes or Artaxerxes; Wehrli, loc. cit. (note 95) comes down for Xerxes but his argument from F 25 is worthless; Laqueur, *Phainias* (*RE* XIX 1565 ff.) does not appear to consider the point. I incline to read the passage as about Artaxerxes, but Plutarch may have adapted it to his preferred solution. Either Phainias thought it was Xerxes, which will damn him for us, or he thought it was Artaxerxes, which is hardly better, since Artabanos will not have survived Artaxerxes' accession by many days. I fear that Artabanos' name is at best a tiny piece of verisimilitude in an unconvincing narrative.
Tithraustes. It is of course encouraging to views about a powerful chiliarch that, a year or so after Conon applies to the chiliarch Tithraustes, Tithraustes is sent to Asia Minor with letters giving him the right to give orders to all satraps and the task of disposing of Tissaphernes (Bruce, *An Historical Commentary on the Hellenica Oxyrhynchia* 90-1, is perhaps the most convenient review of the evidence, but I dissent from the phrase 'commander-in-chief'). If we accept Aelian, his tenure of office will cover at least thirty years. But his only other appearance is as one of three commanders against Egypt in 385-3 with Pharnabazos and Abrokomas (Isoc. IV 140). If there is a temptation to say that his normal place will be at the King's side, it becomes even more disquieting that this major figure of the reign of Artaxerxes II makes no appearance whatever in Plutarch's life of that monarch; contrast the frequent appearances of Tiribazos.

[97] Aesch. *Pers.* 980, Hdt. I 114.2, Ar. *Ach.* 92-3. I concur with Fornara *JHS* 91, 1971, 27 that Aristophanes did not need Herodotus for the information; I cannot understand why he adds *Pers.* 44.

in 401.[98] He is not as yet visible in Persian texts, though there is some evidence for the King's Ears, who seem to be on a rather lower plane.[99] The Greeks were very ready to believe in such an extensive Royal Intelligence Service.[100]

It is understandable that virtually any officer who had access to the King might be in a position to exert influence or secure a favour. Our most notable example is Nehemiah, cup-bearer to Artaxerxes I in 445, who, after ruminating on the problems of Jerusalem for four or five months, made himself visibly sad in the King's presence in order to provoke an occasion for making his request;[101] he was then made governor of Judah. Tradition makes him an eunuch.[102] If so, this is the earliest case of an eunuch's getting a substantial position away from the court. At the court, individual eunuchs are recorded, at least by Ktesias, as holding great influence in practically every reign. The practice of using them is attributed to Cyrus the Great and defended by Xenophon, who makes the clearly unexpected point that there is no particular reason to think eunuchs less courageous than whole men.[103] Eduard Meyer held that no post was closed to eunuchs except the military career,[104] an exclusion which curiously overlooks the career of Bagoas towards the end of the empire.[105]

The first really substantial eunuch in Ktesias starts, like Nehemiah, under Artaxerxes I. He is Artoxares the Paphlagonian, who is entrusted with diplomatic missions at the age of twenty. At one stage he makes a wrong guess about internal politics and is banished to Armenia, without apparent full disgrace. He returns

---

[98] Plut. *Art.* 12.1, Artasyras. For other persons of the name see note 96. X. *Cyr.* VIII 2.11 denies that there is only one official of this name.

[99] See Eilers *IBKU* 22-3.

[100] X. *Cyr.* VIII 2.10-12. Cf. Median κατάσκοποι and κατήκοοι in Hdt. I 100.2, 112.1.

[101] Nehemiah I-II. For the small chronological problem, see e.g. Brockington, *Ezra, Nehemiah and Esther* (1969) 126-7, but note further that the 19th year had an intercalary Addaru II (Parker and Dubberstein, *Babylonian Chronology*³ (1956)) 8). The only other cup-bearer I know is the son of Prexaspes, Cambyses' 'message-carrier' (Hdt. III 34.1); τιμὴ δὲ καὶ αὕτη οὐ σμικρή, Herodotus remarks. This ceremonial position is probably not to be confused with the *Hofkellerwart* (Hinz, *Zeitschrift für Assyriologie* 61, 1971, 290-4), who frequently changes.

[102] Cf. the variant in LXX II Esdras 11.11 and Origen on Matthew XIX 12.

[103] X. *Cyr.* VII 5.59-65.

[104] *GdA* IV² 1 37.

[105] D.S. XVI 47.3-4, 49.4-6, 50, XVII 5.3-6.

in 424 as king-maker for Darius II and exercises great influence until he conceives the idea of pretending to the throne himself.[106] No other Greek source knows about him, apparently, but Ktesias' view of his position becomes more credible if we identify him, as I think we must, with an Artaḥsarû whose large staff of officers is visible in at least eleven Babylonian texts, mostly from the late 420s, and who has villages of his own.[107] The thought has crossed my mind that the silence of the Greek sources is only apparent and that, if in 424 we find Aristophanes portraying Kleon as a slave who has won great influence with his master by flattery, the reason for choosing to call him a Paphlagonian may owe something to knowledge of the greatest Paphlagonian of the day rather than simply to the desire to find a suitable barbarian ethnic which will allow a pun on the word παφλάζω.[108]

It is customary to make fun of Ktesias when he attributes great importance to eunuchs and queens and to say that his point of view is bound to the harem. I am not sure that he in fact implies more by his attitude than Xenophon, for example, takes for granted when he depicts a seeker after a favour from the satrap Pharnabazos taking gifts for Pharnabazos himself, his concubines and those who had the greatest power with Pharnabazos.[109] I am myself disposed to take seriously stories of the irrational caprice and wanton cruelty of monarchs. Nothing is reported of Periander, tyrant of Corinth, which does not find ready parallels in well-attested information about Ali Pasha of Iannina at the beginning of the nineteenth century,[110] and, allowing for some differences of institutions, the Persian court will be subject to the same kind of pressures and insecurities which have afflicted the courts of absolute monarchs

---

[106] Ktesias 39, 40, 47, 49, 53.

[107] The identification was first made by Hüsing, *Bericht des Forschungsinstitut für Osten u. Orient* 2, 1918, 140, an earlier edition, which I have not seen, of Hüsing *Porysatis*. König, in *Reallexicon der Assyriologie* I 156 b, collects the evidence. For the linguistics of the identification see Eilers, *ZDMG* 90, 1936, 174, and cf. Eilers *IBKU* 52 n. 2, 89-90.

The villages are in *UM* II/1 84. König's dates are not correct. The earliest text (*BE* IX 4) belongs to February 442; the latest (*UM* II/1 109) is of January 418, which will provide a terminus post quem for Ktesias 53.

[108] The pun in *Knights* 919, *Peace* 314. As far as I know, the evidence for real Paphlagonian slaves in fifth-century Athens lies in two appearances of the name Τίβειος in 405 (IG II² 1951. 69, 145); that name is said by Strabo to be characteristically Paphlagonian (VII 3.12).

[109] X. *Hell.* III 1.10.

[110] W. Plomer, *The Diamond of Iannina* (1970).

down to the time of Stalin[111] and perhaps beyond. It seems unlikely that Greek fascination with the Queens of Persia[112] is solely
due to the fact that they were hidden in harems. At any rate the
tradition of their independent wealth is securely based. Besides
the Greek sources for that of Amestris, consort of Xerxes, and of
Parysatis, consort of Darius II,[113] Parysatis' extensive holdings in
Babylonia have been known from cuneiform evidence for many
years.[114] This is not a practice which begins in degenerate days.
Herodotus[115] tells us that Darius I's favourite wife was Artystone, daughter of Cyrus; she was of course also useful to him in securing his dynastic claim, though she is not the mother of his heir.
She now turns up in 500 with an estate at Kuknaka in Persis.[116]
Hinz[117] has pointed out that this is presumably the Kukannakan of
the Behistun inscription, from which arose a Persian pretender in
Darius' first year; we can perhaps deduce further that the pretender's estates went to Darius' new queen. It is perhaps likely that
queens are more interested in personalities than in policies, and I
would doubt propositions about Parysatis' being a champion of
Zoroastrianism.[118] I am not clear why Nehemiah draws attention
to the fact that the queen was present when he was sent to
Jerusalem.[119]

When Ezra goes to Jerusalem 47 years later, under Artaxerxes
II,[120] there is no mention of the queen, but we are told that he goes
on the orders of the King and his seven counsellors.[121] Meyer
thought that this was a regular institution and made some sugges-

---

[111] Bialer (ed.), *Stalin and his Generals* (1969) is rich in instances.
[112] Cf. e.g. Plato, *I Alc.* 121c, 123cd.
[113] Plato, loc. cit., X. *Anab.* I 4.9, II 4.27. Cf. Anthylla in Egypt which
provides the Queen's shoes, Hdt. II 98.1.
[114] First seen by Meissner, *OLZ* 1904 col. 385. See Hüsing *Porysatis*,
passim, and Cardascia *Archives* 7 n. 1 who lists the texts.
[115] Hdt. VII 69.2.
[116] *PF* 1836-7, cf. 718 where we have Artystone's village and intendant,
but the King's seal.
[117] *Orientalia* 39, 1970, 423, where further evidence is collected for Artystone and her son Arsames (cf. Hdt. VII 69.2); add the missing references,
PF 733-4, 2035.
[118] Hüsing *Porysatis* 23 ff.
[119] II 6.
[120] I am satisfied with the chronology argued most cogently by Rowley,
The Servant of the Lord (1965) 135-68; see also his *Men of God* (1963) 228-42.
[121] Ezra VII 14. There is some evidence that this document has been
reworked; Rowley, *Men of God* 217-9.

tions about its composition.[122] Those whose knowledge of Herodotus is at second hand are liable to say that this has something to do with the Seven who killed the false Smerdis,[123] despite the facts that the later King was himself one of the Seven, that Herodotus gives them only particular marks of honour and rights of audience[124] and that Darius himself goes no further.[125] These seven counsellors are surely to be distinguished from the βασιλήιοι δικασταί who make fairly frequent appearances but are indefinite in number.[126] There is a passage nearly contemporary with Ezra which gives us another seven, the seven best Persians in attendance on the younger Cyrus who are summoned to judge his enemy Orontas;[127] we cannot be sure whether their advisory or their judicial function is uppermost.[128] No Greek author seems to be aware of a regular royal council. The most famous of all councils, summoned to decide on Xerxes' expedition to Greece,[129] is simply a gathering of the best of the Persians, so that Xerxes may learn their opinions and he may declare his wishes in public. Of the two speakers, one is the son of one of the Seven, the other is the King's uncle. It will be prudent to agree with Frye[130] that it is doubtful whether a council of seven was a regular bureaucratic institution and that the council was an indefinite advisory group to the ruler.

We will not doubt that descent from the Seven remains a social and political asset,[131] but it must be said that the Achaemenid royal family was itself so philoprogenitive that there rapidly came to be

---

[122] *GdA* IV² 1 39.

[123] E.g. *Daniel, Ezra, Nehemiah* ed. Slotki p. 152.

[124] Hdt. III 84.

[125] Kent *OP* Db IV 86-88 "Saith Darius the King; Thou who shalt be king hereafter, protect well the family of these men."

[126] Meyer *GdA* IV² 1 30-1; Hdt. III 14.5, 31.3, V 25, VII 194.1, Plut. *Art.* 29.8-12, Aelian *V.H.* I 34. The first three passages antedate Darius, and none of those named have anything to do with the Seven. Judges and seven counsellors may be identified in Esther I 13-14, for what that is worth; Eissfeldt, *Festschrift für W. Eilers* (1967) 164-6, shows that they should probably be distinguished even there. A trial by three judges, D.S. XV 10-11.

[127] X. *Anab.* I 6.4-11.

[128] Eissfeldt's view that δικασταί declare the law and others make the judgement only fits one of the Herodotus passages about δικασταί (III 14.5) at all well.

[129] Hdt. VII 8 ff.

[130] Ap. Walser (ed.) *Beiträge zur Achämenidengeschichte* (1972) 88. The silence of the *Cyropaedia* about a regular institution seems to me noteworthy.

[131] Cf. as late as 344 Rhosakes (D.S. XVI 47.2).

a very large class of royal princes,[132] which was amply sufficient to fill high military commands[133] and to form a pool from which the King could seek advice.[134]

At a lower level, there is some evidence that the King may have at his disposal persons who can give expert advice on peoples with whom he may come into contact. Much of our evidence is of course about Greeks whose importance their fellow-countrymen may have exaggerated. Histiaios of Miletos needs no introduction, and the value to Cambyses of the Egyptian knowledge of Phanes of Halikarnassos may only have been temporary.[135] The Persians will have had better Egyptian advisers later, and we can name one, Oujahorresne, summoned to court by Darius at the beginning of his reign.[136] A stray reference in Nehemiah is helpful. After recording a peculiarly knowledgable royal edict about the Temple service, he adds, apparently in explanation, "Pethaḥiah son of Meshezabel, of the children of Zeraḥ, the son of Judah, was at the King's hand in all matters concerning the people".[137] Such sources of information may have been relatively numerous, though not always impartial or reliable.

I should at least raise the question of central records. We do after all hear of missions of inspection and reporting, including one on the Greek coastline.[138] Even in Herodotus, we hear of scribes recording army and fleet numbers and taking down the names of

---

[132] In Akkadian, a *mâr-bîti* of the King (Eilers *IBKU* 91). In Aramaic, bny byt' (Cowley *AP* 30.3 (408) "The health of your lordship may the God of Heaven seek after exceedingly at all times and give you favour before Darius the King and the princes of the palace . . . ."). The class covers such remote relations as Arsames, satrap of Egypt, grandson or greatgrandson of Darius I, Manuštanŭ (see note 94), grandson of Xerxes, and the difficult Arrišittu. Eilers *IBKU* 65 n. 3, 125 denies the identification with the Arsites of Ktesias 50-51, full brother of Darius II, since he survives until December 417 (*UM* II/1 137, *TMHC* II/III 190); I agree that it is unlikely that the chronological gap between Ktesias 49 and 50 should be so long, but see Chapter Three note 192.

[133] Cf. Burn, *Persia and the Greeks* 333-6 for their dominance in the expedition of 480.

[134] At least true for the earlier phases of the empire; compare the role of Artabanos in 480. Later, troubles about the succession tended to thin the ranks of the King's immediate relations more drastically.

[135] Hdt. III 4. The importance which has sometimes been attached to him is somewhat diminished by the removal from him of his coinage by E. S. G. Robinson, *American Numismatic Society Centennial Volume* (1958) 586-8.

[136] See e.g. Drioton and Vandier, *L'Égypte*³ (1952) 600-2, 619.

[137] Neh. XI 23-24.

[138] Hdt. III 135.1.

good fighters.[139] How efficient all this was is anybody's guess. Even the tight world of the Persepolis ration-tablets shows signs of inefficiency.[140] The problems of what we call information-retrieval must have been immense and certainly not made easier by the fact that there was more than one royal capital. In Ezra [141] we hear of a search made for a text of only twenty years back. The search started in Babylon and the document was eventually found in Ecbatana, three hundred miles away and an uncertain number of weeks or months later.

Up-to-date information is always likely to have been preferred. I have already spoken of the King's eyes and ears. We should not forget that, apart from the satraps, whose relations to the King will demand treatment later, the King has personal representatives in the provinces responsible to him directly. Major fortresses were in the hands of his commanders[142] and it appears that he had his own secretariat at satrapal courts.[143] These sources can provide information, including information on satrapal behaviour, in cases where the King has reason to distrust the satrap's judgement or loyalty.

We are only just beginning to be able to estimate the role of bureaucracy in the running of the empire and there will be revaluations to come about the influence of its heavy machinery. What is clear is that we are dealing with a despotism where the views of the despot are important. Much will depend on the character and predilections of the King himself. This is a topic on which, by the nature of our evidence, we can have very little material, but sometimes we can infer predispositions. That Xerxes inherited a grudge against Athens is a natural view of our Greek sources, tempered, we may think, by the evidence of the diplomatic overtures to her in the winter of 480/79. That Darius II was in general ill-disposed to Athens for supporting revolt against him may come

---

[139] Hdt. VII 100.1-2, VIII 90.4.
[140] Hallock *Evidence* 31.
[141] Ezra V 17-VI 2.
[142] X. *Cyr.* VIII 6.1, 14. See Chapter Three note 21.
[143] Hdt. III 128.3 γραμματιστὰς δὲ βασιληίους οἱ πάντες ὕπαρχοι ἔχουσι. To this reference we should, I think, add Megaphernes, the φοινικιστὴς βασίλειος executed for plotting by Cyrus the Younger (X. *Anab.* I 2.20). Various interpretations have been offered (see Masqueray ad loc.), but now that ποινικαστὰς is attested as a Greek word for a scribe (Davies and Jeffery, *Kadmos* 9, 1970, 132-3), I see no reason to look beyond the explanation already offered by a scholiast.

later to seem likely. That Artaxerxes II in the 390s was deeply hostile
to the Spartans is something I firmly believe, not merely because
Deinon tells us so,[144] but because he persists in an anti-Spartan
policy for four years after he was rightly advised to the contrary.
I have no doubt in my own mind that the reason for this is essentially personal to him and that he could not forgive the Spartans for
having backed his brother against him.

---

[144] *FGH* 690 F 19 ap. Plut. *Art.* 22.1.

CHAPTER TWO

I turn now to contemplating the Sparta which had produced the
contradictory messages of which Artaxerxes was complaining in 425.
Here the evidence has not increased noticeably for many years,[1]
but some of the recent scholarly discussion has contributed considerably to our understanding. I shall try in this lecture to pick
out some aspects which have particular bearing on the making of
foreign policy.

The major determining fact about Sparta, which in the last
analysis affects every other aspect, is the existence of a large subject
population of helots and Messenians. Curiously, despite the fact
that one clear functional purpose of Thucydides Book I is to introduce us to Sparta and Athens, this factor is far from prominent in
that book and is even glossed over when Thucydides describes the
slowness of Spartan reaction to Athenian imperialism.[2] The book
nevertheless contains material hearing on it in the description of
the Helot Revolt in the 460s[3] and the importance in the Spartan
worries about the regent Pausanias of the possibility that he was
plotting with the helots.[4] The matter becomes dramatic and
relevant after the Athenian landing at Pylos in 425, and Thucydides,
despite his general complaints about the difficulty of probing
Spartan institutions and behaviour,[5] had picked up a fair amount
about it. Clear hints about Spartan worries start appearing almost
immediately.[6] Before long we learn more explicitly that the
Spartans are normally intensely cautious about the helots and that
this crisis makes them more willing to get some out of the country

---

[1] The new text published by Peek, *Abh. Ak. Leipzig*, Phil.-Hist. Kl.
65.3 (1974) 3-15 (see Cartledge, *Liverpool Classical Monthly* 1, 1976, 87-92) is
however a substantial acquisition for the light it throws on the development
of Spartan alliance-formulae. For a new fragment of Theophrastos see note 88.

[2] Thuc. I 118.2, where οἰκείοις πολέμοις has more to cover than helot
revolt.

[3] Thuc. I 101 ff.

[4] Thuc. I 132.4; for doubts about the accuracy of the charge, see Rhodes,
Historia 19, 1970, 391-2, but Spartan preoccupations are what concern us,
even if they are only bogeys. See also Lotze, *Klio* 52, 1970, 271-4.

[5] Thuc. V 68.2 τῆς πολιτείας τὸ κρυπτὸν.

[6] Thuc. IV 41.3, 55.1.

with Brasidas and conduct an extensive purge of others.[7] Thucydides eventually asserts that fears about the helots were a determining reason for the Spartans' making the Peace of Nikias.[8] How far this was clear from the outside is uncertain; they are at least once said to wish to conceal it from the Athenians.[9] From our point of view, it seems clear, although modern books are shy of saying it, that the Athenians would have had no difficulty in winning the Peloponnesian War decisively, had they done a little more to promote helot revolt.[10] That they did not is a problem about Athens which is easily soluble in Marxist terms, but the solution would presuppose, wrongly in my view, that the Athenians were as scared of their slaves as the Spartans were of theirs.[11] Even after the Spartans had made their fears explicit in 421 by making the Athenians swear to come and help in the event of a servile uprising,[12] the Athenians apparently do not see the point.[13] The most illuminating information about the relations of Sparta to her unprivileged population comes in 399 with the conspiracy of Kinadon. Xenophon's narrative[14] is remarkable both for the frankness of its

---

[7] Thuc. IV 80. It is not clear what the Spartan fear about the helots besides their πλῆθος. On my view of the textual tradition, the mss. combination which gives σκαιότητα has no authority and νεότητα makes difficulties as well (see Classen-Steup and note the immediately preceding νεωτερίσωσιν as a possible cause of error). I agree with Gomme against Classen-Steup that αἰεὶ γὰρ τὰ πολλὰ Λακεδαιμονίοις πρὸς τοὺς Εἵλωτας τῆς φυλακῆς πέρι μάλιστα καθειστήκει does not mean "most of the Lacedaemonian institutions were intended especially to guard against the Helots" but "Spartan policy with regard to the Helots had always been based almost entirely on the idea of security".

[8] Thuc. V 14.3.

[9] Thuc. IV 41.3.

[10] The description of Spartan morale in Thuc. IV 55 is too often overlooked.

[11] There is a similar problem about Syracuse, where Nikias' view that nothing is to be expected from internal revolution in Syracuse is endorsed by Thucydides himself (Thuc. VI 20.2, VII 55.2), despite our other evidence that there was a servile insurrection during the siege (Polyaen. I 43.1, not noticed e.g. by Dover *HCT*; see Busolt GG III 2 756 n. 1, 1339, who does not however ask whether the Athenians could have known about it or why they should have ignored it if they did).

[12] Thuc. V 23.3.

[13] Even Demosthenes' fortification in 413 of a post opposite Kythera (Thuc. VII 26.2) is only said to be to receive helot deserters, not to promote helot revolt. It would not be a secure inference from Thuc. VI 105.2 that the Argives did see the point. No Argive motives are required there other than a wish to get Athens to commit herself to open hostilities with Sparta.

[14] X. *Hell.* III 3.

acknowledgment of the subjects' attitude and for the light it throws on the mechanism of repression. Thereafter we hear nothing until 370/69, when Epaminondas had no great difficulty in restoring an independent Messenia,[15] but I shall be arguing in my last lecture that the threat was of great importance to Sparta even before then.

To this permanent threat, the peculiar Spartan training, the *agoge*, and Spartan discipline in general are designed to provide an answer. Professor Finley has given us an excellent analysis[16] of the various ways in which Spartan life is organised to produce concentration on the service of the state, habits of obedience and deference to commanders and also, in more general terms, the way in which this discipline did not succeed in producing people who could cope with the strains of contact with the outside world and the new requirements of flexibility and imagination demanded by Sparta's emergence as a great power. Thucydides was well aware of this, even though most of the major manifestations recorded despairingly by the laconophile Xenophon[17] are after his time. The key passages are the foreboding references in the Athenian speech at Sparta in 432 to the way Spartans behave outside Sparta[18] and the analysis of Sparta's good fortune in its having been Brasidas who first made substantial contact with the outside world in the Peloponnesian War. "For he was the first to go out and, seeming to be a good man in all respects, he left a firm expectation that the others too were like him."[19] We are surely meant to understand that they were not.

I should add at this point that the restrictions of Spartan life may have produced, not merely an inability to get on with other Greeks, but also some ignorance about them outside fairly narrow frontiers. Information about personal friendships between Spartans and citizens of other cities, copious enough on the mainland,[20] seems to thin out fairly sharply as we move further east and, before

---

[15] D.S. XV 66.1, notoriously not in Xenophon. Xenophon's account only has Spartan worries, ultimately unjustified, about arming helots (*Hell.* VI 5.29) and a concession that some perioikoi joined the invaders (VI 5.32). Much more unrest in Laconia appears in X. *Ages.* 2.24, Plut. *Ages.* 32.

[16] Finley *Sparta*.

[17] X. *Lac. Pol.* 14.

[18] Thuc. I 77.6, not, I think, simply a generalisation from Pausanias; cf. Raubitschek in Stadter (ed.), *The Speeches in Thucydides* (1973) 45-6.

[19] Thuc. IV 81.2-3.

[20] Cf. the friends of Boeotia and Corinth (note 55) and the Athens-experts (note 65).

Sparta gets fully involved in Asia, I see no case beyond Samos.[21] Meetings at Panhellenic festivals will have done something to plug the gap, but I think it possible that for the Spartan of the 420s knowledge of what lay beyond the Aegean was rather vague.

The Spartan way of life produced, as Finley has reminded us, losers as well as winners at every stage. A system designed to produce uniformity and conformity will nevertheless produce constant psychological tensions as to the right way of pleasing one's superiors. I remember very clearly how, even in the relatively mild atmosphere of a peacetime English Officer Cadet School, where the only really powerful sanction was the threat of being 'returned to unit' to serve out the remainder of one's National Service in the ranks, there were sharp differences of theory and practice as to whether it was best to remain as inconspicuous as possible, with the danger of being accused of lack of leadership qualities, or to risk doing things which might bring one attention, which could be unfavourable. The sanctions in Spartan life were all-pervasive.[22] There were ceremonies designed to discourage bachelors,[23] and failure even in this respect could downgrade you. The individualist Derkyllidas found that a younger man would not stand up for him, saying "you have not begotten anyone to give place to me".[24] On an even more essential point, Xenophon[25] gives us a general sketch of marks of disgrace given to cowards; for example, they are not chosen when teams are picked up and they are given bad places in choruses.

The first individual cowards we hear much about are Pantites and Aristodemos, who, partly by accident, failed to get killed at Thermopylae.[26] They received not only reproach, but ἀτιμίη, loss of civic rights. Pantites seems to have hanged himself fairly quickly.[27]

---

[21] Hdt. III 55.2, cf. Mitchell, *JHS* 95, 1975, 78-9.

[22] Useful material in Gernet, *Anthropologie de la Grece ancienne* (1968) 288-301, Latte, *Hermes* 66, 1931, 155-8.

[23] Plut. *Lyc.* 15.2, Ath. 555 c.

[24] Plut. *Lyc.* 15.3. For a general statement of Derkyllidas' abnormality, see Ephoros *FGH* 70 F 71.

[25] X. *Lac. Pol.* 9.5.

[26] Hdt. VII 229-232; IX 71.

[27] Clearly the conditions of Spartan life could be so intolerable, actually or potentially, that suicide was an obvious answer, but I find no text which describes it as particularly Spartan. Some gallant deaths in battle may have this element in it, besides that of Aristodemos (Hirzel, *Selbstmord* 54 n. 4 thinks that Aristodemos' offence was to have left the ranks and contrasts

Aristodemos was called 'the man who ran away'; noone lit a fire
for him or talked to him and, when he finally got himself killed,
fighting exceptionally gallantly at Plataea, it was not counted to
his posthumous merit, since he had obviously wanted to die to
escape his state of reproach. Complications arose when the group
affected was larger, and the story of the Sphakteria prisoners is
particularly enlightening about tensions between Spartan traditions
and other factors. It might well be thought that they had originally
had responsibility thrust on them unfairly. They had asked
whether they should surrender and received the unhelpful reply
"The Spartans ask you to make your own decision doing nothing
disgraceful".[28] After they surrender, the Spartans move heaven
and earth to get them back, another major factor in the making
of the Peace of Nikias.[29] They have been back for a year when there
is a suspicion that they may have an inferiority complex because
of their defeat and cause trouble if they have full citizen rights (some
are already holding office). So they are made *atimoi*, incapable of
holding office or making a valid sale or purchase. Later on their
rights are restored.[30] We may suspect that some of this uncertainty
is due to the high social position of some of them.[31] Even the glow
of a successful battle like Mantinea did not save two polemarchs
who had disobeyed orders from exile for cowardice.[32] Other things
can happen which will leave a mark on you, even if your career is
not ruined, and they may even be relevant to Spartan-Persian
relations. Derkyllidas is particularly hostile to Pharnabazos the
Persian, since, as a result of an accusation made by him, he was
made to stand, for how long or where we do not know, holding his

---

Anaxibios, X. *Hell*. IV 8.38), and suicide is specifically attested for Timo-
krates (Thuc. II 92.3). Political suicide is at least a possibility for king
Kleomenes I (I am not unaware that Luria, *Phil. Woch*. 48, 1928, 27-9,
thought it ritual) and is specifically attested for Antalkidas (Plut. *Art*. 22.7),
made fun of by his enemies and fearing the ephors. Kleomenes III put up a
very determined resistance to a perfectly logical suggestion of suicide
(Plut. *Cleom*. 52 (31)) before yielding to it at a later stage (ibid., 58 (37)).
The generalities about the Spartan attitude in Cic. *Tusc*. 5.42, Sen. *Ep*.
77.14, Stob. 7.59 are not helpful.

[28] Thuc. IV 38.3.

[29] See e.g. Thuc. V 15.

[30] Thuc. V 34.2.

[31] Thuc. V 15.1.

[32] Thuc. V 72.1. No doubt Agis was particularly cross with them, but his
views must have been shared.

shield, a mark of disgrace for σπουδαῖοι, since it is a punishment for indiscipline.[33]

Spartan society was both conformist and highly competitive. Xenophon's mythical Cyrus [34] institutes a competition in good actions among his Persians. Xenophon notes that this, as in cities, produces intense jealousies, and justifies it in this particular case by the advantages that it gives the king to have his best men promoting the welfare of the king rather than of each other. That there was corresponding advantage at Sparta for the welfare of the state is doubtful. Finley [35] has advocated seeing the leit-motif of Spartan politics, not in the institutional clashes which have sometimes been seen as fundamental, but in a conflict between men of energy and ambition and the rest. Without going as far as that, I think we can certainly say that an atmosphere of competition may spill over into policy-making. I will cite at this stage only two examples: Thucydides' belief that Brasidas was an obstacle to peace in the late 420s because of his good fortune and because war brought him honour,[36] and Alcibiades' evidently correct assumption that the ephor Endios will prefer one policy-line to another because he will wish to have the credit for a diplomatic coup which will otherwise go to the king Agis.[37]

The individual Spartan's desire for honour is something that we are not likely to overlook, but there is another respect in which recent work [38] has brought out again an aspect of Spartan society about which the sources are fairly clear, but which had fallen into the background. The Spartan *homoioi* are only notionally equal. Some people go into the *agoge* with clear inherited advantages. Some of these advantages are advantages of birth and descent. The nature of our evidence for Spartan prosopography is such that we cannot document this in very much detail, but we have several general references.[39] More can be said about wealth. The well-known

---

[33] X. *Hell.* III 1.9. One of the features of Pausanias' conduct which alienated the allies was his adaptation of this practice by making defaulters stand all day holding an iron anchor (Plut. *Arist.* 23.2).

[34] X. *Cyr.* VIII 2. 26-28.

[35] Finley *Sparta* 151.

[36] Thuc. V 16.1.

[37] Thuc. VIII 12.2.

[38] Finley *Sparta* 150-2, De Ste Croix, *OPW* 137.

[39] Hdt. VII 134.2 (φύσι γεγονότες εὖ); Arist. *Pol.* 1270 b 24 (καλοὶ κἀγαθοί contrasted to δῆμος, whatever the precise implications of ἀρετή).

prohibition on the ownership of coined money has led people to think almost in terms of state communism and I find in a large book published as late as 1965 the observation "There appears to have been little temptation to amass wealth"[40]. Aristotle's general remarks on the economic deficiencies of the Spartan system[41] have been referred almost entirely to later developments. Nevertheless, the existence of wealthy Spartans is always assumed,[42] even in contexts where the point is that the Spartan system discouraged their making a display of their wealth.[43] Finley and De Ste Croix, in collecting the material about birth and wealth, have been principally concerned with illuminating the nature of the *gerousia*, but there is no doubt that there may well be instances not known to us where wealth and birth give an individual definable political influence. I do not suppose it to be mere coincidence that the late-fifth-century Spartan for whose wealth we have the clearest evidence is the Lichas whom we shall find throwing his weight about so conspicuously on his mission to Asia Minor in 412/1.[44]

The existence of hereditary wealth is an incentive to the less wealthy to improve their position, and, as Sparta moves into the outside world, opportunities arise for making money by bribery. Finley has pointed out that there are, even in Herodotus, six references to the possibility of Spartans' being bribed,[45] all of them, we may add, in matters of foreign policy, and the accusation or suggestion is frequently revived.[46] Aristotle regards it as a notorious danger in the case of poor ephors,[47] and presumably it is at least

---

[40] Tigerstedt, *The Legend of Sparta in Classical Antiquity* I 74.

[41] Arist. *Pol.* 1270 a 11 ff.

[42] Hdt. VI 61.3, VII 134.2, Thuc. I 6.4, X. *Lac. Pol.* 5.3, *Hell.* VI 4.11, Arist. *Pol.* 1294 b 22, 26. All these references are from De Ste Croix, loc. cit., and add Plat. *I Alc.* 123 a, where exaggeration may be expected.

[43] Thuc. I 6.4, Arist. *Pol.* 1294 b 22, 26. De Ste Croix overlooks this. X. *Lac. Pol.* 14.3 says that display is a relatively recent development, but how recent ? Lichas is certainly not reticent about his wealth.

[44] Thuc. VIII passim. For the wealth, passages collected by De Ste Croix, loc. cit., but add Plut. *Mor.* 823 D-E, a positive denial that Lichas' wealth brought him as much influence as Lysander had, which I would not deny. His father's name Arkesilas is interesting; had the family married into the royal house of Cyrene at some stage ? A possible sixth-century ancestor, Hdt. I 67.5.

[45] III 148, V 51.2, VI 50.2, 72, 82.1, VIII 5.1.

[46] Thuc. I 109.2, II 21.1 (with Plut. *Per.* 22.2); Plut. *Per.* 22.4, *Lys.* 16-17.1; Eur. *And.* 451; Arist. fr. 544.

[47] Arist. *Pol.* 1270 b 10-12.

an element in Xenophon's complaint about the fourth-century Spartan's passion for overseas service.[48]

For Aristotle, the subject of wealth is intimately connected with that of the position of women,[49] but this is a topic on which our sources fail us almost completely. What Aristotle has to say about the property-position of women, which ends with the assertion that two-fifths of the land belongs to women, is clear enough, but I am utterly defeated by his assertion [50] that many things were managed by women in the time of the Spartan hegemony. Plato seems to agree with his worries about the position of women in Sparta when he says that the Spartans have, disastrously, gone only half way in their liberation of women's education.[51] Both of them are surely thinking of more than the notorious bad behaviour of the Spartan women at the time of Epaminondas' invasion of Laconia,[52] but I know of no text which suggests political influence by any Spartan women in the main period of Spartan power.[53]

Such a failure of our sources should encourage us at any rate to bear in mind further possible alignments of society and politics in Sparta which do not happen to be attested. Besides groupings which we do hear about, like friends of individual kings [54] and vaguer groupings like friends of Boeotia and Corinth,[55] which may be purely political, I find myself wondering whether the communal messes, designed, as Finley suggests,[56] to cut across family and age-group, did not form nuclei of political discussion and activity as well. The only Spartan dinner-conversation about which we happen to hear is that of the royal mess,[57] and no doubt the other messes, like that one, spent much of their time on horses, hunting and boy-friends,[58] but most of the political gossip reported by Xenophon must be

---

[48] X. *Lac. Pol.* 14.

[49] Arist. *Pol.* 1269 b 12 ff.

[50] 1269 b 31.

[51] *Laws* 806 c.

[52] Arist. *Pol.* 1269 b 37-39, X. *Hell.* VI 5.28, Plut. *Ages.* 31.5.

[53] Plut. *Ages.* 20.1, where Agesilaos induces his sister to compete successfully for an Olympic chariot-victory in order to show that such success has nothing to do with ἀρετή, might be held to be against it. There are affinities between this and *Mor.* 823 D-E (see note 44).

[54] The most important passage is X. *Hell.* V 4.32.

[55] Thuc. V 37.1, 37.3-4, 38.3.

[56] *Sparta* 148.

[57] X. *Hell.* V 3.20. I am not sure that I can distinguish between ἡβητικοὶ and παιδικοὶ λόγοι.

[58] X. *Lac. Pol.* 5.6 is too good to be true.

mess-conversation, and political attitudes will certainly have been formed there.

Politics will have included personalities, often to the exclusion of principles, and it is worth devoting a moment's thought to the question of how people get jobs. The most obvious fact is that Agesilaos' relatives tend to get good ones. His half-brother Teleutias has a whole succession of them, despite the original family poverty.[59] Plutarch puts it frankly;[60] since Agesilaos had the greatest power in the city, he arranged for his half-brother Teleutias to get command of the fleet. Teleutias at least, according to Xenophon,[61] did well, but Agesilaos' brother-in-law, Peisandros, put in the same position earlier, had been a disaster, "a lover of honour and firm in spirit, but incapable of organisation",[62] and he proceeded to lose the battle of Knidos. The kings are not the only source of patronage. In 389, though there is no criticism of Derkyllidas' conduct,[63] Anaxibios, since the ephors are friends of his, gets himself sent as harmost to Abydos.[64] Occasional glimpses of successful individuals show us careers where not only ability, but hereditary connexions will play a part.[65]

---

[59] X. *Ages.* 4.5.

[60] Plut. *Ages.* 21.1.

[61] X. *Hell.* V 1.3-4.

[62] X. *Hell.* III 4.29.

[63] But it will be recalled that Derkyllidas' record is neither orthodox nor immaculate.

[64] X. *Hell.* IV 8.32.

[65] I take two cases, which both happen to illustrate the fact that the kind of career which consists of being given jobs need not at first pass through the ephorate. (1) Endios' ephorate of 413/2 (Thuc. VIII 6.3; his alleged second ephorate of 404/3, X. *Hell.* II 3.1, depends on emendation) comes seven years after he appears on the stage at Thuc. V 44.3. That appearance is no doubt due to the fact that he belongs to the category of Athens-experts (Mosley, *TAPA* 96, 1965, 256-7, *Envoys and Diplomacy in Ancient Greece* (1973) 50-1), but that expertise is presumably in its turn a by-product of a birth high enough to have brought the family international connections with the house of Alcibiades of Athens (Thuc. VIII 6.3). It is not surprising that, in a year when he is ephor as well, he becomes one of the very few ephors or indeed private Spartans who is credited with the possibility of competing in τιμή with a king (Thuc. VIII 12.2). (2) Antalkidas is not ephor until 370/69 (Plut. *Ages.* 32.1), 23 years after his first major diplomatic mission. To give him a family requires manipulation which perhaps goes beyond the evidence but not, I think, beyond the realities of Spartan life. If all the Leons of the period are the same, his father won an Olympic victory in 440 (Eustath. ad Hom. Il. II 852), was oikist of Heraklea in 426 (Thuc. III 92.5) and ephor in 419/8 (X. *Hell.* II 3.1) and his brother was the Pedaritos of Thucydides VIII; the cause for suspicion is the Leon who succeeds Pedaritos in 411 (Thuc. VIII 61.2).

I turn now to the political institutions through which this complex society took its political decisions. I shall be attempting to see what features may account for instability of policy and where ultimate power may lie. Here there has been recent disagreement between Andrewes[66] and De Ste Croix[67] which has focussed the issues more sharply. Part of the difficulty is caused by Aristotle, since it is unclear how far in the *Politics* he is talking about his own day and how far about the past. It is also unfortunate that the main passage[68] is not even trying to be a balanced account of how the Spartan constitution actually works, but is rather reviewing the main criticisms which can be made of that constitution and of those of Crete and Carthage; some of what he has to say about Sparta is in rather obscurely phrased comparison with the other two. Fortunately there is a good deal of material to be derived from actual practice; Xenophon is particularly helpful here.

The main point in dispute is originally an Aristotelian point. Aristotle lays substantial weight on the *gerousia*, the council of 28 men over 60 years of age, elected for life by acclamation, and suggests that he thought that the assembly was of no great account. Andrewes pointed out that the historical sources, by contrast, have very little to say about the *gerousia*, but do have quite a lot to say about the assembly and frequently speak as if its view was decisive. De Ste Croix has done much to restore the importance of the *gerousia* by putting weight on its actual or likely importance in the case of political trials,[69] and I have no wish to modify this picture substantially. Strictly, this will only give the *gerousia* a voice over actions already past and does not tell us much about its role in initiating action, but of course it does make the likely attitude of the *gerousia* a matter of some importance. As far as the assembly goes,[70] De Ste Croix draws attention to the fact that, in the assemblies collected by Andrewes, most of the speeches are made by foreign ambassadors; there is only one case where a Spartan speaker is named who cannot instantly be shown to occupy an

---

[66] *The Government of Classical Sparta* in *Studies* .... *Ehrenberg* (1966) 1-20.
[67] *OPW*, passim.
[68] *Pol.* 1269-1271.
[69] *OPW* 132-6 with Appendices XXV-XXVI.
[70] *OPW* 126-31.

official position.[71] He holds that, despite the evidence apparently provided by the Great Rhetra,[72] the Spartan assembly had no power of spontaneous amendment to a motion put before it, still less of initiative, the ability to put a new motion forward, and that individual Spartiates had no power to speak. They could do so only if they were kings, ephors or *gerontes* or were invited to do so by the presiding ephor. His view then is that, as a general rule, there was no doubt about what the assembly would decide, since the issue had been decided in advance by the most prominent men, in fact, as we shall go on to see, generally by a king. If we want to seek the sources of Spartan policy, we should not be looking in the assembly. The prominence of foreign ambassadors in our sources for assemblies is due to the fact that they alone had a real chance of influencing the assembly because they might have some new proposals or unfamiliar arguments to put forward.[73]

This last point seems to me to be an admission which in fact destroys a large part of De Ste Croix's case. If what the foreign ambassadors are putting forward is identical with the proposal put before the assembly by the authorities, then it cannot be said that they are influencing policy by influencing the assembly; they are only supporting what, for De Ste Croix, has already been decided. If what the foreign ambassadors put forward and the assembly accepts is not in line with the official proposal, it is inescapable that the assembly must have some powers of amendment or initiative. I see one clear case along these lines, the assembly addressed by Alcibiades in 415/4 when the Spartans are wondering what to do about the Athenian invasion of Sicily.[74] Thucydides tells us what the official view was.[75] The ephors and οἱ ἐν τέλει (and whatever that means,[76] it is a fair equivalent for De Ste Croix's 'most prominent men') were intending to send ambassadors to Syracuse to counsel resistance but were not eager to send assistance themselves. We

---

[71] Prothoos in X. *Hell.* VI 4.2 (cf. Plut. *Ages.* 28.6) before the Leuctra campaign. Nothing else is known of him, and there is no foundation for the guess of Poralla (*Prosopographie der Lakedaimonier*, 1913, 110, 169) that he was an ephor at the time.

[72] Plut. *Lyc.* 6-7, cf. Andrewes, op. cit., n. 24. I do not fully understand the objections of De Ste Croix, *OPW* 128 n. 103.

[73] *OPW* 129.

[74] Thuc. VI 88-93.

[75] VI 88.10.

[76] Andrewes' notes on Thuc. V 27.2 and 77.1 will be found clearer on this ambiguous phrase than Dover's note here.

then get Alcibiades' advice: Syracuse should be helped, Attica should be invaded and Decelea fortified. After the speech, we are told that the Spartans, which is certainly a wider expression than that we had before, had been previously intending to invade Attica, but were delaying and considering. As a result of Alcibiades' speech they paid attention to the fortification of Decelea and to immediate help for Sicily, though not much is actually done except the appointment of Gylippos as commander to consider, along with the Corinthians and Syracusans, what practical steps should be taken to provide that help. It would appear that the result of this assembly, at any rate, was a shade different from the previous views of the ephors and οἱ ἐν τέλει and the possibility that some amendment came out of the assembly seems very strong. There is a further possibility, that there are more cases than one might suppose where the assembly had been given no positive recommendation, a possibility already suggested by Andrewes [77] for the assembly of 432 which decided whether to make war on Athens, where nothing is said of a formal motion before the assembly. This assembly is a nice case anyway. It is, I find, positively worrying that the most fully-described of all Spartan assemblies should have eventually to be described by De Ste Croix [78] as having taken place in an atmosphere which was altogether exceptional.

I am not of course arguing that the views of the most prominent men are unimportant to the assembly, and I know of no evidence to speak of which confutes De Ste Croix's view of who was allowed to speak in the assembly. Finley [79] does well to put the question "Can we imagine that the obedient, disciplined Spartan soldier dropped his normal habits on those occasions when he was assembled not as a soldier but as a citizen, while he listened to debates among those from whom he otherwise was taught to take orders without criticism or hesitation?" and to offer the guess that the function and psychology of the Spartan assembly was much closer to the Homeric than to the Athenian. It is further likely that the assembly did not have nearly as much regular business referred to it as in Athens, even allowing for the much greater complexity of administration at Athens. But, however true it is that decisions were often taken within the Spartan leadership, it is obvious that that

---

[77] Op. cit. (note 66) 4.
[78] *OPW* 130.
[79] *Sparta* 152-3.

leadership was sometimes split. "When the leadership was divided over policy, someone had to make the decision, and that was the *damos*".[80] At that point, not only personal allegiances, but argument, rational or irrational, must have come into play.

I take here one further instance which has a bearing both on the assembly's power of initiative and on its habits of deference. In the summer of 418 the Spartan army found itself in a position, as it seemed, to inflict a major defeat on its old enemy Argos, but King Agis preferred to embark on diplomacy rather than a battle. The Spartans and their allies followed him home because of the law, that is, the law that a Spartan king is supreme in the field, but were very dissatisfied with his conduct.[81] After they had got home, news came in which seemed to show that his policy was wrong. The Spartans became even crosser and considered immediately in anger against their character the possibility of demolishing his house and fining him 100,000 drachmai.[82] Agis requested them not to do these things, at least until he had had the opportunity of redeeming his conduct. They held back on the fine and the demolition, but passed a law which involved some restrictions on his powers as commander.[83] The passage raises difficulties for De Ste Croix's views both of the *gerousia* as the only body which could try the king and of the unimportance of the assembly, and his treatment of it is uncertain.[84] He makes an effort to introduce the *gerousia* into the story, but it seems clear to me that, if the Spartans are passing a law, we are dealing with the assembly, and I cannot really believe that Thucydides' language allows of anything else throughout the whole episode. Who was doing the speaking and proposing, I do not know. On the face of it, this is a major manifestation of popular sentiment, frustrated at being robbed of a victory to no avail.[85]

---

[80] Finley, loc. cit.

[81] Thuc. V 60.2, cf. 63.1.

[82] Gomme points out that the Attic equivalent would be over 23 talents, and this is a figure higher than most Athenian estates of the time. (The figure recurs at Plut. *Pel.* 6.1 for the fine on Phoibidas; the 15-talent fine on Pleistoanax of Ephorus *FGH* 70 F 193 could be a rounding of 16 2/3 Aeginetan talents.). Doubtless, as Andrewes says, ad loc., the fine was not meant to be payable, cf. Plut. *Per.* 22.3, D.S. XV 27.3. Passages on fines at Sparta (not including this one) in Kahrstedt 325.

[83] Thuc. V 63.2-4.

[84] *OPW* 133, 351.

[85] For the point at issue, see Busolt *GG* III 1241, Andrewes, *HCT* IV 89. It is agreed between them that Agis' main motive will be the possibility of achieving the main object of Spartan policy, the detachment and neutrali-

As I have said, Aristotle did not think the assembly very important. For him it is the ephorate which is the democratic part of the constitution and of such excessive importance that it has turned aristocracy into democracy.[86] It controls the greatest affairs, it has tyrannical powers. Unlike the *gerousia*, ephors are elected from everybody, so that very poor persons are often elected, and it is this power and universal eligibility which satisfies the *demos* with the constitution. About the powers of the ephorate there can be no doubt. Andrewes [87] has collected the material which shows that decisions to call up even allied contingents for war and instructions to commanders in the field, not necessarily all originated by them, are normal functions of the ephorate, and we should add a fair amount of jurisdiction as well.[88]

Although De Ste Croix accepts Andrewes' statement about the powers of the ephorate, he tends to devalue the ephorate as well as the assembly.[89] His main reason is the difficulty of finding many names of people who held it, and he says that there was a contrast between the great powers of the office and the often insignificant people who held it. These insignificant people are unlikely to get very far against strong kings. This is an acceptable proposition, but,

---

sation of Argos (cf. Thuc. V 36.1, 41.3), without a battle. Busolt's further guesses, that a hard-fought battle might damage the prestige of the kingship and that Agis wished to settle the matter without a clash with Athens, are without much foundation. There were in fact no Athenians present, as Agis could have found during the negotiations, had he not known earlier. The 'hereditary general' does seem to be engaged in diplomatic thinking, but the failure to consult the allies cannot be described as anything but tactless, and I doubt whether he can ever have had enough prestige to impose his solution. It is clearly not unreasonable that the general Spartan feeling should be that, after the troubles of the last seven years which have tarnished their military reputation, what was really needed, for their own self-respect and their own reputation, was a really big military victory (cf. Thuc. VI 11.6).

[86] *Pol.* 1270 b 6-1271 a 8.

[87] Op. cit. (note 66) 10-14.

[88] κρίσεών εἰσι μεγάλων κύριοι (Arist. *Pol.* 1270 b 28), not much emphasised by De Ste Croix in the main text of *OPW*, but see 350, 352-3 and add the important discussion of the Vatican palimpsest of Theophrastus by Keaney, *TAPA* 104, 1974, 189-91, who makes a strong case for preliminary enquiry (ἀνάκρισις) being a function of the ephors even in cases where ultimate decision lies with the *gerousia*. It should be emphasised that, according to Paus. III 5.2, the ephors join the *gerousia* for the trial of kings and their five votes were decisive on the occasion recorded there (the trial of king Pausanias in 403/2).

[89] *OPW* 148-9.

since we could also define strong kings in terms of their ability to
enforce their will even on the ephors, not a very helpful one. We
have, I hope, moved for ever out of the long phase in which Spartan
history was viewed as a perpetual tug-of-war between kings and
ephors.[90] There is no such thing as an ephorate policy, since not all
ephors of the same year need agree on policy,[91] still less ephors of
successive years.[92] There still seems to me to be scope for a view by
which the ephorate is of major importance, at least in part because
it is not permanent and is therefore more likely to be produced by
and to be sensitive to the changing views of the *demos* as a whole.
It may come as a surprise in view of the extensive scholarly literature on the Athenian elections of generals during the Peloponnesian
War, but Thucydides never thinks a change of Athenian generals
by election worthy of mention [93] but does once draw attention to
the importance for policy of a change of composition in the board of
ephors.[94] Aristotle says that something should be done about the
method of election which is excessively childish.[95] This is what he
says about election to the *gerousia* as well.[96] For this we do know
the method [97] and the two were probably the same. Candidates
came before the assembly one by one and were greeted by shouts.
Judges, removed from view, recorded the loudness of the shouts.
Despite De Ste Croix's view that the system shows how un-
democratic the Spartan assembly was,[98] we should perhaps consider

[90] Dickins, *JHS* 32, 1912, 1-42 is the classic statement of this view.
[91] X. *Hell.* II 4.29 (Pausanias persuades three ephors only, but this is
enough; De Ste Croix compares II 3.34). Cf. Hamilton, *AJP* 91, 1970, 308-9.
[92] The ephors of 422/1 swear to the Peace of Nikias (Thuc. V 19.2) and
to the alliance which follows (Thuc. V 24.1); two of the ephors of 421/0 are
opposed to it (Thuc. V 36.1).
[93] Depositions are another matter.
[94] V 36.1. ἔτυχον is a Thucydidean mannerism with no necessary implication of chance, cf. Gomme, *HCT* III 488-9. In the Syracusan case
(VI 103.4) the deposition is more important than those newly elected. I am
speaking only of Thucydides' attitude and am not myself denying that
Athenian and Syracusan elections were sometimes of importance.
Hamilton, *AJP* 91, 1970, 303, 306, 311, attaches importance to the
elections of 404 and 403, though they are for him an anomaly in the general
situation by which elections give the Spartans a chance to choose between
ephors committed to one king or another (295). In Chapter Four we shall
have occasion to consider the change of ephors in 412.
[95] *Pol.* 1270 b 27.
[96] *Pol.* 1271 a 10.
[97] Plut. *Lyc.* 26.3-5.
[98] *OPW* Appendix XXIV.

that the anonymity of the system might have made it relatively
free from external pressures; Athenian elections were not conducted by secret ballot either. When Sthenelaidas, abnormally,
asked the assembly of 432 to divide themselves physically rather
than shout, his aim was not to expose the size of his majority [99]
but to apply moral pressure to possible waverers.[100] De Ste Croix
is doubtless right to suggest that, in normal circumstances, known
allegiance of a candidate to a king or a powerful person might be of
use to him, but the only evidence of royal manipulation of the
choice is third-century.[101] There is perhaps one good example to
show that elections might be particularly influenced by enthusiasms
of the moment. In 431 Brasidas saved Methone in Messenia from
the Athenian fleet and for this gallant action was the first person
in the war to be praised in Sparta.[102] Since the eponymous ephor
who entered office in September 431 was called Brasidas,[103] it seems
captious to deny that it is the same man.[104] Whether this is real
evidence for the independence of the assembly's judgement, I do
not know.[105] [106]

---

[99] So Gomme ad Thuc. I 87.2.

[100] For φανερῶς Classen-Steup rightly compare Thuc. IV 74.3 (on which
Gomme, rightly this time, adds X. *Hell.* II 4.9, to which Lys. XIII 37 is
relevant). 'Er wollte die Zustimmenden durch das Gefühl ihrer Majorität
ermutigen, die Abgeneigten durch die Überzahl der Gegner terrorisieren.'

[101] Plut. *Agis* 8.1 διαπραξάμενος ὁ Ἆγις ἔφορον γενέσθαι τὸν Λύσανδρον in
the same language as Agesilaos' arranging for Teleutias to become nauarch
(Plus. *Ages.* 21.1).

[102] Thuc. II 25.2. The language suggests some formal institutionalised
ἔπαινος, for which I know of no Spartan parallel (Thuc. VIII 28.2, cited by
Classen-Steup, seems totally irrelevant).

[103] X. *Hell* II 3. 10.

[104] The connection is very rarely made. I have not found it before Poralla,
op. cit. (note 71) s.v.

[105] That Brasidas' relations with the πρῶτοι were bad later (Thuc. IV
108.6-7) has of course no bearing on whether he would be an acceptable
'official' candidate in 431. He is already of a position to hold minor command
before this. That his father Tellis seems to appear among the negotiators
of the Peace of Nikias (Thuc. V 19.2; Andrewes and Lewis, *JHS* 77, 1957,
177-80) is capable of various interpretations; neither his social status nor
his political attitude could be safely deduced.

[106] I have nothing to add on the question of whether the ephorate could
be repeated. De Ste Croix (*OPW* 148) simply assumes that it could not, and
Kahrstedt's view (162) that it could rests on emendation (cf. note 65 on
Endios). It suffices to say that Agesilaos' attempt in 241 to stand again
immediately (Plut. *Agis* 16.3) is revolutionary in character and that it at
least occurred to no one before him to turn the ephorate into a permanent
power-base. The problem is purely theoretical.

I turn now to the position of the two kings. It seems relatively clear that Aristotle [107] is to some extent misleading and that he substantially undervalues at least the potentialities of the position, no doubt, as De Ste Croix says,[108] because the kings of his adult life were of no great quality. A king is permanently there, unless he gets into serious trouble. No doubt he has some kind of inherited *clientela* and possibly has the opportunity of creating more by patronage.[109] He is certainly in a position to acquire considerable prestige and *auctoritas*, as is demonstrated above all by Agesilaos. It seems to be largely Agesilaos who forms De Ste Croix's view of the influential nature of the Spartan kingship.[110] It may however be doubted whether Agesilaos is quite as typical as De Ste Croix suggests. Not all Spartan kings had the qualities to enable them to make use of their advantages, and if they failed or departed too far from public policy, they were vulnerable. When De Ste Croix is rehabilitating the *gerousia*, he collects all the material about the trials of kings, but the topic falls curiously into the background when he is contemplating the kingship. Let us consider the fifth century record.[111] 491: Demaratos deposed. C. 490: Kleomenes retires into exile, returns and dies in suspicious circumstances; Leotychidas condemned to humiliating situation. C. 476: Leotychidas deposed. C. 470: Pausanias the Regent dismissed from office and in effect executed. 446: Pleistoanax exiled and deposed for

---

[107] The relevant passages are *Pol.* 1271 a 18-26, 40, 1272 b 38-1273 a 2, 1285 a 3-15, 1285 b 33-37.

[108] *OPW* 138-9. I am in full agreement with De Ste Croix, Appendix XXX, on the qualities of Agis III. For qualifications about Archidamos III, see Thomas, *Historia* 23, 1974, 263-4.

[109] The only appointments known to be formally in the kings' gift are those of proxenoi and the Pythioi (Hdt. VI 57.2), but we have virtually no information about minor military ranks and a king must have some influence about them, at least when in the field. As far as non-Spartiates and allies are concerned, notice the impressive list of volunteers 'wishing to become known to Agesipolis' in X. *Hell.* V 3.9. The kings' jurisdiction about unawarded heiresses and public roads (Hdt. VI 57.4) may occasionally have been of use, but Ar. *Pol.* 1270 a 26-29 suggests that the rights about heiresses did not exist in the fourth century.

[110] *OPW* 138-49. Recent rehabilitation of the kingship starts with Cloché, *Les Études Classiques* 17, 1949, 113-38, 343-81. See also Thomas, *Historia* 23, 1974, 257-70, who, starting from Cloché's groundwork, argues that the successful kings were those who understood Sparta's military needs; despite its date, this article is independent of De Ste Croix. That the kingship was potentially disruptive by definition (Finley, *Sparta* 151) is true, but not relevant to specific situations.

[111] I only give one more recondite reference.

19 years. 418: Agis narrowly escapes disgrace and probable exile.[112]
403: Pausanias acquitted by 19 votes to 15.[113] 395: Pausanias
deposed. Much has been written about the vulnerability of Athenian
strategoi, but they seldom attain this casualty rate. Unlike Athenian
strategoi, Spartan kings have official watchdogs permanently with
them, since they are accompanied in the field by two of the ephors.[114]
De Ste Croix tells us [115] that, in the relationship between kings and
ephors, "both parties must have well known in whose hands the
real, longterm influence lay. An ephor who used his constitutional
powers unwisely against an Agesilaos might find himself, after
the expiry of his year of office, uncomfortably exposed to the retaliation of a man of far greater influence than himself". Agreed, I
think, for an Agesilaos, though I do not happen to know a case
which illustrates the point, but how many Spartan kings were like
Agesilaos?

Let us consider the kingship in Sparta in 432. First the Agiads,
as is their right, since Herodotus surprisingly describes the Eurypontids as the inferior house.[116] Leonidas had died in 480, leaving
an infant son Pleistarchos. Pleistarchos seems to have died in 458
and may not have become adult many years before that date.[117]
From spring 479 to 470 or later [118] his cousin Pausanias was regent,
but for much of his regency he was out of Sparta or in trouble.
However, it is his son Pleistoanax who succeeds Pleistarchos.
Professor White [119] has shown us that he is also young when he
comes to the throne and cannot have reached his majority more
than ten years before his exile in 446/5. His son Pausanias, whenever precisely he was born, was still too young to command in

---

[112] Cf. note 82.

[113] Paus. III 5.2.

[114] X. *Hell.* II 4.36, *Lac. Pol.* 13.5. The fact that in the first passage the
ephors are supporters of Pausanias has perhaps obscured (*OPW* 146) the
threat that the custom posed to a king who failed. Extra 'advisers' could be
attached to kings or nauarchs whose morale was suspect (Thuc. II 85.1,
III 69.1, V 65.4, VIII 39.2) or who were thought unduly young (Plut. *Per.*
22.2).

[115] *OPW* 149.

[116] VI 51.

[117] D.S. XIII 75.1, Paus. III 5.1, Beloch *GG* I 2 175 (where misprints
have affected not only the Diodorus reference but the date of death of the
regent Kleombrotos).

[118] White, *JHS* 84, 1964, 140-52.

[119] Ibid., 141-2.

427.[120] We therefore have the result that, in the 48 years from 480 to 432, the Agiads will not have possessed an adult king for more than fifteen years at the outside and never one of age and experience.

The Eurypontids are superficially much better off, but some points must be borne in mind. The king in 480 is Leotychidas. He had come to the throne 11 years before, but had not been in the direct line of succession. The uncontradicted story in the time of Herodotus [121] was that he owed the throne to a determined coup by Kleomenes, the Agiad king, which had involved the bribery of the Delphic oracle. Shortly after his accession a court found him guilty of *hybris* to allies and handed him over to the Aeginetans in disgrace, though the Aeginetans prudently failed to take him on these terms, but invited him to assist them in a diplomatic mission to Athens in which he failed.[122] His general status in Sparta is determinable from the fact that he plays no part at all in the crisis year 480. The Spartan force which goes to Tempe is commanded by a non-royal polemarch,[123] the Agiad Leonidas goes to Thermopylae, a nauarch commands the fleet. Leonidas' brother Kleombrotos, in his late fifties,[124] supervises wall-building at the Isthmus until he dies of a heart-attack.[125] In 479 the major command, that of the army, goes to the young Pausanias, and Leotychidas is sent off with the fleet. No other Spartan king ever commands a fleet, although Pausanias the regent does next year.[126] I have sometimes wondered whether the nauarchy may not owe its origin to some kind of tabu against the king going to sea and whether Leotychidas' appointment on this occasion does not almost imply that he is not considered a proper king. However this may be, it is clear that he is not given the fleet in 480 when it might matter and that he gets the inferior command in 479.[127] When, at some time in the 470s, he is eventually allowed into the field on an ex-

---

[120] Thuc. III 26.2.

[121] VI 61-72.

[122] Hdt. VI 85-86.

[123] Hdt. VII 173.2.

[124] White, op. cit. (n. 118) 151.

[125] Hdt. VIII 71.1, IX 10.2-3.

[126] White, op. cit., 141 n. 6 holds that it was normal for the Agiad king or regent to be given the more important command unless unsuitable. The principle is nowhere stated and does not easily fit early fourth century practice. It will not explain the failure to employ Leotychidas at all in 480, and White evidently has little faith in it herself (see note 138).

[127] Hdt. VIII 131, IX 10.2.

pedition to Thessaly, he immediately gets into trouble, is condemned for bribery and goes into exile.[128] As De Ste Croix says,[129]
we know virtually nothing of him; that in itself is significant.

He is succeeded by his grandson Archidamos. De Ste Croix tells
us that he is always spoken of with respect.[130] Let us look at the
record. He seems to have had his regnal years counted from 469 [131]
and he was the only Spartan king of age at the time of the helot
revolt, in the context of which he is mentioned several times
(though not by Thucydides), particularly for having had the
presence of mind to have the rally-trumpet blown in the middle of
the earthquake.[132] In 432 he is said to be experienced in many
wars,[133] but in fact we have heard nothing of him for thirty years,
and he is manifestly not heading the major Spartan expeditions
of those years, that of 458 which ended in the battle of Tanagra,
which is commanded by an otherwise unknown Nikomedes, regent
for Pleistoanax,[134] and the invasion of Attica in 446, led so disastrously by Pleistoanax himself. Those of us who believe that the
helot revolt lasted until 455 [135] can explain his absence from the first
by the supposition that he is still sitting on the foothills of Ithome
waiting to starve the helots out.[136] Those who believe that the
Tanagra campaign was directed against Athens from the first [137] can
explain his absence from both by the assumption that he was
credited with being pro-Athenian.[138] The only evidence for his being
pro-Athenian, rather than simply cautious and realistic,[139] is that

---

[128] Hdt. VI 72.2.

[129] *OPW* 141.

[130] Ibid., but n. 138 does not amount to much.

[131] Beloch's conclusions (*GG* I 2 184-7) are impeccable, though the mechanism of error remains doubtful.

[132] Plut. *Cim.* 16.6.

[133] Thuc. I 80.1.

[134] Thuc. I 107.2.

[135] I have long since ceased to believe much of what I said in *Historia* 2,
1953-4, 412-8.

[136] So White, op. cit., 140 n. 3.

[137] Cf. the references in De Ste Croix *OPW* 190 n. 80.

[138] So, at least for 446, Andrewes ap. White, loc. cit., De Ste Croix *OPW*
142. In view of the doctrine developed by White, 141 n. 6 (see note 127), it is
strange that she does not simply say here that the Agiad had prior claim
to command, even though a regent or a young and inexperienced king.

[139] De Ste Croix *OPW* 142 wants us to allow for the possibility that
Archidamos did not really want war with Athens at all when he advocated
delay in 432, but thought it politic to be not entirely frank in public about
this. I do not see how we can know.

he was a *xenos* of Pericles.[140] I have found no speculation anywhere as to how this *xenia* arose, but no speculation is needed; we should only recall that Archidamos' grandfather Leotychidas and Pericles' father Xanthippos were joint commanders of the Greek fleet of 479.[141] It would in any case be a misunderstanding of the nature of *xenia* to suppose that it connoted necessarily approval of the policies of one's *xenos*, let alone of his state.[142]

Thucydides, in introducing Archidamos at the Spartan assembly of 432 which will decide on war with Athens, describes him as a man who seemed to be both intelligent and moderate.[143] I agree with Westlake [144] that Thucydides does not necessarily endorse this statement. I further agree with him[145] that there is much in the speech of Archidamos which follows which Archidamos is unlikely to have formulated himself, but Westlake does not consider how likely it is that Thucydides will have put these thoughts in the mouth of someone of whom he disapproved. On the basis of Book II, Westlake[146] holds that Thucydides had a low opinion of Archidamos in that emphasis is laid on his slowness and that his predictions are always wrong.[147] Westlake eventually hedges considerably and I do not myself think it possible to determine what Thucydides thought of Archidamos' conduct in 431.[148] However, what Thucydides thought of Archidamos is not in point here. I am concerned with what the Spartans thought of Archidamos. I do not see how De Ste Croix can be right in holding Archidamos both to have a position of preponderant influence and to be deeply unwilling to

---

[140] Thuc. II 13.1.

[141] Hdt. VIII 131.2-3.

[142] X. *Hell.* IV 1.34 is the clearest statement of the irrelevance of *xenia* in time of war. *Proxenia* is in general another matter, see Perlman, *CQ* n.s. 8, 1958, 185-91, but even there the proxenos can be the bearer of an unpleasant ultimatum to the state of which he is proxenos (Thuc. V 76.3).

[143] Thuc. I 79.2.

[144] *Individuals in Thucydides* (1968) 6-7, 123.

[145] Ibid., 124-5; cf. Badian ap. Thomas, *Historia* 23, 1974, 267 n. 49.

[146] Ibid., 125-31.

[147] In II 12.1-4, 18.5 he thinks that the Athenians will come to terms before their land is devastated; in 20.5 he thinks that the Athenians will now come cut and that, if they do not, the Acharnians will be less willing to fight in future.

[148] It does occur to me that Thucydides considered himself remarkably well-informed about Archidamos' thinking. I have no explanation for this.

get involved in hostilities with Athens,[149] a dove rather than a hawk. We have no evidence that Archidamos lifted a finger to save Pleistoanax in 445.[150] He was unable or unwilling to stop the summoning of a League Congress to consider war against Athens in 440.[151] He was unable to stop the declaration of war in 432. He was subjected to a barrage of criticism for his conduct of the war in 431,[152] though it must be admitted that he is allowed to continue in command in 430, 429 and 428.

It seems to me that, if we contemplate both royal houses together, Aristotle's generalisation was right for 432 and for a considerable time before. The kings were little more than hereditary generals and there were many other sources of power in the state.[153] After the death of Archidamos in about 428 the kingship will have sunk still lower. No great importance is to be attributed to Agis before 413, and, even after the restoration of Pleistoanax in 427, his position was bitterly controversial.[154] The hereditary general, even if spared final disgrace, is never immune from criticism. The kind of criticism made of Archidamos in 431 recurs for Agis in 418 and, above all, for Kleombrotos in the 370s.[155]

If I argue that the fifth-century kingship was lacking in political influence, it makes the instability of Spartan policy of which Arta-xerxes was complaining in 425 even more understandable. De Ste Croix and Brunt[156] have given more detailed accounts of the ways

---

[149] OPW 138, 142-3, 204-7. I came near to writing that, for De Ste Croix, Archidamos was in favour of Athens-Sparta dualism, but the possibility, adumbrated on p. 138, is treated more cautiously later.

[150] Archidamos does not enter into De Ste Croix's calculations about this trial on p. 199, though even then a mature king with a good military record (p. 197).

[151] 'surely against the will of Archidamos' (OPW 143). I follow the view of Jones, Proc. Camb. Phil. Soc. n.s. 2, 1952-3, 43-6, and De Ste Croix OPW 200-3, that a vote of the Spartan assembly for war preceded the League congress, but notice the interesting dissenting opinion of Adcock in Adcock and Mosley, Diplomacy in Ancient Greece (1975) 40 that Sparta may have summoned a congress merely in order to show loyalty to the Thirty Years' Peace by voting against intervention. The tantalising reference to Pelopon-nesians in ML 56.7 should be kept in mind in this context.

[152] Thuc. II 18.3-5.

[153] The statement of the position by Brunt, Phoenix 19, 1965, 278-80, seems to me essentially correct.

[154] Thuc. V 16.

[155] X. Hell. V 4.16, VI 4.5. The other king of his time was a competent general, which made matters worse for him.

[156] See note 153.

in which Spartan policy varies,[157] and rightly seek the origins of this in party-struggle, the details of which it is seldom possible to ascertain. We should remember that issues which seem to us important may not be those which the Spartans themselves found most interesting. Doubtless in the early 420s they will have found policy about the exiled king Pleistoanax a good deal more engrossing a topic than policy towards Persia. We should also beware of seeking party-struggle everywhere. As Wesley Thompson has recently reminded us,[158] there are many occasions when policy and actions are attributed to the Spartans and there is no reason to assume that their views were anything but unanimous. It may be true that Agesilaos was capable of carrying policy through in defiance of public opinion,[159] though this will have not been common. It is even more likely that the top men kept many issues away from the assembly altogether. Of course we should allow full weight to birth, wealth and experience in the originating of Spartan policies, but we should never neglect the opinions and sentiments of Spartans in general. We should remember that, when the leadership was divided in policy, the assembly will have had a substantial part to play.

[157] I add a gloss. Despite De Ste Croix's general picture of hawks in control of Spartan policy in the run-up to war in 432, he rightly inclines (322) to see a more conciliatory note in the embassy reported by Thuc. I 139.1 (the appearance of Archidamos' influence here, apparently arbitrary, is partly justified by Plut. *Per*. 29.7, though I doubt the presence of genuine tradition in that passage). More evidence for this view can be adduced. The anecdote in Plut. *Per*. 30.1 about the Spartan ambassador Polyalkes who replied to Pericles' assertion that there was a law preventing the repeal (κωλύοντα καθελεῖν) of the Megarian decree with the suggestion that its face could be turned to the wall (στρέψον εἴσω τὸ πινάκιον) is proved to be authentic by the extraordinary word μεταστραφείη applied to the same thing in Ar. *Ach*. 537. (The observation was made at least twice independently in the nineteenth century and appears in the editions of the *Acharnians* by Rennie, Starkie and Van Leeuwen, but seems to have evaded historians.) At least one Spartan embassy is engaged in serious negotiations even after the assembly decision to make war.

[158] *Rivista Storica dell' Antichità* 3, 1973, 47-58.

[159] The obvious case is that of Phoibidas' seizure of the Cadmeia, opposed by the ephors and τῆς πόλεως τὸ πλῆθος (X. *Hell*. V 2.32), but it should be noted that, despite Xenophon's silence on the point, Phoibidas does seem to have been heavily fined (D.S. XV 20.2, Plut. *Pel*. 6.1), though his career was not thereby ended. If, though not an only son, he managed to pay 100,000 drachmai, he was very ὄλβιος indeed. We have no patronymic. I have no opinion as to whether his brother Eudamidas is the eponymous ephor of *IG* V 1.1232.

CHAPTER THREE

When Artaxerxes sent Artaphernes to Sparta, he had been on the throne for forty years, but such evidence as we can muster suggests that he was still only in his late fifties.[1] It is pretty hard to form any coherent picture of him[2] or his main preoccupations, and it is always necessary to consider that Persians may have problems in the east which do not come out in Greek sources. When he came to the throne, the counter-offensive of Xerxes' last years had been resoundingly defeated by Kimon at the Eurymedon. After five years or so, things had gone from bad to worse, and a major Egyptian revolt, supported by Athens, took six years to suppress. We should note that, during this revolt, he had already tried the policy of making trouble for Athens in Greece by sending Megabazos to Sparta with money to persuade the Spartans to invade Attica and make the Athenians withdraw from Egypt;[3] Artaphernes would not have been the first Persian to have been seen in Sparta. The mission was unsuccessful, and Artaxerxes fell back on straight military operations. The Egyptian revolt was suppressed and the Athenian fleet destroyed, leaving Athens in a state of marked weakness for three or four years until Kimon's last Cyprus expedition restored the balance. It seems that at this point both Athens and Persia agreed that there was no point in carrying on. The balance of scholarly opinion and, to my mind, the weight of the evidence is in favour of accepting Diodorus' Peace of Kallias

---

[1] The implication of Ktesias 20 is that Xerxes' marriage follows his accession and that Artaxerxes was the third son. Darius was certainly the eldest son (ibid., and D.S. XI 69.2) and evidently the expected heir (cf. Ktesias 29-30) and, if the principle of Hdt. VII 3, that the heir is the eldest son born after the father's accession, was followed, Artaxerxes can hardly have been born before 482. But that principle is said to be a Spartan one, which does not in fact work very well for Sparta.

[2] His posthumous reputation for πραότης and μεγαλοψυχία, Plut. *Art.* 1.1, 4.4, does not amount to much, and Nepos' source for *De regibus* 1.4 would be more credible in asserting his *amplissima pulcherrimaque corporis forma*, if he did not add his *incredibilis virtus belli* as well; there is no evidence that he ever fought a battle. On the origins of his Greek nickname Μακρόχειρ, nothing has been added to Nöldeke, *RE* II 1312.

[3] Thuc. I 109.2; for a possible identification of Megabazos, see Burn, *Persia and the Greeks* 385, but the name Bakabaduš is common; there are at least three in Hallock *PFT*, of very different social levels.

in 449. I have no objection to a view that the treaty was not fully formalised. There is, for example, no suggestion that Artaxerxes was forced to the formality of oath-taking. But it seems clear that a firm understanding was arrived at. The Athenian decision to commit large resources to a building-programme on the Acropolis which, in general and in detail, carried strong implications of being a victory-dedication can have no other explanation. It is true that we continue to find a good deal of friction between Athens and Persia, but I do not think that the evidence supports a recent view[4] that war broke out again, in a cold form, a year or so after peace was made. What seems to be happening are a number of isolated troubles at a lower level, with the King not necessarily operative. For what the evidence of Ktesias is worth, Artaxerxes has at least one major preoccupation after the peace, the revolt of his commander in Egypt, Megabyxos, the satrap of Syria, and some trouble continues in Egypt.[5] In any case, responsibility for relations with Greeks now devolves in the first instance on the western satraps.

In our period there tend to be two main satraps in western Asia Minor, though occasionally one of them or a third party has special powers. Over what the Persians called something like the People by the Sea[6] and we tend to call Hellespontine Phrygia, is a satrap whose seat is at Daskyleion on the shore of a lake south of Kyzikos; the Greeks sometimes referred to the satrapy by that name.[7] The palace at Daskyleion has been excavated, but not published,[8] apart from the sealings which are all that is left of what must have

---

[4] Eddy, *Class. Phil.* 68, 1973, 241-53.

[5] For Megabyxos, Ktesias 37-39; for Egypt, Thuc. I 112.3, Philochoros *FGH* 328 F 119, Kienitz, *Die politische Geschichte Ägyptens* (1953) 72-3 (the evidence slightly over-pressed). Chronology is difficult. Philochoros is reasonable evidence that trouble in some part of Egypt continues at least until 443, but Wadi-Hammamat in the south is the scene of normal quarrying operations in 450 and 449 (Posener, *La première domination perse en Égypte*, 1936, nn. 32-33); I do not know where Hdt. III 15.3 fits in. No word of these troubles enters the story of Nehemiah, whose first stay in Judah is 445-433. I incline to think that Megabyxos' revolt must be over by 445. It clearly cannot be excluded that some imperial calculation lies behind Nehemiah's mission. Olmstead *HPE* 313-7 sets it and the preceding troubles of Ezra IV 8-23 (for which see Rowley, *Men of God*, 211-45) in the context of Megabyxos' revolt and its failure, but sees Nehemiah as acting against imperial interests; I could spin another story, I think. See Chapter Six note 118.

[6] Schmitt, *Historia* 21, 1972, 522-7.

[7] Hdt. III 120.2, Thuc. I 129.1.

[8] See e.g. J. M. Cook in *Archaeological Reports for 1959-60* 34-5.

been a substantial archive.[9] Reliefs, some long-known and some comparatively recent, illustrate the fusion of Greek and Persian art in the area.[10] The most vivid description is likely to remain that of Xenophon.[11] "Round the palace are many large villages with ample supplies, with excellent hunting-grounds, some in fenced paradises, some in open ground. A river ran round full of all kinds of fish, and there was ample wildfowl for those capable of catching them." Daskyleion became a more or less hereditary satrapy under the descendents of our acquaintance Parnaka, who is, you will recall, of royal blood. Artabazos, his son, took it over after 479, was in charge of negotiations with Pausanias in the 470s [12] and seems to have survived at least until 449.[13] His grandson, Pharnakes son of Pharnabazos, was in office at the end of 430 [14] and is apparently still alive in 414.[15] By 412 he seems to be dead and his son Pharnabazos in control,[16] though we have one reference to the sons of Pharnakes which may suggest a collective period.[17]

There is a marked contrast between this relatively rural satrapy and the other satrapy, based on Sardis. Lydia had, after all, been a substantial kingdom and its institutions and culture continued to some extent.[18] I think we can take it that the satrapy was always more important in the eyes of the King. For one thing, it brought in more revenue [19] and must have controlled considerably larger

---

[9] Balkan, *Anatolia* 4, 1959, 123-8.

[10] Private funerary reliefs: Dupont-Sommer, *CRAI* 1966, 44-58, Cross, *BASOR* 184, 1966, 7-10. A possible satrapal tomb: Bernard, *Rev. arch.* 1969, 1, 17-28.

[11] *Hell.* IV 1 15-16, cf. 33, and Hell. Oxy. 22.3.

[12] Thuc. I 129.1.

[13] D.S. XII 3-4.

[14] Thuc. II 67.1.

[15] Ar. *Birds* 1028-30; his name is evidently familiar in Athens. Was the fertile breed of wild mules imported from Syria to Phrygia by him or only in his time (Arist. *Hist. An.* 580 b 1-9) ? If the former, it would make a good match for the plantbreeding activities of Gadatas (*ML* 12).

[16] Thuc. VIII 6.1. Pharnabazos, older than Agesilaos (X. *Hell.* IV 1.31), was born before 444.

[17] Thuc. VIII 58.1. They are perhaps witnesses rather than office-holders (Krumbholz, *De Asiae Minoris Satrapis Persicis*, Diss. Leipzig 1883, 39 n. 3), but cf. Delaiah and Shelemiah the sons of Sanballat governor of Samaria, Cowley *AP* 30.29. Pharnabazos' only known brother Bagaios is illegitimate (X. *Hell.* III 4.13, Plut. *Alc.* 39, Nep. *Alc.* 10).

[18] Cf. Arr. I 17.4.

[19] If we look at the financial *nomoi* of Hdt. III 90, Daskyleion will not contribute all that much to the 360 talents of the third *nomos*, whereas Sardis will control, not only all the 500 talents of the second *nomos*, but what

resources. An independent satrap of Sardis, Oroites, had caused Darius considerable trouble at the beginning of his reign and had had to be removed by stealth.[20] Possibly for this reason, we find from time to time that the Sardis garrison is independent of the satrap and its commander responsible directly to the King.[21] There was a fair-sized Persian settlement in Sardis as early as the Ionian revolt,[22] and a very recent inscription now attests a cult of Ahura-mazda there of some exclusivity.[23] The probability is that Sardis is the normal residence or urban centre for Persians who have royal land-grants in Lydia. We have no details of these for the Persian period in Lydia, but I doubt if they will have looked much different from a substantial estate in the area which happens to be attested for the Hellenistic period [24] and which comprised a large village and a separate group of three villages, worth nearly as much, together with various smaller villages and *kleroi*, the peasants, their household, their belongings, and various rights to produce and labour-service.

These large estates, entailing, no doubt, some feudal obligations,

---

remains after 449 of the 400 talents of the first *nomos*. (I fear I do not share the belief of Altheim and Stiehl, *Die Aramäische Sprache unter den Achaimeniden* I, 1963, 132-7, that they have disproved the documentary basis of this list; for their howler about Hdt. V 49.6, see Murray, *Historia* 15, 1966, 147 n. 22).

[20] Hdt. III 126-128.

[21] For a generalised statement about the separation of garrison-commanders from satrapies, see X. *Cyr.* VIII 6.1-14; the dependence of garrisons on the King seems to be a general feature of the account in *Oec.* 4.5-11, but problems are caused there by the doubtful reference of the last sentence about the satrap. It should not, I think, be expected that all garrisons are dependent on the King, and we shall be lucky if our sources have occasion to mention that they are. I note the royal garrison at the Cilician gates in 401 (X. *Anab.* I 4.4) and a royal appointee at Miletos in 334 (Arr. I 18.4), and there may be more. As far as Sardis itself is concerned, Artaphernes the satrap seems to be holding the acropolis himself in 498 (Hdt. V 100), but at the end of the century we find it held by Orontas, of royal blood, taking his orders direct from the King (X. *Anab.* I 6.1, 6). In 334 Mithrenes is *phrourarchos* of the acropolis and in a position to hand over the treasury as well (Arr. I 17.3; Spithridates had been satrap of Lydia, I 16.3); Alexander also separates the garrison-command from the satrapy, I 17.7. It cannot, of course, be excluded that the institution of a separate command of the Sardis garrison is occasioned by the revolt of Pissouthnes rather than that of Oroites.

[22] Hdt. V 101, VI 4. It is not clear how they are related to Oroites' body-guard of 1000 Persians (Hdt. III 127-128).

[23] Robert, *CRAI* 1975, 306-30.

[24] *Sardis* VII i no. 1 (cf. Atkinson, *Historia* 21, 1972, 45-74).

and their fortified castles, will have been common in western Asia Minor,[25] and their owners are collectively described in 498 as the Persians who dwell within the river Halys.[26] But these holdings are not confined to Persians. We hear of Assyrians and Hyrcanians as well[27] and also of various Greeks who have rendered good service to the King. Themistocles' cities are the most familiar,[28] but there is also the family of Gongylos the Eretrian at the mouth of the Kaikos valley [29] and that of the exiled Spartan king Demaratos further up it.[30] The best-known later grant is that to Memnon in the Troad.[31] It is not clear how far these estates had to contribute their share of the royal tribute. I see no reason to doubt that at any rate the bulk of them did, but there is little direct evidence.[32]

---

[25] The foundation for their study was laid by Rostovtseff, *Studien zur Geschichte des römischen Kolonates* (1910) 240 ff. and in *Anatolian Studies . . . . Ramsay* (1923) 372-5. Some references collected by De Ste Croix *OPW* 37-9 and by Lane Fox, *Alexander the Great* (1973) 515-6. Rostovtseff and Lane Fox rightly lay stress on Asidates' large estate in the Kaikos valley plundered by Xenophon (X. *Anab.* VII 8). No doubt many landowners were absentees (X. *Cyr.* VIII 6.5).

[26] Hdt. V 102.1. Cf. the apparently wider phrase πάντες ὅσοι εἰς Καστωλοῦ πέδιον ἀθροίζονται (X. *Anab.* I 1.2, cf. 9.7, *Hell.* I 4.4).

[27] Also in the Kaikos valley (X. *Anab.* VII 8.15).

[28] Thuc. I 138. 5, Plut. *Them.* 29.5-11.

[29] X. *Hell.* III 1.6 (Gambreion, Palaegambreion, Myrina, Gryneion). The discussion in *ATL* III 200-2 overlooks X. *Anab.* VII 8.8 which makes it possible that Gongylos had lived at Pergamon rather than at Gambreion, even though Pergamon technically belonged to the family of Demaratos (see note 30). The families are obviously intimately associated in 400 and shortly after (X. *Anab.* VII 8.17, *Hell.* III 1.6) and there is clear evidence that they intermarried at least once (*SIG*³ 381, cf. Durrbach, *Choix d'inscriptions de Délos*, 1921, 21-3).

[30] X. *Hell.* III 1.6 (Pergamon, Teuthrania, Halisarna), cf. *Anab.* II 1.3, 2.1, VII 8.17. The earlier *Anab.* references explain their later behaviour; deeply committed to Cyrus, they do not rate their chances of making their peace with Artaxerxes very high; unlike Ariaios, who managed it, they were after all Greeks. They disappear from the scene when Agesilaos arrives. Proud of their ancestry (they were named Eurysthenes and Prokles), they will not have forgotten that his great-grandfather had usurped their family's throne. Later a member of the family married Aristotle's daughter (Sext. Emp. I 258), a shocking mésalliance. Herodotus (II 10.1) knows the Kaikos valley as Teuthrania and had surely passed this way, to learn much from the Demaratid family tradition (Jacoby, *RE* Suppl. II 412, cf. 442-3 etc.). For coins of both families, see Babelon, *Monnaies grecques et romaines* II 79-98.

[31] Arr. I 17.8, Str. XIII 1.11, Polyaen. IV 3.15. For a fifth-century case further east, cf. Amyntas the Macedonian at 'Alabanda' in Phrygia (Hdt. VIII 136.1).

In any case, their security will be a major concern of the satrap.[33]

There is a long gap in our evidence about the satrapy of Sardis, but we find it in 440 under the control of Pissouthnes son of Hystaspes.[34] On the face of it, he is even closer to the throne than Pharnakes of Daskyleion, since his father should be the Hystaspes who commanded the Bactrians in 480, full brother of Xerxes, son of Darius and Atossa.[35]

We should not, I think, consider these satraps as in full control of territory contiguous to each other and tied to the rest of the empire in a tight provincial system like that of the Roman empire. That is not true even in the centre of the empire, where, three days' march outside Susa on the way to Persepolis, there were, at any rate in the fourth century,[36] mountaineers who regularly levied a tribute from the King on his way through.[37] The two satrapies

---

[32] The Seleucid estate of note 24 had by that time a regular tribute-assessment. Both this case and that of the Coan settler in Caria who is granted, while the Achaemenid empire still exists, exemption from all taxation except τὰ βασιλικὰ τέλη (*Labraunda* III 2 no. 42) would be more helpful if the origins of the holdings were clearer. The new text from Lagina (*Anatolia* 17, 1973, 190) is very obscurely worded, but it is likely that the exemption from all taxation except the φόροι βασιλικοί applies to some ground which has just been dedicated.

Note also Zenis of Dardanos and his wife Mania, 'satraps' of Pharnabazos in 'his' Aeolis. They are certainly dependent on him and tribute-paying, which does not stop them being very wealthy, X. *Hell.* III 1.10-28. But there is no suggestion of a royal grant here.

[33] Eventually the vested interests of their owners formed a serious obstacle to the conduct of operations against Alexander's invasion (Arr. I 12. 9-10 with the comments of Lane Fox, *Alexander the Great* 118-9, but see also D.S. XVII 18.3 for another, perfectly credible, motive, that Memnon's scorched earth policy was unworthy of Persian μεγαλοψυχία; a similar disagreement about the proper way for Persians to make war seems to underlie Hdt. IX 41.3-4).

[34] Thuc. I 115.4.

[35] Hdt. VII 64.2. If D.S. XI 69.2 is right to assert that there was a Hystaspes son of Xerxes in Bactria in 465 (see Chapter One note 96), Pissouthnes could be his son, which would reduce his age considerably.

[36] I see no trace of difficulty about the Susa-Persepolis road in *PFT*, where small parties are frequent and armed escorts have not yet been identified, even for apparently valuable goods (e.g. *PF* 1357). Other roads may have been more dangerous; cf. the 31 men needed to take the 'tax of Udana' from Barrikana to Susa in *PF* 1495. In the light of what will be said about conditions in Asia Minor, notice the relatively large size of parties originating in Sardis (35 in *PF* 1404, 13 in *PF* 1455); but one party going to Sardis is only 3 in number (*PF* 1321).

[37] Arr. III 17.2. This slur on the Persian monarchy does not appear in D.S. XVII 67 or Q.C. V 3.

of the west were substantially divided from one another by independent tribes in Mysia.[38] Further south, Pisidians caused the
same trouble. Pharnabazos is credited with frequent campaigns
against them both.[39] The younger Cyrus' first campaign in Asia is
against them [40] and he used the project of an expedition against
them to cover his recruitment of Greek mercenaries and his initial
moves.[41] When Tissaphernes succeeds Cyrus, he is expected to
renew the campaign.[42] Further to the south-east Lykaonia is clearly
totally out of Persian control in 401[43] and Cilicia is not a satrapy,
but a dependent kingdom, normally left to itself, if it does its duty.[44]
Paphlagonia may also be an uncertain quantity,[45] and Pharnabazos'
control of the Bithynian Thracians was clearly not complete.[46]

We have in effect seen why the Royal Road described by Herodotus [47] runs to the north of the desert area of central Anatolia.
It is not the only possible route for armies, as we see from Cyrus'
movements, but we need not doubt that it is the normal route for
communications in the fifth century,[48] probably the only one

---

[38] Hell. Oxy. 21.1 εἰσὶ γὰρ οἱ πολλοὶ τῶν Μυσῶν αὐτόνομοι καὶ βασιλέως
οὐχ ὑπακούοντες, cf. X. Anab. III 2.23 for an assertion of their prosperity and
independence. Some of them may take the side of a stray Persian who
offers them booty, X. Anab. I 6.7. Cf. also X. Mem III 5.26 for both Mysians
and Pisidians.

[39] X. Hell. III 1.13. What Pharnabazos has to do with Pisidia, I cannot
imagine. I doubt Underhill's explanation (ad loc.) that he has been called up
by the karanos, and suspect that Xenophon is carelessly grouping the usual
pair.

[40] X. Anab. I 9.14. He is credited with some success.

[41] X. Anab. I 1.11, 2.1, 4.

[42] X. Anab. II 5.13.

[43] X. Anab. I 2.19 (hostile territory), III 2.23.

[44] Cf. the negotiations, X. Anab. I 2.21-27; D.S. XIV 19.3, 6 (cf. 20.3)
may bear the implication that Syennesis has not yet entered Artaxerxes'
allegiance. The large cavalry garrison of Hdt. III 90.3 has long since disappeared, but it mysteriously plays no part in the year 480 either. The Cilician
contribution in 480 is 100 ships (Hdt. VII 91) and they continue to make
their contribution to the Persian fleet (D.S. XI 60.5, 75.2, 77.1, XII 3.3;
Thuc. I 112.4).

[45] In 395 Otys has declined a summons from the King (X. Hell. IV 1.3,
cf. Anab. V 6.8).

[46] X. Hell. III 2.2.

[47] V 52-54.

[48] But see Ramsay, Historical Geography of Asia Minor (1890) 27-43. I
do not really understand the movements of Alcibiades at the time of his
assassination; cf. Hatzfeld, Alcibiade 344-6, which lacks Arist. Hist. An.
578 b 26. For further thoughts by Ramsay on Persian routes, see JHS 40,
1920, 89-98; for attempts to correct Herodotus, see e.g. Calder, CR 39,
1925, 7-11.

covered by the system of way-stations described by Herodotus and Xenophon [49] and now illuminated by the Persepolis tablets. Communications are crucial to the viability of an empire, and we should be glad to know how fast instructions could get from the King to his satraps. There is some very depressing evidence for the Seleucid empire,[50] but we need not doubt that the Persian post was a great deal more efficient. You will recall that Herodotus' comment "Neither snow nor rain nor heat nor gloom of night stays these couriers from the swift completion of their appointed rounds" has been adopted by the United States Post. The most optimistic calculations that I know for Susa to Sardis bring them within 7 days of each other,[51] but I suspect that this is a little on the low side. That fire-signals made it possible for the Persian King to know on the same day any troubles in the whole of Asia is, I fear, romance of the Roman period.[52]

---

[49] Hdt. VIII 98, X. *Cyr.* VIII 6.17-18.

[50] See the comments of Aymard, *REA* 1949, 340-2 on Robert, *Hellenica* VII p. 7. An edict of Antiochos III made (but where?) before 18 March 193 was published in Phrygia on 6 May and north-west of Susa on 26 June. The gaps are considerable, even though the governors concerned may have been otherwise engaged when the messengers arrived. That local delay was part of the trouble is shown by the third copy, *CRAI* 1967, 283-93, which was sent out on 19 June by the same Menedemos who despatched the copy of 26 June.

[51] Bengtson, *The Greeks and the Persians* (1969) 13. More elaborate calculations giving 8 to 10 days are quoted from Droysen, *Geschichte des Hellenismus*, II 2. 372, by Riepl, *Das Nachrichtenwesen des Altertums* (1913) 194; I have as yet not traced them in any edition of Droysen. Riepl, 188-96, has the richest collection of comparative material, but it will be seen that his sources need checking (the dromedaries which brought death to Parmenio in a third of the usual time are in Str. XV 2.10, not in Diodorus); more summary treatment by Reincke, *RE* XVI 1522-3, 1537-8. For the evidence of the Persepolis tablets, see Hallock, *PFT* p. 6, but I do not think that he need be right to suppose that their comparatively rare references to rations for horses imply that most travellers went on foot. The implication might rather be that horses are part of the road-system and not normally attached to the rider, with their fodder accounted for by such texts as *PF* 1672 or more elaborate journal-texts. In calculating speeds, it should be recalled that both Herodotus and Xenophon are firm that horses are only changed once a day, even though post-stations were a good deal more closely set than this. For the Ptolemaic system, certainly descended from the Persian, which involved regular changes of rider, see P. Hib. 110 = Wilcken, *Chrestomathie* I 2 n. 435 (cf. Preisigke, *Klio* 7, 1907, 241-77).

[52] Arist. *de Mundo* 398 a 11 ff. A thorough discussion by Riepl, op. cit. 46-74. Clearly only the most simple messages would be possible, and Riepl (65) is over-optimistic in saying that the point of origin of the message could be deduced from the signal-line itself. There may be some develop-

Opinions may legitimately differ as to the extent to which satraps could pursue policies without reference to the King and how far they kept the King in close touch with what was going on, and doubtless the position varied from time to time. New arrivals in western Asia Minor tend to arrive with general instructions.[53] We generally hear of specific references to the King when Greeks are told of them. We may suspect some of these of being bluff on the satrap's part, a means of stalling on an unwelcome request,[54] or simply to gain time to work on a predetermined policy.[55] But there is at least one general statement for the fourth century of the propensity of the King's generals to refer even the smallest details to him and await his replies,[56] and we certainly need not doubt that major changes of policy affecting the King's pride or pocket would be regularly referred.[57] At one point, in 392, we shall find Tiribazos reflecting that it would not be safe to change the policy without reference to the King and going to argue the point himself.[58] As it turned out, it was not safe even to raise the point. He lost his command for four years, and the episode does not seem to have been forgotten.[59] We can also safely say that the King's authorisation would be needed to draw on resources outside the satrap's control, particularly if he needed a fleet.[60]

---

ment between Hdt. IX 3.1, when Mardonios may have been hoping to signal the fall of Athens to Sardis (but, as Macan points out, he did not hold the islands; similar messages went to Susa by horse the previous year, Hdt. VIII 54, 98-99), and D.S. XIX 57.5, when Antigonos mobilises with fire-signals and βυβλιαφόροι, but in Persis at the same period they simply shouted across the valleys (D.S. XIX 17.7).

[53] Tissaphernes, Thuc. VIII 5.5, cf. 28.3; Cyrus, X. *Hell.* I 4.3, cf. 5.3; Tithraustes, ibid., III 4.28.

[54] E.g. it seems clear that Tissaphernes in Thuc. VIII 29.1 may be as much trying to save his own money (cf. 45.6) as anything else when he says he will need royal instructions to pay a wage of more than three obols a day.

[55] Agesilaos and Xenophon thought Tissaphernes' offer at X. *Hell.* III 4.5 a clear case of this.

[56] D.S. XV 41.5.

[57] Hdt. V 31.4; the King's consent needed for the attack on Naxos. X. *Hell.* I 3.8 ff.; Pharnabazos agrees that an Athenian embassy shall go to the King; ibid. III 2.20; Derkyllidas, Tissaphernes and Pharnabazos kave worked out the makings of an agreement.

[58] X. *Hell.* IV 8.16.

[59] D.S. XV 8.4, 10.2. I doubt if there is more than rumour behind the assertion of XV 9.4-5 that his son-in-law Glos did come to some arrangement with the Spartans in the 380s, accepted uncritically by Judeich, *Kleinasiatische Studien* (1892) 190.

[60] Cf. e.g. Thuc. VIII 87.5, without going into the tangled story of the origins of Konon's fleet in the 390s.

To return to the period after the Peace of Kallias, there is really no evidence [61] that the northern satrapy made any trouble for Athens before 412, although Pharnakes is prepared to assist Spartan ambassadors in 430 [62] and provide a home for Delians exiled by Athens in 422.[63] It seems to me particularly noticeable that possible Persian help does not seem to come into the calculations of Mytilene in her revolt in 428/7.[64]

But even before the Peloponnesian War begins, Pissouthnes' behaviour is a good deal more equivocal. The Samian exiles in 440 who wish to overthrow the democracy newly imposed by Athens are said by Thucydides to have an alliance with Pissouthnes,[65] and at the least Pissouthnes accepts the custody of the Athenian garrison and magistrates when the revolt is temporarily successful. It is clear that Persia is a factor in Athenian calculations in 440, and Athenian naval movements are partly dictated by a succession of rumours that the Phoenician fleet is on its way.[66] Nothing in fact seems to have happened,[67] and to my mind one source gives a

---

[61] Eddy, *Class. Phil.* 68, 1973, 247-51, presses too hard scattered evidence about absences from the tribute-lists in the 40s, and attempts to bring back the casualty-list *ML* 48 to 440 on the ground that this is the only year in which deaths can have occurred at Byzantion. But Meiggs has explained how there could have been deaths at Byzantion in 447 (*The Athenian Empire* 161) and I do not see how the casualties in the Chersonese fit 440; the Chersonese tribute is unaffected in that year. Bradeen, *CQ* n.s. 19, 1969, 152 n. 7, found Meiggs' dating plausible.

[62] Thuc. II 67.1.

[63] Thuc. V 1.1.

[64] Pharnakes does not do anything visibly for the Mytilenaean exiles at Antandros either (Thuc. IV 52, 75).

[65] Thuc. I 115.4. Eddy, op. cit., 250 with n. 51, following D.S. XII 27.3, holds that the 700 mercenaries raised by the exiles are a present from Pissouthnes and that there is unimpeachable evidence that Persia acted against Athens and broke the treaty. "Foreigners could scarcely obtain troops in the satrap's territory without the satrap's consent." There is no evidence that these mercenaries came from Pissouthnes' territory, and I do not think it sound method to expand Thucydides by Diodorus when there is no other evidence in the chapter of anything but paraphrased Thucydides. Pissouthnes will surely have been more careful than that to begin with. Notice Plut. *Per.* 25.3: Pissouthnes tries to buy Pericles off imposing democracy on Samos.

[66] Thuc. I 116.1, 3.

[67] *Contra* Eddy "It appears that their navy made a demonstration along the Phaselis line, or even to the west of it, to draw Athenian triremes away from Samos." D.S. XII 27.5 and the πλεῖστοι of Plut. *Per.* 26.1 also believe in the fleet.

positive statement that Pericles found no fleet.[68] If there had been a fleet, we could, as I have just said, hardly acquit the King of complicity, but the timetable is very tight and this would have been by far the fastest Phoenician naval mobilisation on record.[69] Something will certainly have to have been done after the failure of the revolt to recover the Athenians in Pissouthnes' hands, and it is possible that some minor rectification of the Peace of Kallias followed.[70]

If the Phoenician navy is not certainly visible, other ships coming from Phoenicia are. In winter 430/29 we find the Athenians attempting to protect from piracy a trade-route from Phaselis, Phoenicia and the mainland in that direction,[71] and the existence of a Phoenicia-Athens trade in dates and *semidalis* (fine wheat-flour) is taken for granted by a contemporary comic poet.[72] Readers of Hippocrates would know that *semidalis*, like groats, when

---

[68] Kallisthenes FGH 124 F 16 ap. Plut. *Cim.* 13.4, where Pericles sails with 50 ships beyond the Chelidonians and finds no barbarian fleet, is normally attributed to the 460s (e.g. Meiggs, *The Athenian Empire* 79 n. 1). I find it impossible to believe that Pericles was general in the 460s, and the difference between Kallisthenes' 50 ships and Thucydides' 60 is hardly important. So Wade-Gery, *Essays* 203 n. 2.

[69] It will not be disputed, I think, that the rumour of the fleet is at its strongest in early summer 440, the year in which Thucydides puts the start of the episode. Can we really believe that it took so little time for Pissouthnes to refer to Artaxerxes, Artaxerxes to make up his mind and send instructions to Phoenicia, for the Phoenicians to mobilise and arrive ?

[70] There is a strong temptation to connect these events with the Athenian abandonment of eastern Caria in 438 attested by the tribute-lists (*ATL* III 212 n. 79). The cities which disappear cannot be simply disaffected (so Eddy, op. cit., 252), since there is a simultaneous reorganisation of the books of the hellenotamiae which unites the rest of Caria with Ionia. It is clearly possible that there was some deal. Adcock in Adcock and Mosley, *Diplomacy in Ancient Greece*, 39 suggests that the deal was between Pericles and the Phoenician admiral, but I prefer to associate it with discussions about the return of the Athenians.

That an Athenian embassy went to Persia precisely in 437/6 is a most unsafe deduction from Ar. *Ach.* 66, but the embassy of Diotimos to Susa (Damastes *FGH* 5 F 8 ap. Str. I 3.1) ought to belong to the 430s.

Little importance for relations between Athens and Persia attaches to Pericles' Black Sea expedition, even if we could date it (Eddy, op. cit., 252, wrongly asserts that Diodorus dates it to 437/6). The Peace of Kallias prohibited the entry of Persian ships into the Propontis (so rightly Oliver, *Historia* 6, 1957, 254-5), but it is not clear that it prohibited the entry of Athenian ships into the Black Sea, if they kept away from the King's *chora*. Sinope (Plut. *Per.* 20.1) is part of the Persian empire 100 years later (Arr. III 24.4), but there is no suggestion in X. *Anab.* V 5-6 that it has anything to do with the King in 400. Cf. Raubitschek, *GRBS* 5, 1964, 155.

[71] Thuc. II 69.1.

[72] Hermippos F 63.22 K.

boiled, particularly in milk, is strengthening and nourishing, but does not pass at stool; it is therefore good for feverish colic.[73]

When the war breaks out, Pissouthnes has more opportunities. Thucydides' approach is curiously backward. In 427 the Ionian exiles and Lesbians who are trying to put some guts into the Spartan admiral Alkidas after his failure to relieve Mytilene advocate the seizure of a coastal city and think it possible to persuade Pissouthnes to join in the war.[74] No reason is given for expecting Pissouthnes to be helpful, but one shortly emerges.[75] We discover that Kolophon has been taken in spring 430 by Itamenes and barbarians who had been brought in in a *stasis* there. Itamenes is unexplained, but he is evidently Persian [76] and a subordinate of Pissouthnes. The Kolophonians have fled to Notion and gone into *stasis* again there. One group has acquired Arcadian and barbarian mercenaries from Pissouthnes. The Athenian admiral Paches removes them from Notion.[77]

Pissouthnes is clearly on the make, but he has only been seen to operate by supporting sides in Greek *stasis*, so that he might have been able to argue if necessary that he was not in actual breach of the Peace of Kallias.[78] Whether external support for internal political strife is aggression is one of the hardest diplomatic problems in all periods down to our own day.[79] We have no clue

[73] *Vict* II 42 fin., *Acut.* (*Sp.*) 53.

[74] Thuc. III 31.1.

[75] Thuc. III 34.

[76] For the name cf. *PF* 1389, X. *Anab.* VII 8.15.

[77] Eddy, op. cit., 254, tries to make the Athenian expedition of winter 430/29 (Thuc. II 69.1) a reprisal for the loss of Kolophon. Clearly Melesandros is going into areas where Athens has not been for some time, but this is perfectly intelligible in the context of suppressing piracy; as we have just seen, the trade concerned is real. Eddy uses König's translation of the Xanthos Stele to show that Melesandros was actually attacking areas under Persian control. Even if the passage does refer to 430/29 and not to a second Melesandros in 414/3 (W. E. Thompson, *Hesperia* 36, 1967, 105-6), it is always folly to trust König for anything, as our increasing knowledge of Lycian makes clear.

Eddy's case, 255-6, based on Ktesias 43, for Persian intervention in Kaunos between 430 and 425 is moderately argued and could be right.

[78] The point is overlooked by Eddy, for whom Pissouthnes is in constant breach since 440.

[79] E.g. Demosthenes habitually claimed that Philip was in breach of the Peace of Philokrates. The truth was much more complicated (Brunt, *CQ* n.s. 19, 1969, 245-65), the possibility of providing for its nuances in a treaty remote. Contemplation of Viet Nam and Angola will suggest that modern diplomacy and international law are no more successful.

as to what had passed between Pissouthnes and Artaxerxes, but the first years of war have shown strains in the Athenian empire, notably in the revolt of Mytilene, and possibilities of stray profit, which can make Artaxerxes in 425 at least interested in the possibility of a substantial change in the situation. It should not be thought that Artaphernes' mission in any way represents coming down on the Spartan side. It is likely that there will be more profit to Artaxerxes in a change in the status quo, but the drift of his letter is an invitation to the Spartans to make their terms clearer. He will wish to know what he is buying.

As far as the Spartans were concerned, their conviction was that for more than a hundred years they had stood for the integrity of all Greek cities against Persia. Whether or not they had really sent a message to this effect to Cyrus the Great before 540,[80] they will certainly have believed it in Herodotus' day. Their actual record on the point before the Persians actually came to mainland Greece is a good deal less impressive,[81] but in 480 and 479 they had done a good deal of which they were rightly proud. After 478 leadership in the Persian War had passed to Athens, and the initial Spartan view that the Greeks of Asia could not be protected[82] was proved erroneous, but this will not have initially softened the Spartan attitude to Persia. Technically, Sparta remained in a state of war with Persia until 412, although no one ever seems to make a point of it.[83] In about 456, as we have seen, the Spartans resisted the invitation of a Persian ambassador to invade Attica, though he was well-supplied with money to encourage them.[84] The episode does

---

[80] Hdt. I 152-153.

[81] I still have some fondness for an old-fashioned view that some Spartans had the Persian threat well in mind even before 491, but that it was seldom possible to do anything about it except when, c. 512 and in 507, Athens looked like medising. Essentially, this becomes a question of whether Herodotus' motives for the Samian expedition of 525 (III 47.1) should be replaced or supplemented by a far-sighted concern for the balance of naval power in the eastern Mediterranean. The view is economically posed and rejected by Forrest, *A History of Sparta* (1968) 80-1.

[82] Hdt. IX 106.3.

[83] Cf. Amit, *Rivista storica dell' antichità* 4, 1974, 55-63, who argues that the point was kept well in mind in the Spartan-Persian treaties of 412/1.

[84] Thuc. I 109.2-3. Thucydides is imprecise about what happened to Megabazos' money, though he clearly knew. Walker's guess (*CAH* V 78) that the bribes were accepted is as worthless as Diodorus' assertion (XI 74.6) that they were not. For the problem of Arthmios of Zelea, see Meiggs, *The Athenian Empire* 508-12.

not much interest De Ste Croix, but we should, I think, consider
the possibility that collaboration with Persia is simply abhorrent
to Sparta at this stage. For De Ste Croix, Sparta is basically hostile
to Athens throughout the First Peloponnesian War and only in-
hibited from offensive action by the difficulty of passing the
Megarid.[85] He is not interested at all in the Five Years' Truce
between Athens and Sparta in 451, and more interested in possible
dissatisfaction at Sparta with the Thirty Years' Peace than in the
fact that Sparta made it at all when Athens was in a weak position.
I have very little evidence to deploy, but it seems to me not impossible, particularly if it was Kimon who made the Five Years'
Truce, that the main argument the Athenians used with the
Spartans on both occasions was that it would be undesirable for
Greece as a whole if the Delian League, the main bulwark against
Persia, were to collapse. I do not think that it would be in the least
out of character for the Spartans, at this stage, to accept this
argument.

In 432 we get the first hint of a possible Spartan change of
policy. Archidamos, arguing for more careful preparation before
war with Athens is embarked on, suggests the acquisition of new
allies, both Greek and barbarian, in the hope of acquiring ships
and money. The reference is unequivocally to Persia, as his apology
makes clear: "no blame can attach to us, since we are being plotted
against by the Athenians, if we seek safety through the aid, not only
of Greeks, but of barbarians".[86] ἀνεπίφθονον [87] makes it clear that
this is a proposal which is on the face of it improper, and only Persia
can be in mind. It is evidently very improper and we hear no more

---

[85] *OPW* 190. I hope to argue elsewhere that the First Peloponnesian War
was in its origins a war between Athens and Corinth and that Sparta was
only marginally and occasionally involved.

[86] Thuc. I 82.1 ἀνεπίφθονον δέ, ὅσοι ὥσπερ καὶ ἡμεῖς ὑπ' Ἀθηναίων ἐπιβου-
λευόμεθα, μὴ Ἕλληνας μόνον, ἀλλὰ καὶ βαρβάρους προσλαβόντας διασωθῆναι.
I find this very hard to translate, though there is no doubt about the grammar (see Classen-Steup). There is no difficulty about the Athenians' plots
against Greece. That is what the Corinthians have asserted at I 68.3 and
earlier in the sentence Archidamos has explicitly endorsed their complaint,
but the καὶ before ἡμεῖς suggests to me plots against barbarians as well, and
of this nothing whatever has been said. It would not be hard to construct
a case about Athenian plots against Macedon, but this can hardly be relevant.
There does seem to be an assumption that Persia will recognise Athens as a
perpetual enemy.

[87] Is he picking up the apology of the Athenian speech πᾶσι δὲ ἀνεπίφθονον
τὰ ξυμφέροντα τῶν μεγίστων πέρι κινδύνων εὖ τίθεσθαι (I 75.5)?

of it in Thucydides I. It plays no part in the very much more detailed plans of the Corinthians [88] who in fact indulge in memories of how their fathers freed Greece.[89]

Archidamos' defence is the only hint we get as to how the idea of seeking the aid of the old enemy could be sold to the Spartans. In the next year we find both sides contemplating sending embassies to the King and to other barbarians in the hope of gaining help,[90] but it is not in fact clear that any embassies went in 431. Owing to the nature of Thucydides' information, we are bound to hear more about embassies which do not get through. When we do hear of one, in the next year, it turns out to be a Peloponnesian League embassy rather than a purely Spartan one,[91] composed of three Spartans, two of whose fathers had been on a mission to Persia and come back with a reputation for independence and heroism,[92] Aristeas, most active of all Corinthians to our knowledge, a Tegeate and a private Argive. It was evidently a fairly well-planned operation, moving by land as far as the Hellespont with a boat ready to take them across and the expectation that Pharnakes would send them up to the King, but they stopped at the Thracian court on the way, were handed over to the Athenians and executed in Athens. That exhausts our direct information before 425, but Artaphernes' mission attests that some embassies had got through.[93]

That Artaxerxes failed to extract a clear message from the various ambassadors who had reached him is of course not necessarily an index of Spartan lack of diplomatic skill. It might point in the contrary direction, and there is some evidence of surprising sophis-

[88] Thuc. I 120-124.

[89] I 122.3.

[90] Thuc. II 7.1 μέλλοντες.

[91] Thuc. II 67, Hdt. VII 137.

[92] The fact is clear, whatever we believe about the previous mission, and fits Spartan patterns of selecting ambassadors; cf. Mosley, *Envoys and Diplomacy in Ancient Greece* 51.

[93] It is a fair inference from Ar. *Ach.* 646-51 that the Athenians knew of at least one Spartan mission which had got through before spring 425 and from the early part of the play in general that the topic of Persian help was a fairly current one. It is not easy to know what to make of the assembly episode (61-127) with its parody of ambassadors' reports and a high Persian official and his speech. The joking is not consistent, since the Persians, though meant to be fraudulent, give the lie to the ambassadors. Dover, *Aristophanic Comedy* (1972), 78 n. 1, is obviously right to say that we need not think any particular embassy is being satirised, but I suppose that at least one embassy has come back from Persia within the last few years; I do not know whether it was accompanied by a Persian.

tication at Sparta in technical diplomacy. I think particularly of
the close of the long siege of Plataea. It emerges [94] that there is
a permanent instruction from Sparta to the blockading force that
Plataea is not to be taken by force. The reason is that it will be
desirable to have some form of capitulation to show, if they ever
have to make a peace treaty which contains a clause providing for
the restoration of places taken by war. We should not put Spartan
diplomacy on too high a plane. They are capable of being double-
crossed, as they were over the surrender of their fleet in the armistice
of 425,[95] and they can be outfaced, as they were by the Argives in
the negotiations of 420, with the result that they were forced to
accept in principle the possibility of an archaic trial by battle for
disputed territory.[96] But among these plain blunt men we can expect
to find some who are more than capable of reading fine print or
even composing it.[97]

We have seen that another factor which made Spartan policy
incomprehensible to Artaxerxes could have been tension between
the various forces which made that policy. But it should also be clear
that there was a major point of principle which will have limited
the negotiating power of Spartan embassies. The Spartans went to
war with Athens with one clear war-aim and battle-cry, the liberation of Greece from Athenian enslavement.[98] In the discussion of
whether to go to war, a link was claimed between past success
in liberating Greece from Persia and the present necessity of
liberating it from Athens.[99] Consequently it is a complaint against
the Plataeans that they make their share in the liberation of Greece
an excuse for sharing in the current Athenian enslavement of it,[100]
and the Mytilenaeans in 428, less loyal to Athens and appealing to
the Peloponnesians for help, assert that they joined Athens to free
the Greeks from the Mede, not to enslave them to the Athenians.[101]

There is of course no indication that Thucydides took the Spartan

---

[94] Thuc. III 52.2.

[95] Thuc. IV 23.1.

[96] Thuc. V 41.2. Of course, it could be further said that the need to make
that particular concession was occasioned by the failure of the ephors
Kleoboulos and Xenares to bring off an abnormally complicated diplomatic
manoeuvre (V 36.1).

[97] Cf. Chapter Two note 157.

[98] Thuc. I 124.3, II 8.4, 12.1, III 32.2, 63.3, IV 85.1, 86.1.

[99] Thuc. I 69.1, 122.3.

[100] Thuc. II 72.1, III 63-64.

[101] Thuc. III 10.3-4.

claim at its face value and his final judgement[102] is that the
Spartans were only moved to act by threats to their own alliance.[103]
It is easy to disparage Spartan claims to be acting on principle, and
we shall see plenty of justification for doing so. The point is put
most bluntly by the Athenians, when the Melians express the view
that honour will make the Spartans come to their help: [104] "We
congratulate you on your innocence, but do not envy your folly.
For the Spartans, in dealings among themselves and in matters
which involve their own country's institutions, practise what is
honourable in the highest degree. One could say plenty about the
way in which they conduct themselves to outsiders; but, to sum
up, it could be demonstrated that they, most of all men we know,
consider what is agreeable to themselves honourable, and what is
expedient just".[105] The Athenians are arguing a case, well in line with
Thucydides' general convictions about international relations.[106] But
whatever conclusions the cynicism of opponents or the considered
judgement of the historian may come to, it is not in the least unlikely that, if the Spartans said they were fighting for Greek liberation, very many Spartans will have believed this account of their
own motives and been unwilling to contradict it too blatantly.[107]
And the claim will certainly provide a yardstick by which others
will judge their actions. To return to Alkidas on the coast of Asia
Minor in 427, he has just casually massacred some prisoners and
is firmly told by observers that he is not liberating Greece in the
right way by killing men who have not raised a finger against him,
who are not enemies, but have been forced to be Athenian allies;
if he does not change his ways, he will win few opponents to his
friendship and turn even more of his friends into enemies.[108]

The claim that what is going on is generous-minded liberation

---

[102] The phrase is considered, since I hold the account of the πεντήκοντα
ἔτεα to have been incorporated by Thucydides at a very late stage of the
composition of the work. Whenever the bulk of it was drafted (for another
purpose than that which it now so inadequately serves), I 118 is linking-
matter written to bring the material into superficial coherence.

[103] Thuc. I 118.2.

[104] Thuc. V 104.

[105] Thuc. V 105.3-4 (mostly De Ste Croix's translation).

[106] De Ste Croix, *OPW* 16-25.

[107] All De Ste Croix's careful work on the complexities of Sparta seems
to go for nothing on p. 158 when he argues that it is obvious that the claim
was 'mere propaganda'. 'Sparta' is a logical construct (cf. ibid. 64).

[108] Thuc. III 32.2.

continues to manifest itself from time to time, and in fact recurs on the last day of the war when the Peloponnesians demolished the walls of Athens to the sound of flutegirls with great enthusiasm, thinking that that day was the beginning of freedom for Greece.[109] It will be my main aim in the rest of these lectures to consider how cynical the claim had by then become, but it cannot, I think, be doubted that, at any rate in this first phase of the war, the claim will constitute a serious embarrassment to power-politics. Whatever Archidamos may have said about its being unobjectionable to negotiate with Persia, the fact remained that Sparta had remarkably little to bargain with. Obviously, it might in the long run be an advantage to Persia to lose so prickly a neighbour as Athens, but we have seen no clear evidence that Artaxerxes had any recent reason to complain of Athenian behaviour. He might well rapidly get on to demanding assurances that Sparta, which had not previously shown itself sympathetic to Persia and which was still living on the fruits of a tradition in which hostility to Persia played a considerable part, would be less determined than Athens about where the boundaries between Spartan and Persian interests lay. Sparta had indeed in the past believed that the Greeks of Asia could not be defended and she was in the present certainly not in a position to defend them navally in the same way as Athens, so that Artaxerxes might well see possibilities for himself in a change of the balance of power. But Sparta's professed aims would make it difficult, perhaps for individual Spartans as a matter of conviction and certainly for Sparta in general as a matter of policy, to do anything very obvious about making concessions to Persia.

This at least seems to me to be where hard thinking about Persia would have led a responsible Spartan between 431 and 425, not that there is very much evidence of such thinking. When it is suggested to Alkidas in 427 that it might be a good idea to raise revolt in Ionia and seek the collaboration of Pissouthnes, he will have nothing to do with it;[110] clearly all this goes far beyond his instructions or interests. What hard thinking is visible goes all the other way, and is considering the possibility of settling for a good deal less than the liberation of Greece. In 430 the Spartans are still turning down Athenian peace offers,[111] no doubt under the influence

---

[109] X. *Hell.* II 2.23; I have supplied a subject for κατέσκαπτον.
[110] Thuc. III 31.
[111] Thuc. II 59.2.

of their original conviction that the Athenians will not last long,[112] but there is clear evidence that, by 427 and probably well before, some people of importance at Sparta are considering the shape of a negotiated peace.[113] In 425 the importance of Sparta's own interests to Sparta becomes manifest. Spartans are in danger on Sphakteria and, without a word to their allies, the Spartans send off ambassadors to Athens about a peace settlement.[114] The champions of freedom offer to the enslavers of Greece peace, alliance, friendship and close ties in return for their men.[115] The rest of Greece is mentioned just twice, firstly in a perfunctory assertion that peace will bring it freedom from toils and then, at the end of the Spartan speech, in the cheerful assurance that, if Sparta and Athens are in agreement, the rest of Greece will do what it is told.[116] It is clear that everything is subordinate to Sparta's interests, a point which had been put less elegantly by Brasidas a few days before when he told the allies that they owed Sparta a great debt of gratitude and should not grudge breaking up their ships.[117] There is some trace of shame. One of the reasons offered by the ambassadors for not wishing to discuss peace terms openly in the Athenian assembly is that, if they offered concessions which were not accepted, it would be bad for their reputation with the allies.[118]

I need not, I think, follow in detail the theme of Spartan selfishness for the rest of the Archidamian War and its final culmination in the Peace of Nikias. Brasidas is allowed to go to Thrace as a liberator,[119] but the motives for sending him are purely Spartan, to relieve Athenian pressure on themselves and to get rid of some helots.[120] It is sufficiently clear to Thucydides that the home government was less interested in him as a liberator than in his potential

---

[112] Thuc. IV 85.2, V 14.3, VII 28.3, legitimately stressed by De Ste Croix *OPW* 207.

[113] Thuc. III 52.2. In 429, however, Archidamos eventually shows no hesitancy about trying to take Plataea by force (Thuc. II 75-77).

[114] Thuc. IV 15 ff. I am disposed, with Classen-Steup, to press the strict grammar of IV 15 and suggest that, once the assembly has sent τὰ τέλη to Pylos, it is they who decide on the embassy to Athens without further reference to the assembly.

[115] Thuc. IV 19.1.

[116] Thuc. IV 20.2, 4.

[117] Thuc. IV 11.4.

[118] Thuc. IV 22.3. Cf. III 109.2 where a more minor bit of selfishness may have had this effect.

[119] Thuc. IV 85.1, 86.1.

[120] Thuc. IV 80.

for establishing some kind of equilibrium for making peace.[121] The new allies which he wins are duly sold out, at least in that they will be expected to resume tribute to Athens, though if they pay it, they will be autonomous and secure from Athenian armed action;[122] the formula is thought unsatisfactory by Brasidas' men.[123] The Peace is pushed through the Peloponnesian League assembly against the wishes of the Boeotians, Corinthians, Eleans and Megarians,[124] and immediately, rather mysteriously for us, amplified by an alliance with Athens.[125] There is bitter resentment in the Peloponnese; now Sparta and Athens will join in enslaving them.[126] We may agree with De Ste Croix[127] that Spartan selfishness is displayed to the full, but it is surely selfishness directed to the narrow security of Sparta and her citizens,[128] not to greed or the development of a Spartan empire. We can, I think, safely say that, if Artaphernes had got through to Sparta in winter 425/4, he would have found them very interested in getting their men back and dispelling the helot threat as quickly as possible and not much interested in putting systematic effort into opening up a new area of operations.

Artaphernes did not get through, but landed up in Athens in that phase of Athenian optimism after the capture of the Spartans on Sphakteria when Spartan peace offers were being contemptuously

---

[121] Thuc. IV 108.7 (with the additional theme of φθόνος from the πρῶτοι ἄνδρες), 117.2, V 13.2, but as far as I can see, Thucydides does not attribute to the Spartans the initial intention of seizing bargaining-counters among Athenian allies for an eventual peace (so Brunt, *Phoenix*, 19, 1965, 275-6; De Ste Croix *OPW* 18 does not appear to go so far); he merely says that this is what Brasidas' gains turned out to be (IV 81.2).

[122] Thuc. V 18.5-8.

[123] Thuc. V 21.2-3.

[124] Thuc. V 17.2.

[125] Thuc. V 22.

[126] Thuc. V 29.3.

[127] *OPW* 158. I confess to finding the whole treatment of Strasburger on pp. 158-9 a little intemperate, not simply because, as will be seen, I disagree with De Ste Croix on Spartan-Persian relations. I find his treatment of Sthenelaidas' speech (Thuc. I 86) totally mysterious. I agree that we are entitled to take it as representative of Spartan opinion because the great majority of Spartans immediately voted in accordance with it, but I do not understand why he is said to be the speaker in Thucydides who concentrates most exclusively on the selfish interests of his own city, in contempt of all other considerations. Every sentence in it lays stress on the need to support Sparta's allies; Sparta's honour is at stake, not her own special interests.

[128] Cf. what I have said about the helots on pages 27-9.

brushed aside,[129] when all projects, possible and impossible, seemed
capable of achievement.[130] The Athenians saw the possibility of
converting Artaphernes' mission to their own purposes, and they
later sent him off in a trireme to Ephesos accompanied by Athenian
ambassadors.[131] They learnt there that Artaxerxes had recently
died (for he died at about this time) and went home. It is, as far as
I know, common ground among all editors and users of Thucydides
that, not only the capture of Artaphernes, but the whole episode
of the Athenian embassy, belongs to the Thucydidean winter of
425/4 and is in fact over before the first event of his summer, the
eclipse of the sun which we can date to March 21, 424.[132] Many
have drawn more comfort than I can from the fact that Diodorus [133]
also enters Artaxerxes' death under 425/4 after a reign of 40 years.

There are, however, terrible complications. It has been known
for many years that at the Babylonian city of Nippur a long and
virtually unbroken series of documents shows Artaxerxes' 41st year
continuing until December 24, 424.[134] At a village somewhere near
it they were still dating by him on February 26, 423.[135] The earliest
dated text of Darius from Nippur is of February 24, 423,[136] and in
the next month they make it more explicit that the 41st year and
Darius' accession year are one and the same.[137] These tablets clearly
have no room for an intermediate King between Artaxerxes and
Darius, but there is Greek evidence for two, spreading over a period
of eight or nine months.[138] These intermediate Kings cannot simply

---

[129] Thuc. IV 41.4.

[130] Thuc. IV 65.4.

[131] Notice the view of Raubitschek, *GRBS* 5, 1964, 155-6, that, whatever
had been going on with Pissouthnes, Athens' relations with the King were
good at this time and that the embassy was intended to complain about
Spartan negotiations.

[132] Thuc. IV 52.1.

[133] D.S. XII 64.1.

[134] Twenty-eight documents are listed in *BE* IX pp. 86-7.

[135] *BE* IX 109. The village is now read as Hašbâ. Its location is still
unknown (Cardascia, *Archives* 3), but eight documents come from it (ibid.
17 n. 5), so it is not insignificant.

[136] *BE* X 2 and 3.

[137] *BE* X 4, VIII 1.127, and, retrospectively, *UM* 3 (transcribed and
translated, Cardascia, *Archives* 112-3).

[138] Ktesias gives Xerxes 45 days (45) and 'Secundianos' 6 months 15
days (48). Diodorus' first entry (XII 64.1) gives Xerxes a year, which is
clearly a chronographic device; his second (XII 71.1) gives an alternative
version of 2 months and goes on to give 'Sogdianos' 7 months. Paus. VI
5.7 gives yet a third version of the name, 'Sogdios', deposed by Darius
ὁμοῦ τῷ Περσῶν δήμῳ.

be discounted. There is too much evidence about them in Ktesias, who is now getting very near his own day, and some of the detail is circumstantial.[139] They were simply not recognised in Babylonia, and it is clearly a tempting thought that Artaxerxes' 41st year is, in part or as a whole,[140] a chronological device protracted after his death to cover uncertainties about the succession.[141]

I fear there is yet worse to come. Very few assyriologists have worried much about texts of the Persian period, and those which are published[142] must represent only a small fraction of what exists in museums, in many cases uncatalogued. Nippur is in a relatively good state, but the situation of Babylon itself is appalling. Only the chance that one text from Babylon is in the Nippur archive had given us the information that Darius was recognized there at least 11 days earlier than in Nippur, in fact the information that he was there on that day, February 13, 423.[143] Twenty years ago

---

[139] We have already seen that at least Menostanes and Artoxares are real figures.

[140] Followers of Thucydides will have to assume that the whole of the 41st year, which started on April 22, 424 (Parker and Dubberstein, *Babylonian Chronology*³ 33), is fictitious, but it seems perfectly possible to me that the sentence beginning with ὕστερον is in the nature of a footnote and refers several months on beyond the winter of 425/4; cf. Thuc. III 68.3 which contains material about the site of Plataea which goes far beyond its chronological context. Kügler, *Sternkunde und Sterndienst in Babel* II (1912) 395-7, knowing only the evidence from the Nippur archive and observing that there was no double-dating of 41st year and accession year in month 11, but only from the 14th day of month 12, held that Artaxerxes had died in between the 15th of the 11th month and the 14th of the 12th month in his 40th year and that the double-dating was introduced in the 12th month to avoid ambiguity. This does not fit the new Babylonian evidence.

[141] So Meyer, *Forschungen zur alten Geschichte* II (1899) 484 with the suggestion that the King was not recognised until after he had performed the βασιλική τελετή of Plut. *Art.* 3.1. I find it simpler to suppose that Xerxes was not recognised in Babylonia at all. If Andrewes, *Historia* 10, 1961, 2, is right to suppose that Xerxes is in Diodorus' list because he was in office on a New Year's Day, I think this will have to be a Persian New Year's day (cf. the rather opaque suggestion by Hinz, *Orientalia* 39, 1970, 423, about a New Year's Feast in Persis in 503).

Cf. Polyaen. VII 17, where Ochos conceals the death of his father Artaxerxes for ten months. I suppose the normal assignment of this to the accession of Artaxerxes III is correct, despite the attractive coincidences of name and dates.

[142] A useful list now in Oelsner, *Welt des Orients* 8, 1976, 310-8.

[143] A lease of a house at Babylon until the going-forth of the King (*BE* X 1, translated, ibid., p. 22 and Köhler-Ungnad, *Hundert ausgewählte Rechtsurkunden* (1911) p. 29; cf. Olmstead *HPE* 356). I doubt Olmstead's view that

the standard book on Babylonian chronology referred incompletely
to a much earlier tablet of Darius,[144] but no one seems to have
noticed. Investigation shows that the tablet is from Babylon and
that Darius was already recognised there, not much over 50 miles
from Nippur, on August 16, 424.[145] If we are to take the eight or
nine months of the intermediate Kings seriously, it is clearly likely
that they are going to overlap the reign of Darius.[146]

These chronological difficulties are only the exterior signs of a
major convulsion, which will have resembled the troubles at the
accession of Darius I, put in the shade the not inconsiderable
difficulties at Artaxerxes' own accession, and which was certainly
far more complex than the familiar, relatively simple, story of the
succession problem at the beginning of the next reign. The Athenian
ambassadors did well to go home on hearing of Artaxerxes' death,
and I suspect that they had at any rate some idea of what was going
to happen. The story is known to us virtually only from Photius'
epitome of Ktesias. Ktesias has always, and rightly,[147] been a less
fashionable source than the Behistun inscription which tells us of

---

the King left immediately for Susa, which seems insecurely based. Consider-
ring Darius' background, we would expect him to remain at Babylon for the
New Year's Day, seven weeks later. We are thus not as totally deprived of
information about where Darius was in spring 423 as Andrewes thinks (op.
cit., 4 n. 7).

[144] Parker and Dubberstein, op. cit., 18, on a report from Sachs.

[145] I am greatly indebted to Mr. C. B. F. Walker and Prof. E. Leichty for
checking this tablet (BM 33342) for me. It is a contract concerning the
reassignment of a debt, dated "Babylon, 4th month, day 29, 41st year,
accession year, Darius, king of lands" (E^Ki itiŠU UD 29-KÁM MU 41-KÁM
MU SAG NAM. LUGAL.LA ¹da-ri-ia-a-muš LUGAL KUR.KUR). Sachs
had read 'day 25 (?)'.

[146] This had already been suggested, in a different form, by Olmstead
HPE 355-6, who took the tablets at their face value, deferred Artaxerxes'
death to the very end of 424, and had Darius recognised in Babylonia during
the reign of 'Secundianos' in Susa.

It is perhaps necessary to add a warning that the timetable worked out by
Meyer, Forschungen II 483 has exercised some authority for longer than he
would have wished; he showed some uneasiness about his solution later,
GdA IV² 2.261 n.1. In 1899 he did not know that there were tablets which
identified Artaxerxes' 41st year with Darius' accession year; in fact he
thought that the institution of the accession year was dead (Forschungen II
484-5). Why did he think the accession year was dead? Because Thucydides
and Diodorus told him Artaxerxes died in 425/4 and his reading of Thuc.
VIII 58.1 told him that February 411 fell within Darius' 13th year; Darius'
first year was therefore 424/3 (for the latter problem see Andrewes, op.
cit., 2 n. 4).

[147] Cf. most recently Bigwood, Phoenix 30, 1976, 1-25.

Darius I's accession or than Xenophon's *Anabasis*, but that is no reason for us to shut our minds to the fact that the Persian empire, at a point when we are expecting it to take once more an active part in Greek affairs, now had to survive a Year of the Four Emperors. Our materials are slender, but we must at any rate try to see what the main factors were.

Artaxerxes had, Ktesias tells us,[148] only one legitimate son, Xerxes. The mother, Damaspia, is named, but we know nothing of her except that she died on the same day as her husband. She is evidently Persian.[149] Whether legitimacy at this point included the qualification that the King must marry a descendant of one of the Seven who slew the false Smerdis, as the Greeks believed,[150] we do not know, but certainly both Xerxes I and Artaxerxes had had Persian mothers. Artaxerxes had seventeen bastard sons. He seems to have done his best for them. One of them, Ochos, later to be Darius II, had been married to his half-sister Parysatis and been made satrap of Hyrcania, and doubtless some of the others also had good jobs.

All three named concubines are Babylonian. For Herodotus Babylonia is the most prosperous part of the empire. Its tribute in actual silver is only about 10% of the royal tribute,[151] but it contributes one-third of the foodstuffs required for the King and his army and the perquisites of its satrap are simply enormous.[152] Xenophon believed that a permanent garrison in Babylonia had been instituted by Cyrus the Great[153] and presumably implies that there was one in his own day. It is clear that it was central to the King's mobilisation in 401. The year we are considering happens to fall into the middle of our most copious evidence for feudal holdings in Babylonia, and the tablets show us military settlements of Armenians, Indians, Urartians, Lydians, Phoenicians and Arabians, apart from local troops and bodies which bear military rather than ethnic titles.[154] Many of the participants in the succession-troubles

---

[148] Ktesias 44.

[149] König, *Die Persika des Ktesias von Knidos* 81, suggests that her name is Zoroastrian, comparing Jamaspa minister of Vištaspa in the Avesta.

[150] Hdt. III 84.2.

[151] Hdt. III 92.1 (including Assyria) with 95.1.

[152] Hdt. I 192. For an analysis of these taxes as they appear in Babylonian tablets, see Cardascia, *Archives* 98-9.

[153] X. *Cyr.* VII 5.69.

[154] Cardascia, *Archives* 7. For the nature of the feudalism involved, see his discussion in *Recueil de la Société Jean Bodin* I² (1958) 55-88; he overlooks

have substantial Babylonian estates [155] and will have been able to draw on feudal levies from them. It will not be unreasonable to suppose that Babylonia, centrally placed geographically in the empire, was militarily of major importance in this year.

Unfortunately, Ktesias is maddeningly inexplicit about where everybody is,[156] and reconstruction is about as difficult as it would be if we had to disentangle the events following the death of Nero without knowing the whereabouts of Galba and Vitellius. It cannot even be assumed that a satrap whose satrapy is named was in that satrapy.[157] We are not clear where Artaxerxes died, except that it was, unsurprisingly,[158] somewhere west of Persepolis.[159] In view of the silence of the tablets about his two successors, it was evidently not in Babylon, but at Susa or Ecbatana, depending on the time of the year at which he died. The Crown Prince Xerxes is obviously near enough to take over immediately. The first pretender, Sogdianos, is obviously not far away, since he matures his plot fast enough to kill Xerxes 45 days after the accession. His collaborators are an eunuch Pharnakyas, of whom we know nothing, and Menostanes his cousin, son of a satrap of Babylon, with substantial Babylonian estates of his own.[160] Menostanes becomes his ἀζαβαρίτης,[161] a certain Arbarios, who has been tentatively, but probably wrongly, identified with Menostanes' father Artarios,[162] his cavalry-commander.[163] However, he evidently does not have a firm grip on his military forces and is said to have upset them by

the earliest evidence, from the reign of Cambyses (Dandamayev in *Festschrift . . . Eilers*, 1967, 37-42). Cardascia's more detailed discussion of the groups. *Le hatru et les collectivités en Babylonie à l'époque perse*, has not yet appeared.

[155] See in general, Hüsing, *Porysatis* 50 ff.

[156] Olmstead, *HPE* 355-7 cheerfully fills all the gaps.

[157] E.g. Arsames, satrap of Egypt, was certainly away from Egypt in 410 (Cowley, *AP* 27, 30, 31) and may well have been more centrally placed in 424 as well.

[158] For the King's routine in this period, cf. X. *Cyr.* VIII 6.22, seven winter months in Babylon, three spring months in Susa, two summer months in Ekbatana.

[159] The bodies have to be removed εἰς Πέρσας (Ktesias 45), which certainly means Persepolis (Cameron, *JNES* 32, 1973, 56).

[160] See Chapter One, note 94.

[161] Ktesias 46.

[162] Hüsing *Porysatis* 52, but the supposed father will rapidly split from his supposed son. Texts of Artarīme run from 431 to 424 (*BE* IX 72, 82, 83, 84).

[163] ὁ τῶν ἱππέων Σεχυνδιανοῦ ἄρχων (Ktesias 47).

the execution of a mysterious Bagorazos, evidently an influential survivor of Artaxerxes' reign.[164]

An *arcanum imperii* has been divulged. One does not need a Persian mother to become King, and, with the only legitimate heir out of the way, there are sixteen other possible sons of Artaxerxes around. Ktesias[165] focusses on Ochos, satrap of Hyrcania. Repeatedly summoned by Sogdianos, he promises compliance, but does not come. He is gathering his own strength, which is apparently substantial. He is joined by Sogdianos' cavalry-commander and by Arsames, satrap of Egypt, whose Babylonian estates alone are so substantial that his agents can lease out 2381 animals in five days for pasture, 1333 in one.[166] The Paphlagonian eunuch Artoxares, relegated to Armenia by Artaxerxes,[167] returns and proclaims Ochos King, though he is ostensibly unwilling.[168] Clearly we can now be in or near Babylon and somewhere round August 424. Sogdianos evidently gets no acquisitions of strength, capitulates, despite Menostanes' protests, and is put to death.[169] For Ktesias, this is the decisive point in Darius' success and he pauses to discuss the influence on Darius of Artoxares and other eunuchs and his wife Parysatis. That influence is visible for us in the estates received

---

[164] Ktesias 46.

[165] Ktesias 47.

[166] The texts are collected by Driver *AD* 88-90 and discussed by Dandamayev in *Problemy socialno-ekonomichekoj istorii drevnego mira* (1963) 138-45. None of them antedates May 26, 423, but this is so early in Darius' reign that I hardly think it likely that the estates are simply a result of his support for Darius. It will be recalled that Driver *AD* VI (quoted here on page 6) implies large holdings in Syria as well.

Despite Driver, *AD* pp. 94-6, I find it very hard to associate Polyaen. VII 28.2 with this Arsames. The Arsames there revolts from the King, admittedly, but Φρυγίας τῆς μεγάλης κρατῶν must surely mean that he is satrap of Greater Phrygia, not merely 'making himself master of it', and a combined satrapy of Egypt and Greater Phrygia seems wildly improbable.

[167] Ktesias 40.

[168] Hüsing *Porysatis* 40 takes Artoxares for satrap of Armenia at this point, which is hardly consistent with the ἐξορίζεται of Ktesias 40, though influence in the region is perhaps possible. How early Artoxares' extensive Babylonian connections are is uncertain. He has a slave who owes dates in February 442 (*BE* IX 4, translated, ibid., p. 33) and a subordinate of his appears in a list of witnesses as early under Darius as April 24, 423 (*UM* 27.20, transcribed in Cardascia, *Archives* pp. 113-4), but I imagine that the four villages who provide him with barley for Darius' first four years (*UM* 84) are recent acquisitions.

[169] Ktesias 48.

by Artoxares [170] and by Parysatis.[171] It may be a reasonable guess that it is the news of Sogdianos' capitulation which induces Nippur to start to date by Darius in February 423.

The evidence of the new tablet that Darius was already recognised in Babylon in August is helpful in considering an Athenian embassy which, on the majority view, went to Persia, conducted successful negotiations with Darius and returned before the end of the archon-year 424/3. The orator Andocides tells us [172] that his uncle Epilykos went on an embassy to the King which concluded *spondai* and friendship for ever with him. This does not fit the Peace of Kallias in either content or date, and it is in any case convenient to have an Athenian treaty with Darius, since the treaty denounced as a forgery by the fourth-century Theopompos was a treaty with Darius.[173] The precise date was argued by Wade-Gery [174] on the basis of an Athenian decree [175] thanking a certain Herakleides for his services to Athenian ambassadors who had made *spondai* with the King.[176] Prosopographic arguments, admittedly not conclusive, can be used to date that text to 424/3,[177] and Wade-Gery argued that it was entirely plausible that the Athenians should wish to repeat their abortive embassy of the previous year as soon as Darius was established. The dating has been questioned[178] and I certainly should not be surprised to find new evidence everthrowing it. The problem is complicated by Andocides' assertion that the

---

[170] See note 168, and Chapter One, note 107.

[171] See Chapter One, notes 113-4. *TMHC* 185 of September 420, translated by Cardascia, *Archives* p. 96, shows how the estates were actually managed.

[172] III 29.

[173] *FGH* 115 F 153-4.

[174] *Essays in Greek History* 207-11, partly following West, *AJP* 56, 1935, 72-6.

[175] *ML* 70.

[176] The attempts to find a fourth-century context for the decree (Foucart, *BCH* 12, 1888, 163-9, Stockton, *Historia* 8, 1959, 74-9) have not found much acceptance.

[177] They have had rough treatment from W. E. Thompson, *Klio* 53, 1971, 119-24, but I dissent from his starting-point, his argument that the Athenian treaty with Halieis (*IG* I² 87= *SEG* X 80) need not belong to a period of war, since I do not think Thuc. V 47.7 a good parallel for the use of ὁ πόλεμος in the Halieis text. ὁ πόλεμος cannot be justified by the preceding ἐ]ὰν δέ τις ἵει π[ολέμιος, since the intermediate sentence does not seem to depend on this hypothetical case.

[178] Raubitschek, *GRBS* 5, 1964, 156-7, goes as late as 'soon before the Sicilian Expedition in 415' without firm argument; Thompson, op. cit., thinks that no closer dating than 424-418 is possible; Blamire, *Phoenix* 29, 1975, 25, opts for 422/1.

new arrangements embodied friendship for ever. This seems to be a new element, as has been recently emphasized,[179] possibly even amounting to alliance. Wesley Thompson, in his recent attempt to move the treaty chronologically, has doubted whether the Athenians would be in a hurry to treat with a newly-established Darius, and our investigations might, I suppose, be held to strengthen the point that Darius' position need not have looked very secure in Athens. He further asks whether Darius would in 423 have been anxious to reciprocate. "He may have held out to secure the best possible terms and only agreed to a treaty when the Peace of Nikias freed Athens to cause him real trouble." The argument could be turned the other way. By winter 424/3 the Athenian position was very different from what it had been earlier in the year. If the embassy was sent, say, after the Athenian defeat at Delion and the start of Brasidas' successes in Thrace, it might have been seeming urgent to mend their diplomatic fences. Darius' position, as we shall continue to see, is not secure, and he may well be anxious to ensure that Athens will keep out of the Persian sphere. I do not think that the current dating of the treaty is obviously wrong, and the new tablet, by advancing the date at which Darius may seem likely to come out on top, usefully relaxes the tightness of the timetable.[180]

Darius is Darius Nothos, Darius the Bastard, though the cognomen only appears in very late sources.[181] His own texts, of

---

[179] Blamire, *Phoenix* 29, 1975, 21-6, but the point was adumbrated by Raubitschek, loc. cit. Amit, *Rivista storica dell' antichità* 4, 1974, 60, rules out all element of alliance here: "the treaty is clearly a peace treaty, σπονδαί being the keyword, whereas φιλία expresses the hope of good (friendly) relations in future '; he does not comment on εἰς τὸν ἅπαντα χρόνον.

[180] The tightness of the timetable was a point made by Thompson (120) and crucial for Blamire (24-5). I do hold *IG* I² 87 to belong to a war-year (note 177), but I recognise that it is possible that *ML* 70 is not from the same year as *IG* I² 87. The *epistates* of *ML* 70 could be [Θ]εοκλείδης as well as [Ν]εοκλείδης; it is not significant that the name is spelt Θουκλείδης in other fifth-century texts.

Wade-Gery *Essays*, 201 n. 2, 210, suggests the possibility that the Peace of Kallias was with Artaxerxes only and would positively need renewal. It might well be alarming to the Athenians if Persia suddenly had a free hand. But very few references to the Peace mention Artaxerxes at all: D.S. XII 4.5, where interpolation has been suspected, Aristodemos *FGH* 104 F 13, 2, Paus. I 8.2, and even Diodorus says the Peace was πρὸς τοὺς Πέρσας.

[181] It is not a cognomen in Paus. VI 5.7, who uses νόθος to contrast with the γνήσιος which he inaccurately applies to his Sogdios. The prevalence of the designation in modern literature is derived from its appearance in the Christian chronographers (sources in *Die Chronik des Hieronymos*, ed. Helm 1956, pp. 115, 358); otherwise, I think, only in Schol. Aesch. *Pers.* 6.

course, lay orthodox stress on his ancestry:[182] "I am Darius the Great King, King of Kings, King of peoples [183] with many kinds of men, King on this great earth far and wide, son of Artaxerxes the King, of Artaxerxes (who was) son of Xerxes the King, of Xerxes (who was) son of Darius the King, an Achaemenid", and, unlike those of his son, they only acknowledge Ahuramazda and not the newfangled Anaitis and Mithras.[184] But he is a bastard and, as I have said, the point is not insignificant. If he can be King, others

---

[182] The only useful published text of Darius II, allegedly from Hamadan, is published by Paper, *Journal of the American Oriental Society* 72, 1952, 169-70, from which I quote. I am not unaware that there has been considerable suspicion attaching to all the finds from Hamadan of this date, and I suppose that this is why the parallel but different texts referred to by Kent, *OP* 218 have not been heard of again. It seems to me a little surprising that a forger would produce two divergent versions of the same text. I have had a copy of one of the others for more than twenty years. I do not think I am under any obligation to anybody to suppress it further, and give here the text as it came to me (I should emphasise that this is a copy of a transcript and that I made no attempt to check the transcript against a photograph I saw at the time): θātiy: Dārayavauš: xšāyaθiya: vazraka: Auramazdā: baga: vazraka: hya: maθišta: baganam: hya: imām: būmim: adā: hya: avam: asmānam: adā: hya: martiyām: adā: hya: šiyātim: adā: martiyahyā: hya: mām: xšāyaθiya: ahyaya: būmiyā: vazrakāyā: akunauš: xšaçam: manā: frābara: aivam: parūnām: xšāyaθiyam: aivam: parūnām: framātāram: karta: adam: Dārayavauš: xšāyaθiya: vazraka: xšāyaθiya: xšāyaθiyānām: xšāyaθiya: dahyūnām: paruzanānām: xšāyaθiya: ahyāyā: būmiyā: vazrakāyā: dūraiy: apiy: Artaxšaçāhya: xšāyaθiyahyā: puça: Artaxšaçāhya: Xšayāršāhyā: xšāyaθiyayhā: puça: Xšayāršāhyā: Dārayavušahyā: xšāyaθiyahyā: puça: Haxāmanišihya: θātiy: Dārayavauš: xšāyaθiya: mām: Auramazdā: pātuv: utāmaiy: viθam: utā: imām: dahyāum: tya: adam: dārayāmiy: utā: avašciy: tyamaiy: Auramazdā: frābara: patuv:

Saith Darius the Great King: a great god is Ahuramazda who (is) the greatest of gods, who created this earth, who created yonder sky: who created man, who created happiness for man, who made me king on this great earth. He bestowed upon me the kingship. He made me one king of many, one lord of many. I am Darius the Great King, King of Kings, King of peoples with many kinds of men, King on this great earth far and wide, son of Artaxerxes the King, of Artaxerxes (who was) son of Xerxes the King, of Xerxes (who was) son of Darius the King, an Achaemenid. Saith Darius the King: may Ahuramazda protect me and my royal house and this land which I hold and also what Ahuramazda bestowed upon me may he protect.

[183] For dahyūnām, I follow Cameron, *JNES* 32, 1973, 47-50. The orthodox translation is "lands containing many kinds of men".

[184] Cf. e.g. Kent *OP* A²Sa. Cf. Berossos *FGH* 680 F 11 for the assertion that Artaxerxes II introduced the worship of Anaitis.

At the last moment before I gave these lectures evidence appeared which perhaps shows Darius as more tolerant of Babylonians than his predecessors. Oelsner, *Welt des Orients* 8, 1976, 316-7, publishes a text showing the Belesys referred to in X. *Anab* I 4.10 as ex-governor of Syria in 401 in that office on June 23, 407 under the name of Bēlšunu.

may see themselves as equally or better qualified, and three more revolts or attempts on the throne follow in Ktesias. It would be valuable to be able to establish their chronology, but the evidence is uncertain. The only clear evidence of trouble in Babylonian tablets is a group of documents which attest that, in early January 421, the King called out his feudal levies to Uruk.[185] It is not clear whether Uruk is the object of the expedition or merely the assembly point.[186] In any case, the trouble is in the south, and not very obviously connected with the revolts of which we know.[187]

The first of these[188] is by Darius' full brother Arsites with the assistance of Artyphios, son of the Megabyxos satrap of Syria who had mounted a long revolt in Artaxerxes' reign. It is clearly not unlikely that the revolt is actually in Syria,[189] particularly since Greek mercenaries are involved, making an ominous first appearance in Persian dynastic struggles.[190] It is a big revolt. The rebels win their first two battles, but lose a third, and their mercenaries are bribed away. Despite the precedent of what had happened to Sogdianos, they unwisely trust the royal mercy, with the same

[185] The evidence is collected by Cardascia, *Archives* 99. Six tablets attest the mobilisation between 16 and 24 Tebet of the 2nd year (Tebet began on December 22, 422). The most remarkable of these texts gives full details of the equipment expected of an armoured cavalryman and some insight into the way in which the feudal system was already breaking down under economic pressures. It is discussed by Ebeling, *Zeitschrift für Assyriologie* 16, 1952, 203-13 and Cardascia, *Recueils de la société Jean Bodin* I² (1958) 55-88; cf. Lane Fox, *Alexander the Great* 158-9 (with an initial error about the King involved).

[186] Cf. Cardascia, ibid., 59-60 n. 2. It is clearly possible that Uruk is a regular assembly-point, as the Plain of Kastolos is for western Asia Minor. It is reasonable to hope for some assistance on Uruk from the publication of the large finds there coming down to this reign (Leuzen, XII-XIII *Vorläufiger Bericht über die … Ausgrabungen in Uruk-Warka*, 1956, 13).

[187] One might mobilise the Babylonian levy at Uruk for a march to, say, Susa, but one would hardly bring troops south from Nippur if the intention was to go north, north-west, or to Syria.

[188] Ktesias 50-51.

[189] So Nöldeke, *Aufsätze zu persische Geschichte* (1887) 58, Prašek, *Geschichte der Meder und Perser* II (1910) 173, Swoboda, *RE* IV 2201. The reason for doubt would lie in the apparent implication of Photius' epitome that the failure of the revolt entailed the destruction of Pharnakyas and Menostanes, though they are not directly said to be involved. They were last seen committed to the cause of Sogdianos, in Elam or Media.

[190] Milesians are specifically named. For this and other early uses of Greek mercenaries see Roy, *Historia* 16, 1967, 322-3. If Megabyxos used Athenians in his earlier revolt, which is not specifically said in Ktesias 37, their presence was accidental.

consequences.[191] I incline to put all this pretty early in the reign. The alternative view, which one could perhaps base on Babylonian tablets, would mean that there was a gap of nearly seven years before Arsites decided to revolt.[192]

Much more important for us is the next revolt. Pissouthnes rose in Sardis.[193] There is no evidence that he made any claim to the throne or how far his aspirations went. At first sight, he looks rather like his predecessor Oroites, satrap of Sardis a hundred years before, who took advantage of the succession troubles of 522 to assert his independence.[194] But, as we have seen,[195] he is grandson of Darius I, and he may well be discontented under the rule of Darius the Bastard. Virtual independence for the satrap of Sardis is surely possible. Darius I had not thought it safe to proceed openly against Oroites, and Pissouthnes has a new weapon at his disposal, a force of Greek mercenaries under an Athenian, Lykon. The size of the force does not appear, but it will surely not be smaller and may well be a great deal larger than the 700 men raised by the Samian exiles in 440. At the end of the century, his successor at Sardis will say, and expect to be believed, that the control of 10,000 Greeks will enable him to wear the tiara on his heart, even if another man wears it on his head.[196] If it occurred to Pissouthnes that he might wear the tiara on his head, there was nothing obviously ridiculous about that. He was a good deal closer to the throne than Darius had been in 522 and probably closer than Darius III was when he succeeded in 336.[197]

Various arguments have been deployed to date the revolt, none of them secure.[198] I am inclined to a fairly early chronology, at a

191 Ktesias allows Darius unwillingness to execute his brother and blames his death on Parysatis.

192 For the possible identification of Arsites with a royal Arrišittu who survives at least until December 417, see Chapter One note 132. It is perhaps unlikely that Pharnakyas and Menostanes, so deeply committed to Sogdianos, would have survived until 416. One would have to suppose that Darius had shown clemency to them (I suppose he must have shown clemency to someone, unless Artyphios and Arsites are perfect fools). But note that the evidence for both Menostanes and his father stops in 424 (Chapter One, note 94, Chapter Three, note 162).

193 Ktesias 52.

194 Hdt. III 127.1.

195 Above, page 55.

196 X. *Anab.* II 5.23.

197 For a genealogy showing Darius I and III, see Kent *OP* 158.

198 The arguments are derived from the brief sojourn of the Delians at Atramytteion, from 422 (Thuc. V 1.1) to late summer 421 (Thuc. V. 32.1). They are settled there by Pharnakes (I do not think anything follows for

time when Darius' position is not fully established, but a date as late as 416/5 does not seem excluded,[199] and there is this to be said for it, that Pissouthnes' own revolt does not seem to be unduly protracted and the revolt of his son Amorges is still in full swing in 413/2. Compression would not be unattractive.

Despite the strength of Pissouthnes' position, Darius survives this revolt as well. An expedition is sent against him under a certain Tissaphernes and two other commanders.[200] There is no mention of any battle. The use of mercenary Greeks proves to be a two-edged weapon and they are bribed away from Pissouthnes, their commander Lykon getting cities and lands in return for his treachery. Pissouthnes' position is evidently thus rendered untenable, and he joins the list of those who trust Darius' mercy and pay the penalty. Tissaphernes is given his satrapy.

The last threat to Darius' position seems to be a purely court matter and is certainly not earlier than 418.[201] The Paphlagonian eunuch is credited with ambitions to the throne.[202] We get no sense

relations between Athens and Persia). While they were there, they were atrociously treated by one Arsakes, who in 411 is described as Tissaphernes' ὕπαρχος (Thuc. VIII 108.4). Wade-Gery, *Essays* 222 n. 1, used this last passage to show both that Atramytteion normally belonged to the southern satrapy (because of the presence of Arsakes) and that, when the Delians were originally settled there, the northern satrap was temporarily disposing of it, possibly a sign that Pissouthnes' revolt had already begun. This is a very complex view, but there may be something in it. I see no clear evidence as to which satrapy Atramytteion belonged to, beyond the fact that the financial divisions of Hdt. III 90.1-2 certainly suggest that the area depends on Sardis, and no other evidence has yet suggested that Pharnakes has interests on the Aegean coast (though Pharnabazos' 'satrap' Mania will busy herself later in acquiring some for him, a good deal further west, X. *Hell.* III 1.13). Andrewes, *Historia* 10, 1961, 5 n. 11, uses only the other side of Wade-Gery's argument: "Thuc. VIII 108.4 seems to imply that Tissaphernes' arrival in the west preceded the return of the Delians to Delos in 421—provided that the Arsakes there mentioned was already Τισσαφέρνους ὕπαρχος at the time", certainly not a necessary inference.

[199] I.e. on the basis of the late chronology for Arsites (note 192).

[200] There is nothing that I can see against identifying Ktesias' Spithradates with the subordinate of Pharnabazos who secedes from him to Agesilaos in 396 (X. *Hell.* III 4.10) and eventually leaves him (ibid., IV 1.26-28), Περσῶν οὐδενὸς ἐνδεέστερος (ibid., IV 1.6), master of 200 cavalry (ibid. III 4.10). We cannot tell whether he is already settled in the northern satrapy at the time of Pissouthnes' revolt. The third commander, Parmises, is otherwise unknown.

[201] After January 418, cf. Chapter One note 107. The episode of Ktesias 53-56 can be at any time in the rest of the reign.

[202] Ktesias 53.

on this from Ktesias at all, merely a picturesque anecdote about his instructing his wife to make him a false beard.[203]

The events after the death of Artaxerxes which I have been describing coincide with a very substantial gap in Thucydides' treatment of Persian affairs.[204] It is clear that there is a real gap in Thucydides' treatment, to be explained by the unfinished nature of his history; at a minimum, it cannot be denied that he gives us insufficient background to the events he describes in Book VIII. As Andrewes has said, we cannot deny the gap on the grounds that there never was a renewed treaty between Athens and Darius or that Thucydides did not mind about the events. But we have seen enough to explain why Persia should have dropped out of the attention of the historian of the Peloponnesian War. For a period the length of which we cannot fix, Darius' attention will have been wholly fixed on his struggle to secure his throne and reestablish control of the empire. Circumstances could not have been less favourable for the renewal of any initiatives which Artaxerxes may have had in mind in 425/4. By the time that Darius will have had leisure to think about the west, the Archidamian War which had presented Artaxerxes with some possibilities for profitable action was at an end. The Athenian empire had survived it to be apparently as strong as ever in areas of interest to Persia. The challenge from Sparta, now fully occupied in the Peloponnese, had subsided. Darius would have to wait for a further opportunity of picking up pieces dropped by a defeated Athens. Had it not been for the Athenian expedition to Sicily, he might have had to wait for a very long time.

---

[203] Fantastic interpretations involving eunuchs not being eunuchs in König, *Die Persika des Ktesias von Knidos* 88.

[204] The topic is treated by Andrewes, *Historia* 10, 1961, 1-18.

CHAPTER FOUR

(Bracketed figures in this chapter are references to Thucydides VIII)

As we saw, the principal beneficiary from the failure of Pissouthnes' revolt was Tissaphernes who, according to Ktesias,[1] received his satrapy. The Greek sources leave us in the dark about his background. The only slight clue is that, by the early 390s his home, his *oikos*, is clearly somewhere in Caria,[2] and I think it not impossible that he owed his original command against Pissouthnes to his having estates somewhere near the scene of the revolt.[3] However, an important detail is supplied by the Lycian text of the Xanthos stele, which clearly describes him as the son of what ought to be the name which appears in Greek sources as Hydarnes.[4] The name suggests a distinguished ancestry. The first Hydarnes was one of the Seven who killed the false Smerdis[5] and served as Darius' general in 522.[6] His sons serve Xerxes in 480, Sisamnes as commander of the Arians[7] and another Hydarnes as commander of the Immortals.[8] It is generally held that this second Hydarnes was 'general of the coast men' later in Xerxes' reign.[9] The coast men ought to indicate the Daskyleion satrapy,[10] but it is hard

---

[1] Ktesias 52.

[2] X. *Hell.* III 2.12, 3.12.

[3] Cf. the similar possibility about Spithradates, Chapter Three, note 200.

[4] *Tituli Asiae Minoris* I 44 c 11-12 *cizzaprñna widrñah*. Bilinguals (ibid., 6.1, 56.2, 45.1-2 (partly restored), *CRAI* 1974, 119) make it clear that the second name is in the genitive, and the -*ah* form, which seems to be confined to proper names, also appears in the extended formula *X Y-ah tideimi* 'X son of Y' when X and Y are separated by a verb (*TAM* I 29.1, 99.1,116.1). The context is still obscure. It is clear that Tissaphernes is mentioned in conjunction with Hieramenes (see note 83) who has no patronymic, and there is some reference to Xanthos (*arñnas* line 13).

[5] Hdt. III 70.3, Kent *OP* DB IV 84 (son of Bagabigna).

[6] DB II 18-29. For possible later appearances see note 14.

[7] Hdt. VII 66.1. The first part of this name is presumably the same as the Tissa/cizza of Tissaphernes.

[8] Hdt. VII 83.1, 211.1 etc.

[9] Hdt. VII 135. Beyond the fact that it was in Xerxes' reign, precise chronology is unattainable for this episode.

[10] Schmitt, *Historia* 21, 1972, 522-7, where this passage is not considered. Accepted e.g. by Burn, *Persia and the Greeks* 321 (cf. 136), without recognition of the conflict with his p. 324. I find it a trifle hard to believe in the consequence, that Herodotus draws a rigid distinction which he does not

to find a place for Hydarnes there among the ancestors of Pharnabazos,[11] and I would prefer to put Hydarnes in Sardis, perhaps
with some overriding command in the west, in the long gap in the
history of that satrapy.[12] There is clearly ground for saying that
Tissaphernes was descended from one of the Seven and had hereditary links with Asia Minor. Others have gone much further in
constructions based on the name Hydarnes. Tissaphernes has been
linked with another family with a hereditary unknown satrapy
elsewhere, which is prominent in Ktesias' account of the reign of
Darius II, linked to the royal family by a double marriage before
it falls into disgrace.[13] I find it hard to believe that Tissaphernes
should have dropped out of this story completely, if it concerns his
family. Names like Hydarnes are in fact relatively common.[14]

---

explain between παραθαλάσσιοι ἄνδρες (V 25.1 and this passage) and ἐπιθα-
λάσσιοι ἄνδρες (V 30.5, where the reference is certainly to Sardis); it is unlikely that only the Daskyleion satrapy is referred to in VI 48.2.

[11] See page 52.

[12] See page 55. The view was held by Arnold ad Thuc. VIII 5, but
rejected by Krumbholz, *De Asiae Minoris Satrapis Persicis* (Diss. Leipzig
1883) 24-5. Krumbholz (ibid., 33) followed the logic of his position by
attributing the episode of Hdt. VII 135 to the very first years of Xerxes and
putting Hydarnes in Daskyleion even before the Megabates of Thuc. I
129.1. It is not clear whether he identified this Hydarnes with the commander
of the Immortals in 480.

[13] Ktesias 53-55, used as relevant by Olmstead *HPE* 364 (I do not understand why he says the satrapy was Hyrcania). Two children of an Idernes
marry children of Darius, but the son Teritouchmes slights his royal wife,
thereby attracting the vengeance of Parysatis not only on himself but on two
named brothers and two sisters. Only Stateira, married to Arsakes (later
Artaxerxes II), is said to survive. "For his great services as a diplomat, the
other brother Tissaphernes was spared for a time, although Parysatis did not
conceal her hatred" (Olmstead). But Tissaphernes still had a brother in 401
(X. *Anab.* II 5.35), and I see no evidence for supposing that Parysatis'
hatred for him need be earlier than his denunciation of Cyrus in 405/4.
Hostility was well-advanced by 401 (X. *Anab.* II 4.27).

[14] The Elamite version of DB shows that the Elamite for OP *Vidarna* is
Miturna. Hallock treats *Miturna* as a parallel form and warns me against
attempting to distinguish between the two; see *PFT* Glossary s.vv. e.g.
Daturšiš, Hatarbanuš, hatarmabattiš, Hatarrikaš, Haturdada, haturmakša.
The Persepolis texts give us a minimum of two, possibly as many as six,
people with these names. High official position and possible identity with
one of the Hydarnes's known from Herodotus is to be inferred for the
Mitarna who issued a sealed travel-document for 150 Thracian workers on
the move in 499 (*PF* 1363, 2055). The point of origin is not given, and I had
noticed that Miltiades was at one time in trouble with a Hydarnes, certainly
while he was in the Thracian Chersonese (Hdt. VI 133.1), but Hallock now
tells me that there is evidence for Mitarna issuing such documents for large
parties going from Media to Persepolis in years 19 and 20 (V-2041, V-2349).

After the Athenian disaster in Sicily in 413, we cease to complain about Thucydides' lack of interest in Persian affairs, and for the better part of two years we enjoy the benefits of his eighth book. This book is in an extremely unfinished state, full of loose ends and with duplicated narratives,[15] and some themes of interest to us are hardly clear. Notoriously, the obvious complaint is that, although we are told almost at once (5.5) that part of Tissaphernes' instructions is to bring in dead or alive Amorges, the bastard son of Pissouthnes who is in revolt in Caria, it does not become clear until half way through the book (54.3) that Amorges has enjoyed Athenian support and that his safety has been an interest of the Athenian state. This is a substantial point to obscure. Not only has the disaster in Sicily made it likely that the Athenian empire is about to fall to pieces, but, even before that disaster, the Athenians have gone back on the friendship for ever which they had made with Darius and started backing a revolt against him. It is likely that not only interest but a desire for revenge will inspire the King's policy towards the west.

Since the first Hydarnes was last seen in Media (DB II 18-29), it is now clearly likely that he remained there as satrap until at least 499. On this social plane, Hallock would have no hesitation in identifying this Mitarna with the Miturna who authorises a smaller party in *PF* 1483 (unknown year). A grain-supplier, always spelt Miturna, operating at Tenukku and Tukras, which should be southeast of Persepolis and not very far from it (Hallock) is well attested between June 499 and April 497 (*PF* 939, 940, 1135, 1150, 1151, Fort. 1638). I see no particular reason to identify him with 1) the Mitarna who appears in cattle-contexts in 506/5 (*PF* 2009) and April 504 (*PF* 2070.21-22), 2) the Miturna travelling with 60 men from the King to Makkas in 500/499 (*PF* 1545), 3) a stray recipient of wine, possibly working for Karkiš (Fort. 3544).

Tissaphernes' relations have been greatly expanded by Hüsing, *Porysatis* 57 ff. who identifies his father, not only with the Idernes of Ktesias, but also with an Uda-ar-na in Babylonia presumably married to a Jewish wife, since he has a son Ha-na-nu-ia-ma (*BE* X 7.14, cf. *BE* IX 69.20), and the Vydrng of the Elephantine papyri (Cowley *AP* 20.4, 25.2, 27.4, 30.5, 6, 16, 31.5, 6, 15, 32.6, 38.3-4), first garrison-commander in Syene, then governor of Elephantine, in which capacity he destroyed the Jewish temple in 410 and was disgraced and apparently killed (*AP* 30.16). After this, it does not come as much of a surprise to find that the family recovered even after Tissaphernes' execution in the person of the great satrap Mazaios, attributed to the family because he has a son Hydarnes (Berve, *Alexanderreich* no. 759, and even he may be two people). The religious and ideological implications of this conglomerate have been carefully worked out by König, *Die Persika von Ktesias von Knidos* 92-8. Unless the name Hydarnes became much less common than it was circa 500, there is nothing to be said for it at all.

[15] These will be fully analysed by Andrewes in *HCT* V.

We are of course in a position to fill part of the gap. The decisive nature of the decision to back Amorges was emphasised by Andocides twenty years later.[16] There is some reason to think that the decision was actually taken in early 414.[17] But we do not know what inspired the decision. It is true that the Athenian assembly was virtually incapable of turning down any alliance offered to it, however unadvantageous.[18] It is likely that anti-Medism was a strong continuing constituent of the Athenian mind.[19] We can guess that there was optimistic talk about the instability and weakness of the Persian empire.[20] But we do not know why support was given to Amorges which had not been given to his father, and our uncertainty about the chronology is such that we do not know whether Amorges was continuing Pissouthnes' revolt or starting a new one.

Ktesias has merely told us that Tissaphernes had received Pissouthnes' satrapy. Thucydides, who generally avoids the word 'satrap', now describes him as 'general of the men below' (5.4). The precise phrase does not recur,[21] but the implication should be that he holds a position different in kind and probably wider in extent than the simple satrapy of Sardis. There is however some difficulty about the extent of his powers, since I see no trace of any subordination of Pharnabazos to him, as is the case later where similar but different phrases are used of Cyrus or himself.[22]

---

[16] Andoc. III 29.

[17] *ML* 77.79 (a general at Ephesos in spring 414); see Wade-Gery, *Essays* 222-3, Andrewes, *Historia* 10, 1961, 5. Without knowing this text, Beloch, *GG* II 1.378 had somehow deduced from Thuc. VIII 19.3 that Tissaphernes had taken over Ephesos before the Athenians backed Amorges, but Ephesos was still paying tribute in spring 414 (*ATL* II List 40. I 26).

[18] Nikias' recommendations (Thuc. VI 13.2) are not conspicuously at variance with the truth καὶ τὸ λοιπὸν ξυμμάχους μὴ ποιεῖσθαι ὥσπερ εἰώθαμεν, οἷς κακῶς μὲν πράξασιν ἀμυνοῦμεν, ὠφελίας δ' αὐτοὶ δεηθέντες οὐ τευξόμεθα.

[19] For recent manifestations of it, cf. Ar. *Knights* 478, *Peace* 107-8, 408. It should be remembered that unfavourable references to the Mede had never been deleted from the assembly's prayers (Ar. *Thesm.* 337, 365, Isoc. IV 157).

[20] Consider the distortions of the state of the Peloponnese and of Sicily in Alcibiades' speech, Thuc. VI 16.6-17. An even more plausible account of Darius' troubles could have been given. On more general topics of barbarian inferiority, we can see the possibility of using material like Hipp. *Airs, Waters, Places* c.16 (Isoc. IV 150-151 can be partly under the influence of later events).

[21] See Busolt *GG* III 1418 with n. 3, Meyer *GdA* IV² 1.69-70, Andrewes, *Historia* 10, 1961, 6 n. 13. Classen-Steup and Weil-de Romilly appear to think that the phrase has no implications beyond 'satrap'.

[22] Pharnabazos' subordination to Cyrus, X. *Hell.* I 4.5, to Tissaphernes, ibid., III 2.13, IV 1.37.

Thucydides (5.5) sketches Tissaphernes' motives in winter 413/2. There is a specific instruction from the King to bring in Amorges, and he has recently been asked by the King for arrears of tribute from the Greek cities in his province which he has not been able to collect because of the Athenians. His wish to do damage to the Athenians and to win the Spartans as allies for the King is presented as a consequence of this, rather than as a direct royal instruction. The passage is a well-known crux. I regard it as well established that Tissaphernes had not been asked for many years' arrears and as at least likely that a Persian claim to the tribute of the Ionian cities had been kept open throughout the century despite the Peace of Kallias.[23] It is also clear to me that the reference is not simply to the recent disturbed state of Ionia and to the Athenian support of Amorges which meant that Tissaphernes was unable to pay tribute on parts of his province from which Pissouthnes had collected.[24] The passage has to be read together with the motives attributed to Pharnabazos and said to be identical (6.1); he wanted to make the cities in his province revolt from the Athenians because of the tribute. The King has, apparently indirectly, served notice on his satraps that the Greek cities of Asia are to be brought back.[25] There is no suggestion that it is part of his instructions that an alliance be made with Sparta, though clearly both satraps think that this will be welcome to him.

---

[23] See Murray, *Historia* 15, 1966, 142-56.

[24] I cannot find this view in print, though it is frequent enough in conversation. Murray's apparent flirtation with it (148) is presumably connected with his considering it possible (147) that the King had always demanded the full tribute of Ionia, however little territory was available to pay it.

[25] I should at least raise the point of what prompted the King's decision and when it was made. The Athenian disaster in Sicily is in late September 413 (cf. Dover, *HCT* IV 449 for the difficulty of establishing a firm chronology after the eclipse of August 27), and it seems unlikely that the King can have had reliable news of it until well on in November. It is perhaps possible that he should have come to his decision and issued his request for tribute in time for Tissaphernes and Pharnabazos to formulate their plans and send their missions to Sparta and for Sparta to send a mission to Chios before the end of Thucydides' winter (whenever that was; Gomme's view, *HCT* III 705-6, that it was in the first week of March does not in fact fit the evidence for the next year; see for the moment Andrewes, *Historia* 10, 1961, 2 n. 4 and *HCT* IV 20-21). But it is likely to be a tight fit, and we should not exclude the possibility that the King was being rather more adventurous than simply waiting for a point when Athens' downfall seemed certain. He can have taken his decision out of fury about Amorges and a conviction that Athens had over-extended herself by reinforcing the Sicilian expedition.

Thucydides (2) draws a picture of the animated state of the Greek world after the disaster in Sicily. Even former neutrals are eager to share in the war; Sparta's allies are revived at the thought that their troubles will soon be over; Athens' allies are eager for revolt. All these factors encourage the Spartans and also the hope of help from Sicily. They will soon be free from danger, and the destruction of Athenian power will leave them secure in the leadership of Greece.[26] However, some force will be needed to attain this end, and the ship-building programme arranged (3.2), optimistic though it is, is fairly pitiful. The sharpest index of what war had meant to the Spartan allies is that Corinth with her naval traditions, which had put 90 ships to sea in 433,[27] is now asked to build 15 ships.

Something would doubtless have been achieved from the allies' own resources, and in fact king Agis at Decelea without reference to the city (5.3) [28] contemplates assisting revolt first in Euboea, then in Lesbos; he evidently does not have resources for both. But it rapidly emerges that the Persians are prepared to take a hand. There appear in Sparta (5.4-5) secret delegations from Chios and Erythrai supported by an unidentified representative of Tissaphernes, who offers pay for ships,[29] and (6.1; 8.1) Greek exiles from the court of Pharnabazos, suggesting an expedition to the Hellespont and bringing with them 25 talents in hard cash. The two Persian missions are in open competition with each other,[30] but the Spartans come down by a substantial majority for going to Ionia, after a cautious mission to explore the situation at Chios (6.3-4).[31] Thucydides attributed importance to the influence of

---

[26] The theme of liberation is barely touched on, it may be agreed, but it should not be thought that τῆς πάσης Ἑλλάδος ἤδη ἀσφαλῶς ἡγήσεσθαι carries any necessary implication of Lysandrian imperialism.

[27] Thuc. I 46.1.

[28] It must remain an open question whether the powers described for Agis at this point are inherent in the hegemonial powers of the King as commander in the field, as Kahrstedt evidently thought (202 has his clearest statement on the point), or derive in part from some additional grant (which Kahrstedt also appears to contemplate on p. 196).

[29] The original offer was evidently the good one of 1 drachma per day per man, as we learn from VIII 29.1, which surely should not be taken as referring simply to an amount of τροφή which had not been quantified at Sparta.

[30] I doubt if τῶν can be defended in 6.2, although Weil and de Romilly try hard.

[31] The choice of Phrynis the perioikos for the mission is presumably not so much an index of his importance, though he must have been thought a reliable man, as of the need for secrecy, not only from the Athenians (7) but from the Chian πολλοί (9.3).

Alcibiades [32] with the ephor Endios, but there can be no doubt that the decisions to make Chios and Erythrai allies and to send them 40 ships were taken in the Spartan assembly.[33] To what extent the assembly discussed alliance with Persia and its possible terms we do not know. The point was certainly raised between Alcibiades and Endios (12.2). No one seems to have been frightened by any mention of Persia that was made, but the presence of Greek states seeking freedom should certainly have seemed more attractive than simple representatives of a satrap, quite apart from the strategic arguments in favour of the Ionian plan. The policy of the assembly was endorsed by Agis and by the allies, meeting at Corinth (8.2-4).[34] Direction of the campaign then passed to the ephors (11.3, 12) and Endios' adviser Alcibiades, who encouraged him to gain credit which might otherwise go to Agis.[35] Competition in the conduct of policy is evidently as possible at Sparta as in Persia.

The Ionian policy is successful. The open revolt of Chios and Erythrai is followed by Klazomenai and Teos. The Athenians abandon the Erythrai peninsula [36] and its hinterland (16).[37] Persian troops now appear under a subordinate of Tissaphernes and assist in the demolition of Teos' landward wall, rebuilt by the Athenians, we may believe, with Persian dangers in mind.[38] There is then (17)

[32] Alcibiades can claim knowledge of the Ionian situation and some influence there; see 17.2 and cf. Plut. *Alc.* 12.1.

[33] οἱ Λακεδαιμόνιοι .... ξυμμάχους ἐποιήσαντο .... ἐψηφίσαντο (6.4) can hardly bear a less formal meaning.

[34] I can find no discussion of this interesting meeting, which bears every appearance of being a meeting of the Peloponnesian League, in De Ste Croix. The need to consult the allies arises from the fact that it is their ships which are going to be used, but they are consulted and they formulate a programme (not indeed essentially different from Sparta's own). What was said about Persia ?

[35] I suppose the notion to be that the ephors should get their fleet going, before Agis' man Thermon (11.2) disengages the ships blockaded at Peiraios. Thermon is not mentioned again, but presumably the credit for the action reported at 20.1 belongs to him. The theme of getting credit for Endios is expanded at 17.2.

[36] But forts at Sidoussa and Pteleon are still held at 24.2.

[37] This withdrawal settles for the moment the attitude of Teos, originally hesitant, but we soon find it hesitant again (20.2) and D.S. XIII 76.4 suggests that it reverted to Athens. Lebedos and Hairai need later Spartan persuasion (19.4).

[38] For this wall see Wade-Gery, *Essays* 219-20, but add 20.2 for Persian concern about it. The other revolting states are engaged in building walls, but as a defence from Athenian reprisals by sea (14.3). The allies are obviously doubtful about Teian firmness, rightly (see note 37).

a jump [39] south to Miletos which also revolts. We are getting very close to Iasos, centre of Amorges' revolt (28.2-3) and therefore of Tissaphernes' immediate interests, and the Spartans now come into actual contact with him for the first time.

With no explanation at all and merely the information that it immediately followed the revolt of Miletos, we now get the first treaty between Sparta and Persia (18), an alliance between the Spartans and their allies on one side and the King and Tissaphernes on the other. Formal alliance, we have seen, had been in the mind of both the ephors and Tissaphernes. The Spartan admiral Chalkideus had been in close touch with the ephors when he sailed and must have had a fairly clear idea of what they had in mind, but nevertheless this is a very simple-minded document. The opening clause "All the land and cities which the King holds and was held by his ancestors shall be the King's" is phrased in a way which sent more experienced diplomats through the roof when they saw it (43.3), but it is unlikely that either party had more than Asia Minor in mind, as is made clearer by the next clause "The King and the Spartans and their allies shall jointly prevent the Athenians from receiving the money or anything else they have been receiving from these cities." The nature of the King's rights is left unspecified. As we have seen, the Persians have probably always maintained a claim to the whole of Asia Minor,[40] and Wade-Gery [41] was of the opinion that the Peace of Kallias had not forced a renunciation of this formal claim. No one seems to be thinking the first clause through to the point of determining, for example, whether Sparta is going to have to go back on her new treaty with Erythrai (6.4). Most of the rest of the treaty is harder headed and

---

[39] The allies have obviously been pulled south by pursuing Strombichides to Samos, and much may be due to Alcibiades' special contacts in Miletos. If it seemed desirable to enter into early touch with Tissaphernes, Thucydides has obscured the point. Yet we may agree with the implication of Beloch (see note 17) that Thucydides is curiously silent about events at Ephesos. It appears to be out of Athenian control at 19.3, but we hear nothing else about it until Tissaphernes goes there in 109. By 409 he seems to have a fair amount of control in the neighbourhood and the Ephesians are firmly anti-Athenian (X. *Hell.* I 2.6-9 and the new fragment of the Hellenica Oxyrhynchia, *Studi Papyrologica* 15, 1976, 55-76). I can only assume that its revolt was early and spontaneous.

[40] The clearest evidence is that Pharnabazos still regards Athenian-held cities as being within his ἀρχή (6.1).

[41] *Essays* 220.

directed to the needs of the moment. That the cities should stop paying Athens tribute is an essential of the Spartan war against her, as had been emphasised by the Corinthians even before the war; [42] for Tissaphernes it is an essential preliminary to their starting to pay him, a point on which the treaty has nothing to say. The new allies will continue the war in common and not make a separate peace. The Peloponnesians will regard those who revolt from the King as their enemies, and no doubt Amorges is principally in mind. The King will do the same for the Peloponnesians; it is hard to see who is in mind, and no doubt this is simply a courteous balancing-clause. Nothing is said to formalise any arrangement which had been come to in Sparta about financial support from Tissaphernes. The Spartans have at the very least recognised Persian suzerainty over Asia Minor for no very obvious return except the vague promise of Persian collaboration in the war. Since Chalkideus, the negotiator of the treaty, soon got killed (24.1), no one was in a position to ask him what he was playing at.

For the rest of the year 412 the war moves into a more evenly balanced phase and both sides have their successes. Tissaphernes actually does some fighting, contributing mercenaries and cavalry to a battle outside Miletos, not that they do very well (25.2, 4). But he has shown good will, and he has no difficulty in persuading the allies to assist him in wiping out Iasos, Amorges' base (28). Amorges is taken alive and handed over to Tissaphernes to take to the King, if he wishes; we hear no more of him. The army collects a good deal of loot and sells the inhabitants to Tissaphernes for a daric apiece, hardly commercial value. Amorges' mercenaries turn out to be mostly from the Peloponnese and the Spartans can make use of them. No fuss is made about handing Iasos over to Tissaphernes, who garrisons it (29.1). There are, of course, no inhabitants left, so this should not be seen, I think, as the first clear case of a Persian garrison in a Greek city.[43] It should be noted that Tissaphernes has

---

[42] Thuc. I 122.1; cf. IV 87.3 for this element in Brasidas' thinking.

[43] The later history of Iasos is obscure. I would now withdraw my suggestion (*BSA* 49, 1954, 33) that *IG* II² 3 belongs to the fifth century, since there is no evidence before the early fourth century of the short formula ἔδοξεν τῶι δήμωι; cf. Rhodes, *The Athenian Boule* (1972) 259. Iasos has been imported by emendation into X. *Hell.* I 1.32 and D.S. XIII 104.7; see Meiggs, *The Athenian Empire* 577-8. If the emendations are correct, and they are very tempting, Iasos did not remain uninhabited or under sole Persian control for very long.

been in action himself further south and caused the revolt of Knidos (35.1).

Tissaphernes has some reason to be gratified, but his immediate reaction is to hedge on his undertakings. In a meeting at Miletos (29) he professed himself unable to pay the Peloponnesians at the full rate promised in Sparta for more than a month and proposed to pay half-rates until he consulted the King about the possibility of paying the whole. This was evidently partly bluff, possibly arising out of unwillingness to spend his own money (45.6), but we later get another point of view.[44] Alcibiades was by now with Tissaphernes as we shall see,[45] and later claimed to have influenced him against too whole-hearted backing of the Peloponnesians which might dangerously increase their confidence and hinder the achievement of Persian ends (45-46) and to have fed him with justificatory data, possibly misleading as it stands,[46] about Athenian rates of pay. Thucydides was by no means disposed to take Alcibiades' claims to have influence over Tissaphernes at their face value, but he did at any rate think it likely that Tissaphernes had political as well as financial reasons for not giving the Spartans too much help (46.5). But his reluctance is partly bargaining technique, and the Syracusan Hermokrates, the toughest negotiator present, argued him into an obscure compromise. The allies, still happy with the spoils of Iasos (29, cf. 36.1), find this satisfactory,[47] but the first signs of disagreement have appeared. However, for the moment collaboration continues to be possible, and we find the new admiral Astyochos joining with one Tamos, who, we happen to know, is an

---

Thucydides describes it as a πόλισμα, but it was paying a tribute of 3 talents in 415 (*ATL* II List 39.I 35). It was still paying in spring 414 (ibid., List 40.I 12); we cannot tell whether Amorges had yet moved in.

[44] At this point I begin to attempt to amalgamate Thucydides' parallel narratives. What stands in his text until the end of 44 is from the Peloponnesian point of view. With chapter 45 a different version starts, in the form rather more of extended commentary than narrative and from a source at least very close to Alcibiades. The revolt of Rhodes, described in 44, is not reached again until 52. For the problems of the parallel narratives, see Wilamowitz, *Hermes* 43, 1908, 578-618, and Andrewes *HCT* V.

[45] Andrewes prefers to defer Alcibiades' arrival and refers 45.1 to a later stage of the arguments about pay.

[46] But see Pritchett, *The Greek State at War* I (1974, but originally *Ancient Greek Military Practices* I, 1971) 14-24.

[47] For the possibility that some Peloponnesian commanders were bribed into acquiescence, see 45.3.

Egyptian in Persian service,[48] and who is described, ominously but perhaps unofficially, as hyparch of Ionia, in an unsuccessful attempt to discipline Klazomenai, which has returned to the Athenian side (31.2-4, cf. 23.6).[49]

Some time later, despite their satisfaction over the financial situation, the Peloponnesians are found considering that the first treaty was inadequate and unfavourable to them and make another one (36-37). There has been plenty of time for the terms to be reported to Sparta and for fresh instructions to have been received, but there is in fact no indication that anything of the kind has been done. Much of the difference between the treaties is a matter of nuance, and at least one clause is desperately obscure to us. The treaty is extended to the King's sons. The word 'alliance' is dropped, though the clause about joint prosecution of the war against Athens and against making a separate peace remains. Instead we have a document about *spondai* and friendship. *Spondai* generally implies the termination of hostilities, and it is possible that someone has woken up to the fact that Sparta and Persia have been at war with each other for seventy years.[50] The definition of the Persian empire is only slightly altered and still contains no explicit limitation to Asia, but the clear statement of the first treaty that it is the King's has been replaced by an undertaking that the Spartans and their allies will not attack it, and, where there had stood the undertaking to stop the Athenians collecting tribute, there now stands a promise that the Spartans will not exact it.[51] In effect, Spartan recognition of Persian control has been exchanged for an undertaking that the Spartans will not attempt to succeed to the Athenian position. We

[48] He reappears as Tissaphernes' hyparch in 87.1, 3. Presumably he is the Egyptian from Memphis who is later in Cyrus' service and sees no possibility of reconciliation with Tissaphernes after his death, X. *Anab.* I 2.21, 4.2, D.S. XIV 19.5, 35.3-5, but it is not clear how he can both be in command of Cyrus' fleet and left in charge of Ionia. See Chapter Five note 74.

[49] Klazomenai has a tangled history, see *ML* 88 and commentary, but the pattern of splits in the citizen body, secessions and changes of allegiance may be a good deal commoner than our sources let us see.

[50] The point is argued by Amit, *Rivista storica dell' antichità* 4, 1974, 55-63. For Thucydides (VIII 57.2) all three treaties are *spondai*, but this is the only one which has the word in the text.

[51] The Milesians have been contributing to war-expenses (36.1), but the Spartans are surely not being required to renounce this. The Milesians are only doing what, according to Alcibiades (45.4-5) speaking on behalf of Tissaphernes, all cities in revolt from Athens ought to be doing.

learn later (46.1-2) [52] that the possibility that they may make the
attempt is one of the things which Alcibiades has been trying to
put into Tissaphernes' mind. The King now offers a reciprocal non-
aggression clause, which seems more realistic than the previous
promise not to support revolts from the Peloponnesian League, and
the pair of non-aggression clauses are indeed appropriate to a
peace treaty. Further negotiations are provided for. This time,
there is a financial clause. The King will pay the expenses of any
expedition in his territory for which he has sent. The principle is
conceded, but the King's liability is limited and hard figures are
avoided.[53] The last clause (37.5) is the obscure and tantalising one,
with a reference to cities which have made agreement with the
King, which can be visualised as possibly going to attack the
King's territory. Current interpretations make it little more than
pleonastic, but Andrewes will argue that the reference is to otherwise unknown agreements made by cities in Asia with the King or
his representatives as to how they are going to live with him after
Athens' departure.[54] We shall hear (45.4-5) that some Greek cities,
certainly including some in Asia, have been in touch with Tissaphernes, in fact they have been asking him for money.[55] There is
no suggestion that he, or Alcibiades on his behalf, has as yet reminded them that they may have an obligation to pay Persia
tribute. So far all that has been said is that they should be prepared
to contribute at least as much, if not more, to the war effort on
their own behalf as they had previously paid to Athens. It would
appear that nothing very decisive has yet been said about their

---

[52] Without explicit mention of Asia at this point, but the rest of the
chapter shows that it is in mind.

[53] If the Peloponnesians or Hermokrates wanted them put in, they were
doubtless put off with the reminder that the King's will was still not known on
this point.

[54] If ἢν δέ τις τῶν πόλεων ὁπόσαι ξυνέθεντο βασιλεῖ refers to the present
treaty, the difference between § 2 and § 5 lies in a) that the Peloponnesians
are only to keep off the χώρα in § 5 whereas they are to keep off χώρα and
πόλεις in § 2, an improbable collocation, b) whatever difference may be
sought between μηδὲ βασιλέα μηδὲ ὧν βασιλεὺς ἄρχει in § 2 and τις τῶν ἐν
τῇ βασιλέως χώρᾳ ἢ ὅσης βασιλεὺς ἄρχει in § 5 as possible aggressors, a delicate
nuance hardly comprehensible to us. Andrewes' interpretation that the
Peloponnesians are to discourage Greek cities of Asia from attacking the
King's chora is much more satisfactory, but the balancing clause will have
to be meaningless courtesy, like the balancing clause in 18.3.

[55] Only the Chians are named and ἐλευθερία is mentioned only to them,
but the other cities must be mostly mainlanders and no sharp distinction is
drawn.

future relations with Persia, and the possibility which now emerges, that some arrangements have been made while the Spartans are still on the spot, does something to soften the picture of Spartan renunciation of Asia. The attitude of the Ionians themselves will occupy us at greater length later, but we should note at this point that, even after the first treaty, the Milesians have been contributing to the war with greater enthusiasm than we should expect if they had thought they were simply being handed over to Persia (36.1).

The treaty is later (43.3, 52) referred to as the treaty of Therimenes, Astyochos' temporary predecessor,[56] though there is no trace of disagreement among the group negotiating and cooperating with Tissaphernes far to the south at Miletos.[57] The new admiral Astyochos had already got on to bad terms with his countryman Pedaritos who was operating further north with the Chians and, even when the situation in Chios became much worse, he declined to come to his help (32-33). Pedaritos' commission is apparently direct from Sparta,[58] and there is some reason to suppose that he is

[56] Cf. Westlake, *Individuals in Thucydides* 296 n. 2.

[57] Those familiar with the literature on the treaties who are missing the customary discussion of their language may here be reminded of my conviction (see page 14) that Tissaphernes should certainly have at his disposal secretaries capable of drafting Greek diplomatic documents; we cannot know their linguistic habits. That the second treaty may have even fewer Ionisms than the first would be pretty weak evidence of the influence of Alcibiades, even if it were true. For Ionisms in the first treaty, Klaffenbach ap. Bengtson, *Staatsverträge des Altertums* p. 142 picks out ἔστων and φοιτάω. There is confusion about the form of the imperative employed in 18.3. The mss. are apparently unanimous for ἔστωσαν in both places. It seems folly to emend this, which stands elsewhere in mss. of Attic literary texts (Eur. *Ion* 1131, Plato *Rep.* 352 a, *Soph.* 231 a, *Laws* 737 e, 762 d, all from *LSJ* Suppl.), even though the normal classical Attic is ὄντων and the earliest epigraphic instance of ἔστωσαν is from late fourth-century Cyrene (*SEG* IX 1.13). Retention of ἔστωσαν would hardly eliminate the possibility of an Ionic draftsman. Admittedly, normal Ionic is ἔστων (instances in Thumb-Scherer, *Griechische Dialekte* II 277) and this was favoured by Hude here, but ἔστωσαν seems to have evaded even his censure at Hdt. I 147.1. There can be no case at all for the normal Attic ὄντων, which stands in the Oxford text with a silent apparatus and is accepted by the Bude editors. φοιτάω of tribute stands in Hdt. III 90.3, V 17.2, but in face of Lys. XXXII 15 it cannot be called an Ionism.

[58] I suppose this to be the force of Λακεδαιμονίων πεμψάντων in 28.5. 32.3 suggests that Astyochos, though nauarch, is not in a position to do more than make suggestions to him. Cf. Kahrstedt 172; this is the only case he can find of a 'harmost' who is not subordinate to a nauarch.

from a wealthy and influential family.[59] He clearly did not feel himself subordinate to Astyochos and sent to Sparta accusing Astyochos
of wrongdoing (38.4). As the result of the letters is said to be suspicion of Astyochos at Sparta (39.2 fin.), we need have no doubt
that Pedaritos suggested pretty broadly that Astyochos was being
bribed to favour Tissaphernes' interests to the detriment of the
general conduct of the war; we get later confirmation that the view
was held in the fleet.[60]

Pedaritos will have known better than we what the state of
politics was in Sparta. New ephors will have come in in September[61]
and the first manifestation of the end of Endios' term of office is
an instruction to Astyochos to execute Endios' *xenos* Alcibiades
(45.1).[62] The grounds given are his general unreliability and the
enmity of Agis. The Tissaphernes policy had been the policy of
Endios and Alcibiades, and there is now a clear change in it.
At the winter solstice, not a normal time for seagoing anywhere,[63]
still less in the Peloponnese, one would have thought, the fleet for
which Pharnabazos' emissaries have been negotiating all year
finally gets going (39.1). There are further signs of some rethinking
at Sparta and it is unlikely that Pedaritos' letters are solely respon-

---

[59] See Chapter Two note 65.

[60] 50.3 as an explanation of why he is soft with Tissaphernes about pay;
cf. 45.3.
I know of no material bearing on Astyochos' background. Nauarchs were
doubtless elected (Kahrstedt, 147 n. 1), at any rate in form, but we know
nothing of the timing and certainly cannot say whether Endios and the
ephors of 413/2 had any effective part in his choice. It is sufficiently evident
that he has no permanent affinity with those most influential in 412/1.

[61] The importance of the change of ephors was seen by Busolt *GG* III
2.1437, but it seems to me to go too far to say that the new ephors belonged to
Agis' party. We know nothing of the eponymous ephor Alexippidas. It is a
possible deduction from X. *Hell.* I 1.35 that Klearchos was Agis' man, but
his main qualification for the northern command will be, now as later, his
Byzantine proxeny (ibid.).

[62] Andrewes is more receptive than I now am to an earlier guess of mine
that Alcibiades invented this order for his execution. His withdrawal will be
at about the beginning of Thucydides' winter if the battle of Miletos referred
to in 45.1 is the battle of 25, but the language of 26.3 suggests to me (but not
to Andrewes) that Alcibiades is already by then detached from the Peloponnesians and the mention of the death of Chalkideus may suggest that the
smaller engagement of 24.1 is in mind. It is impossible to say where Astyochos
was himself or in relation to Alcibiades when he received the instruction, if he
did. The timing is further dependent on the question of whether 45.2 refers
to the discussions of 29 or not; see note 45.

[63] For some material see Dover *HCT* IV 258.

sible. The fleet is accompanied by eleven *sumbouloi*, most prominent of whom is Lichas, son of Arkesilas,[64] the wealthiest man in Sparta, a member of the *gerousia* of long standing, seasoned by diplomatic negotiations at least with Argos, and provided, it might be hoped, with useful relationships with foreigners won by his generosity to visitors to Sparta. The advisers have been instructed to go first to Miletos and examine the situation in the south, to consider the size of the squadron which should be sent to Pharnabazos in the Hellespont, and to look into Pedaritos' charges against Astyochos (39.2). They are empowered to depose Astyochos if they see fit, and they have a replacement ready with them.[65] They take a very circuitous route to Miletos by way of Crete, incidentally distracting Astyochos when he is at last about to eat his words and go to the help of Pedaritos and the Chians (40.3-41.1). He finally meets them in Knidos and has something of a recent victory to exhibit.

There is a peculiar fitness about Knidos for the discussion which followed. The Spartans should have remembered that Knidos was traditionally a Spartan colony [66] and, if they did not, the Knidians, noted for their powers of memory,[67] will certainly have reminded them.[68] But the revolt of this Spartan colony from Athens had been promoted by Tissaphernes (35.1), not by Sparta, and, although there has been no difficulty about using it as a base (35.2), it looks as if at this time it was garrisoned by him (109.1). The difficulty of coming to terms with Persia which would be both profitable and honourable could hardly be put more sharply to the Spartan delegation. However, Tissaphernes was present and had to be talked to.

---

[64] See page 33. Was it thought that he, at any rate, would be unbribable ?

[65] Antisthenes has no previous experience that we know of and gets none to speak of this year. In 398 he is evidently regarded as a very safe and sober man (X. *Hell.* III 2.6-9). For the possibility that his ἐπιβάτης Leon is Pedaritos' father, see Chapter II, note 65; to be an ἐπιβάτης is not a lowly position (X. *Hell.* I 3.17, Hell. Oxy. 22.4) but I agree that he may be a little old for it.

[66] Hdt. I 174.2.

[67] Plut. *GQ* 4.

[68] For friendly relations between Knidos and two other Spartan colonies, Cyrene and Taras, see Hdt. IV 164.2, III 138.1, with Jeffery, *Archaic Greece* (1976) 199. Unlike them, Knidos has not produced any Laconian pottery that I know of (some may have disappeared in the looting described in *BSA* 47, 1952, 175) and most of the links with Sparta which one might suggest are trivial. That Knidos had *aphesteres* has been seen to have some bearing on the Great Rhetra since Grote, III 119 n. 2 (Everyman), but there are no other links in political organisation. An early dedication to the Dioskoroi (*BSA*, loc. cit.), a stray onomastic link (ibid., 190), one shared letter with the Melian alphabet (ibid., 193) do not amount to much.

Tissaphernes will have been doing a good deal of thinking on his own, but we are not fully in a position to distinguish it from what Alcibiades said he had been telling him. We have already seen a certain amount of this, Tissaphernes' likely acceptance of the view that an excessive strengthening of the Spartans would present him with a serious threat, and the influence of this acceptance on the formulation of the second treaty. If financial help were dealt out more economically, there would be a better prospect of Sparta and Athens wearing each other down (46.2). Alcibiades further (46.3) put forward a more surprising view, that Tissaphernes would find the Athenians better partners, to judge by their professions and performance; they were less interested in land power and, in return for help in enslaving part of the sea, they would assist him in enslaving the Greeks in the King's sphere. The Spartans, on the other hand, had come as liberators, and it was not likely that they would merely liberate the Greeks from the Athenians and not liberate them from the Persians as well. The correct course of action for Tissaphernes, then, was to strip as much as possible from the Athenians and then try to get rid of the Spartans (46.4). Tissaphernes will have reserved his judgement on the possible eventual switch to Athens, a policy which he would certainly have to sell to a surprised and reluctant King. To go slow on the Spartans for the moment was economical, congenial and sufficient (46.5).

His perceptible reluctance was also sufficient for Alcibiades' further personal plans. To stave off the defeat of Athens and to be seen doing it by influence on Tissaphernes offered him the possibility of securing his return to Athens (47.1), and he opened up communications with some members of the Athenian fleet at Samos, suggesting that he would be able to secure friendship and financial support for Athens from Tissaphernes and the King, if only the Athenians would do away with democracy (47.2-48.2). In Athens' uncomfortable situation, most of those who heard the idea managed to find it plausible and practical; only the cynical Phrynichos maintained that the Spartans already had a considerable grip on the mainland and that there was no reason for the King to abandon friendship with the Peloponnesians, from whom he had suffered no harm, and exert himself on behalf of the Athenians, whom he did not trust (48.4). There had ensued, not only a mission to Athens to put the idea over there, but some very complicated intrigue in which Phrynichos had endeavoured to put Astyochos on his guard against Alcibiades' plans and Alcibiades had tried to discredit Phrynichos at Samos. The net result was, temporarily, to improve Astyochos' relations with Tissaphernes and weaken Alcibiades' reputation at Samos (49-51).

The meeting at Knidos was to be one of the occasions on which the views of Alcibiades and Phrynichos would be tested. Phrynichos was in fact holding that there was no point of principle which would separate Sparta and Persia; Alcibiades had maintained that the Spartans would not forget that they were the liberators of Greece. It is not clear how much Lichas and his colleagues had known when they set out from Sparta. They had certainly been authorised to take a more independent line with Tissaphernes and possibly to transfer some forces to the north, but the principle of alliance had not been questioned. They had matters to complain of in past actions, but the task of the conference was to see how the war was to be best and most profitably conducted in the future for both parties (43.2). It never got on to this point, for Lichas repudiated both treaties, on the issue of the definition of the King's sphere (43.3-4). It was frightful if the King was now to claim control of all land ever held by himself or his ancestors. This would imply the return to slavery of all the islands and the whole of Northern Greece as far as Boeotia. The Spartans would be bringing the Greeks not freedom, but Persian rule. Another better treaty would have to be made or the alliance was at an end. The Spartans had no need of Persian money on these terms. Territorially, Lichas' complaint is obviously highly selective, and it is doubtful that Tissaphernes had ever thought the treaties extended so far [69] or

---

[69] Since we do not have and are never likely to have a Persian 'List of Peoples' from the year 480, we are not likely to know whether Persian attitudes can ever have remotely corresponded to Lichas' extravagant interpretation. We can say that the throne-bearers depicted on the tomb of Darius I became a canonical group for the remainder of the dynasty (full documentation in Schmidt, *Persepolis*, III 108 ff.). Apart from the vexed problems about Scythians, only two of them can belong to Europe, the Thracian and the petasos-wearing Ionian (or, in the Accadian version, the second Ionians bearing shields on their heads), who may well be a Macedonian. That they both appear on the tomb of Artaxerxes II (labeled) and on that of Artaxerxes III (unlabeled) perhaps indicates the limit of Persian theoretical claims. Hdt. I 4.4 τὴν γὰρ Ἀσίην καὶ τὰ ἐνοικέοντα ἔθνεα βάρβαρα οἰκηιεῦνται οἱ Πέρσαι, τὴν δὲ Εὐρώπην καὶ τὸ Ἑλληνικὸν ἥγηνται κεχωρίσθαι seems over-restrictive; IX 116.3 τὴν Ἀσίην πᾶσαν νομίζουσι ἑαυτῶν εἶναι Πέρσαι καὶ τοῦ αἰεὶ βασιλεύοντος is a better statement.

had clear ideas about how the loose formulation could be turned
to practical ends. The more serious aspect was the talk of freedom
for the Greeks, and Tissaphernes chose to storm off in a huff
without testing Lichas' mind further (43.4). Lichas' remarks, he
thought, had confirmed Alcibiades' observation that the Spartans
were liberating all the cities (52).[70]

As it happened, the consequence of this breach was not a Spartan
move to the north,[71] but one further south still to Rhodes, from
which an offer of revolt had been received. It seemed a good offer
and encouraged the belief that they were in fact perfectly capable
of conducting the war without Tissaphernes' money. Rhodes did
indeed revolt, did provide money, and they remained there for some
time (44).

Tissaphernes turned doubtfully to a consideration of the policy
of cooperation with Athens recommended by Alcibiades, who had
been proved right at least on the Spartan attitude, as it seemed.
At first, according to Thucydides (52), his fear of the Spartans,
who now had nearly a hundred ships in the area, was outweighed
by his dislike of Lichas' talk of freedom, and Alcibiades did his
best to confirm his view. Athens was indeed more cooperative than
might have been expected, and the Athenian assembly authorised
the opening of negotiations with Tissaphernes (53-54.2). However,
by the time the ambassadors arrived, it seemed unlikely to Alcibiades that Tissaphernes could really be pushed on to the Athenian
side, since his fear of the Spartans was greater and he was still
attracted by Alcibiades' own advice to wear down both sides. On
Alcibiades' own account (56.2), he decided to arrange for the
negotiations to fail by making Tissaphernes appear to be setting
his terms too high. Thucydides himself agrees (56.3) that Tissaphernes was too frightened to come to terms with Athens, but
adds the nuance that Alcibiades knew perfectly well that Tissaphernes would not come over to the Athenian side and wanted to
conceal his lack of influence with Tissaphernes from the Athenians

---

[70] ἁπάσας is important. The version of Lichas' remarks given at 43.3
spoke of χώρα, though both treaties spoke of χώρα and πόλεις. At 52 nothing
but πόλεις is in mind.

[71] The commission is evidently reading its instructions (39.2) very freely
and is not deeply committed to what we would have thought to be Agis'
plan. In effect, it has also acquitted Astyochos, perhaps an indication of his
general innocence rather than of their sloth (Westlake, *Individuals in
Thucydides* 299, is unsatisfactory here).

by throwing the responsibility for the breakdown of negotiations on them. Neither account makes the slightest allowance for another factor which we may think not insignificant. How was Tissaphernes going to explain to the King, to whom he will have initially triumphantly reported his alliance with the Spartans and their far-reaching, though vague, concessions, that he had transferred his support to the Athenians, who had kept the King out of his rights for so long, had cast aside his promised friendship and backed the rebel Amorges?

There was only one chance, and that a slim one: to secure from the Athenians concessions so specific and dramatic that even the King would be convinced. The stage was thus set for the conference (56.4). Tissaphernes was present and listening,[72] and Alcibiades spoke on his behalf. He seems to have begun by assurances of Tissaphernes' willingness to come to an agreement, and then stated his terms. After two meetings, the Athenians had conceded the whole of Ionia and the neighbouring islands, whatever is meant by that,[73] and other unspecified conditions. They had done more than enough to justify Alcibiades' prediction that the Athenians were not essentially interested in land power, but the screw was turned still tighter, whether, as Thucydides thought, to break off the negotiations, or because one remaining provision of the peace of Kallias was felt particularly irksome. At the third meeting, it was suggested that the King be allowed complete freedom of ship-building and navigation on his own coast.[74] This is to endanger

[72] Direct statements about Greek-speaking Persians are rare; cf. Hdt. IX 16.2. No clear testimony exists to Tissaphernes' knowledge of Greek, and no doubt most of, if not all, his formal speeches in Xenophon were made through an interpreter, though this only happens to be attested at X. *Anab.* II 3.17. But it never seems to occur to anybody that this may be a handicap in negotiation or that misunderstanding is possible. I would guess that, even as early in his career as this, he was perfectly well aware of everything which was being said.

[73] The King's Peace will add Cyprus and Klazomenai to Asia, but Cyprus will not as yet be an issue, and more must be meant here. Grote suggested Lesbos, Chios and Samos. Others have been wisely less specific. I get no assistance from other Thucydidean uses of the phrase.

[74] It was no particular secret that ms. C had ἑαυτῶν even before the recent article of Goldstein, *Cal. Stud. Class. Ant.* 7, 1974, 155-62, and the reading was preferred, not only by Krüger and Hude, but as late as Hatzfeld, *Alcibiade* 238 n. 4, about whom Goldstein is ungenerous. The odds seem to me heavily against it. 1) After VI 92.5, the presumption must be for concurrences of B and the hyparchetype β against C, though VIII 76.6, 82.1, 92.4, 101.2 show that good material can get through. 2) This would

even Athens' command of the sea,[75] and the Athenian ambassadors, furious with what they considered to be Alcibiades' deceit, broke off negotiations and went back to Samos.

The authority of Thucydides is such that I find that I have only one predecessor [76] in even considering the possibility that Tissaphernes was in the least serious in entering into these negotiations, but there seems to me to be something in it. He certainly cannot leave the situation as it was after his meeting with Lichas at Knidos and allow the King to be for long in the position, perhaps already known to him, that he has no Greek allies at all. His chances of getting an agreement out of Athens which will satisfy the King were, we have seen, always slim, but the negotiations will certainly have served one useful purpose. The Spartans have started to behave as if they were his only possible partners. He has now demonstrated that they are not, and he can produce a detailed account of how far the Athenians on their side have been prepared to go.

These are points which are not considered by Thucydides when

----

be for me the most difficult use of a reflexive in Thucydides. Goldstein seems to have misread Powell, *CQ* 28, 1934, 162 note a. This is merely a correction of a total to be derived from Hude and Powell does not return to a consideration of ἑαυτῶν. Cases like II 7.1, 92.4 are due to the dominance of the subject of the sentence. I see no case in Powell's survey of Thucydidean reflexives, or indeed in Kuhner-Gerth II 1.561-2, where the point of reference of the reflexive is neither the subject of the sentence (Alcibiades in this case) or that of the immediate verb controlling the reflexive (the King), but that of an intermediate verb (the Athenians, not even directly expressed). I think Thucydides would have written αὐτῶν. 3) Arnold pointed out what seems to have been forgotten, that Thuc. IV 118.5 is a perfectly adequate parallel for a Greek treaty (an armistice, admittedly, in this case) where a state accepts restrictions on freedom of navigation on her own coastline. There is no parallel that I know of for a reference to the other party's coast. Sea-limits, for which, besides the Peace of Kallias, compare Pol. III 22.5, are another matter, and so is entrance to harbours (Thuc. II 7.2, VI 52.1).

[75] Alcibiades himself had suggested that she be allowed this at VIII 46.3. Cf. II 26.2, V 56.2 for the attitude of Athenians and others. It should be observed that the proposed relaxation of restrictions on Persia will coincide with a situation in which the Athenians will be reconciled to a major loss of revenue with which to maintain their own fleet. "It extinguished the maritime empire of Athens, and compromised the security of all the coasts and islands of the Aegean. To see Lesbos, Chios, and Samos, etc. in possession of Persia, was sufficiently painful; but if there came to be powerful Persian fleets on these islands, it would be the certain precursor and means of further conquests to the westward, and would revive the aggressive dispositions of the Great King as they had stood at the beginning of the reign of Xerxes" (Grote, VIII 19, Everyman).

[76] Hatzfeld, *Alcibiade* 239.

he comes to discuss Tissaphernes' motives after the departure of
the Athenian ambassadors (57).[77] He is evidently aware that Tissaphernes was under pressure, since he makes him move with some
speed (εὐθύς) and ready for compromise with Sparta,[78] but he sees
as the cause of the pressure a deterioration in the Spartans' ability
to keep their fleet going, which is alluded to, rather than described
or accounted for. The consequence might be that they are forced
to fight the Athenians on unfavourable terms or that their rowers
may leave them entirely. They may also, and here we see more
clearly what has been meant by previous references to his fear of
the Spartans, be led in their need for money to sack the mainland.
If his policy of keeping the Greeks on a level with each other is to
be maintained, the Spartans must be supported. The Spartans are
summoned, they are given aid, and a third treaty is made (58).

You will see that I think Thucydides' account of Tissaphernes'
motives for making this treaty is inadequate, and for the Spartans
we are given no background at all. We can certainly deduce that
their high hopes of financing themselves had been dashed. It can
be calculated that the 32 talents they had received on Rhodes
would have paid their 94 ships for about 20 days and they were
there for 80 days (44.4).[79] This will certainly have made them more
conciliatory, and I believe that the news that an Athenian embassy
had been with Tissaphernes and of how far it had been prepared
to go will also have put considerable pressure on them. That Athens
and her fleet were about to be torn by revolution will not have yet
appeared, and, if Thucydides was not able to see that Tissaphernes
was, as I have argued, under some compulsion to exhibit a new
treaty to the King, it is perhaps unlikely that the Spartans appreci-
ated that this might give them something of a lever. If realities

---

[77] Thucydides tiresomely fails to say where the meeting with the Athenians
took place. Busolt *GG* III 1471 guesses Magnesia, evidently from 50.3 (Oroites,
though satrap of Sardis, was to be found at Magnesia in the 520s, Hdt. III
122.1). This is certainly handy for Samos and not inconsistent with παρέρχε-
ται ἐς τὴν Καῦνον. But Tissaphernes was surely at Knidos later than he was
at Magnesia, and I suspect that he may have been at his Carian οἶκος,
wherever that was.

[78] ξυνθήκας ἔτι ἄλλας ποιησόμενος (to be preferred to ποιησάμενος), ἃς ἂν
δύνηται.

[79] Cf. Busolt 1450. To believe in the 80 days has its difficulties, which
Andrewes will discuss, for those who believe that Thucydides was consistent
about the end of his winter, But so does the apparent fact that the treaty
is dated to Darius' 13th year which ought to have begun on March 29
(Andrewes, *Historia* 10, 1961, 2 n. 4).

alone are considered, the third treaty is rather worse for Sparta than the second.

There is some reason to think that the King had a hand in the treaty, though he in fact drops out of the list of participants and the text is merely described as about the King's affairs and those of the Spartans and their allies.[80] On the Persian side, the participants are, besides Tissaphernes, Hieramenes and the sons of Pharnakes. The last phrase presumably means in effect Pharnabazos, although the greater part of the treaty is about collaboration between the Spartans and Tissaphernes. It has been held[81] that his inclusion is due to Spartan insistence. It seems to me a shade more likely that the King thought his presence desirable if the status of Asia was going to be dealt with. Hieramenes is more of a puzzle. He is associated with Tissaphernes in a Lycian text which we cannot translate,[82] and may be the same as the Hieramenes who appears in an interpolation in Xenophon apparently as Darius' brother-in-law.[83] If so, he would not be unsuitable as a visiting representative of the King.

The other reasons for believing the King to be involved are internal. The question of the rate of pay had been referred to the King (29.1); it has now evidently been settled (58.5), though we are not told on what terms.[84] The Phoenician fleet, which I have so far been deliberately avoiding, makes repeated appearances in the treaty under the designation of 'the King's ships'; there can be no doubt that their mobilisation is a royal matter.[85] Lastly, I find it hard to believe that the King has not heard of Lichas' objections

---

[80] For an explanation of the problem that the text suggests that the negotiations were at Kaunos and the heading of the treaty says that the agreement was made in the plain of the Maeander, see Kirchhoff, *Thukydides und sein Urkundenmaterial* (1895) 139.

[81] Kirchhoff, op. cit., 140 (the Spartans are bound by their original instructions), Busolt 1451-2. Effective Spartan help for him does start shortly afterwards (62.1).

[82] See Chapter Four, note 4.

[83] X. *Hell*. II 1.8-9 (from Ktesias?). If Hieramenes is not the father of the executed youths, the reason for his indignation is not clear. There is nothing which can be done to make sense of τῆς τοῦ Ξέρξου τοῦ Δαρείου πατρὸς, but it is curious that virtually the identical mistake is made about Parysatis in Ktesias 44.

For some highly unlikely thoughts about the role of Hieramenes, see Altheim and Stiehl, *Die Aramäische Sprache unter den Achaimeniden* I 151-2.

[84] κατὰ τὰ ξυγκείμενα leaves us with no choice but to believe that the reference is to 29.2, but this may not be right.

[85] Formal proof at 87.5; cf. Hdt. V 31.4, where admittedly royal consent goes beyond the mere question of the number of ships.

to the definition of his empire in the first two treaties. Since that definition is now modified and restricted, it seems wildly improbable that the King has not given his views.

The King's empire is now explicitly limited to Asia, but we now get, not only a return to the forthright statement of the first treaty that it shall be the King's, but also a reinforcing clause that he may deliberate about his own territory as he wishes. There is a further change which may be of significance. The first two treaties had spoken of χώρα καὶ πόλεις, land and cities; this one only speaks about χώρα. The distinction between χώρα and πόλεις is an important one in Asia Minor at least from the time of Alexander[86] and it would certainly not be surprising to find it extending much further back.[87] There is an initial temptation to think that the Greek cities of Asia may be silently omitted from this document and that Spartan recognition is only being extended to areas under the King's direct rule.[88] But a later passage (84.5)[89] seems to prove that, even in the mind of Lichas, Miletos and therefore presumably all cities on the mainland were in the King's χώρα and were bound by the treaty.[90]

The reinforcing clause, in effect that the King may do as he likes with his own, prompts speculation about its origins. Andrewes once suggested[91] that there is an implicit reference to the Peace of Kallias and that such a clause is strong evidence for the existence

---

[86] Tod II 185. See e.g. Jones, *The Greek City* 95-6.

[87] So De Ste Croix *OPW* 313-4.

[88] De Ste Croix, loc. cit., considers the possibility that the Spartan negotiators were hoping to maintain, after the war was over, that they had only recognised the King's right to the χώρα in the narrower sense.

[89] ἔφη τε χρῆναι Τισσαφέρνει καὶ δουλεύειν Μιλησίους καὶ τοὺς ἄλλους ἐν τῇ βασιλέως τὰ μέτρια καὶ ἐπιθεραπεύειν, ἕως ἂν τὸν πόλεμον εὖ θῶνται.

[90] De Ste Croix *OPW* 155. χώρᾳ certainly has to be supplied with the feminine article; γῇ, which sometimes has to be understood in such phrases (e.g. I 44.1), is not suitable here and would make no difference anyway. De Ste Croix compares 43.3 for similar thinking on Lichas' part. Andrewes has considered a line of escape from this conclusion, that Lichas' mind at 84.5 is not on the third treaty, but on the separate agreements between the King and the cities to be deduced from 37.5 (see page 94 and note 54). If the agreements had stipulated that there were to be no Persian garrisons, Lichas could simply be telling them not to insist on their rights. This is clearly possible, but a good deal less likely than the normal interpretation.

[91] *Historia* 10, 1961, 15-6, doubted by Meiggs, *The Athenian Empire* 142 n. 2. Andrewes would now be prepared to accept the King's bad temper as an adequate explanation and withdraw reference to the Peace of Kallias.

of this Peace which contained, according to the sources, substantial
limitations on the King's freedom, not only of navigation on his
coasts, but of military movement on the mainland; what will be
being stressed is the dissimilarity of this treaty with that predecessor. It is clearly also possible that the clause is a reaction to specific
Spartan proposals, perhaps about the status of the Greek cities.[92]
But it may simply reflect an angry outburst of the King when faced
with the difficulty about the definition of his empire. If he is going
to accept an explicit limitation to Asia, it must in any case be made
clear that there is to be no quibbling about his rights there.

The slight changes in the non-aggression clauses and those about
the joint conduct of the war and of peace-negotiations and some new
mutual assistance clauses need not detain us, but we must consider
the references to the royal fleet. This has so far played no part in
that strand of Thucydides' narrative which reflects the Spartan
point of view. Its first appearance is in discussions between Tissaphernes and Alcibiades (46.1) which may go back before the making
of the second treaty, though there is no mention of the fleet in that
treaty. Tissaphernes was preparing to bring in Phoenician ships and
Alcibiades advised against it as likely to produce too speedy an
end to the war.[93] Tissaphernes, in adopting Alcibiades' general
advice about wearing both sides down, simply uses the future
arrival of the ships as an argument to the Spartans against seeking
a premature naval battle (46.5).[94] In the third treaty the ships are
coming and it is moreover made clear to the Spartans that they will
reduce Persia's need of the Peloponnesian fleet. Tissaphernes will
only pay their fleet [95] until the King's ships come. After the King's
ships come, Tissaphernes will go on paying the Peloponnesians if they
wish to stay, but only as a loan to be repaid at the end of the war.

---

[92] Goldstein, *Cal. Stud. Class. Ant.* 7, 1974, 162-4 thinks that the clause is
a restatement of 37.2 as against 18.1, reaffirming the King's sole right to
tribute in Asia.

[93] The logic of the use of participles and infinitives in this sentence is not
impeccable. It is unclear how the arrival of Phoenician ships would have the
effect of giving the Spartans control of land and sea, except in so far as they
might ensure the destruction of Athenian sea-power.

[94] The timing is obscure. The most likely occasion for this advice to the
Spartans is during the stalemate at 38.5, when the Spartans do not respond
to an Athenian naval challenge, but the advice may have been given more
than once.

[95] And only those of them which are now present, ταῖς νῦν παρούσαις. The
theoretical possibility left by the second treaty (37.4) that the King may
send for more is now withdrawn.

We can hardly disentangle the Persian side of this or determine whether it was really in the King's mind or that of Tissaphernes that it would be preferable to use their own resources for their own purposes rather than to rely on the Spartans.[96] Lichas' outburst at Knidos will certainly have done something to create an impression that the Spartans were fundamentally unreliable. Our task is certainly not made easier by Thucydides' conviction[97] that, at any rate on Tissaphernes' part (he virtually never considers the King at all),[98] the whole of the business of the Phoenician fleet was a gigantic bluff, that there never was any intention of using it, and that Tissaphernes' consistent policy was to wear down both sides. We can, I think, say that the firm intentions now expressed by Tissaphernes that the fleet was now going to arrive, perhaps strengthened by the appearance of a royal representative in the person of Hieramenes, will have played their part in convincing the Spartans that they had better make a treaty quickly and get their pay. What reservations they may have had about the permanence of their concessions we do not know,[99] but on the face of it the Spartan professional negotiators have not improved on the performance of the amateurs. We may seek excuses for them in their financial difficulties and in their need to match the Athenians' bids, but, despite their wriggling, the liberators have conceded Asia to the King.[100]

---

[96] We cannot tell how efficient a machine the royal fleet will be or, rather, how efficient the King thinks it will be. We know that the successful creation of a Persian fleet in the 390s involved a considerable amount of Greek manpower, particularly in the skilled ranks; cf. the Athenian ὑπηρεσίαι of Hell. Oxy. 7.1 and Isoc. IV 142 (the latter a determined effort to minimise the importance of that fleet). We may reflect on the long gap since it has had any battle experience. But there may have been advice available to the Persians which would stress the long tale of Spartan naval incompetence and point out that the Sicilian expedition had severely damaged Athenian naval power and skill. Much could have been gained from conversation with Alcibiades and, if Tissaphernes had an infantry expert later (Chapter One, note 69), he can have a naval expert now; Tamos (see note 48) is a possibility, but there must have been Carians and Cypriotes whe tried to keep up with naval matters.

[97] Expressed most fully at 87.

[98] 87.5 at least reflects a belief that the King will like economical policies.

[99] 84.5 (cf. note 89) ἕως ἂν τὸν πόλεμον εὖ θῶνται suggests that there were some.

[100] The bleak conclusion is partly rhetorical, partly making a maximum concession to an opposite view before the argument of the next chapter. But if 37.5 does mean that the cities had already been protecting themselves by agreements with Persia, the Spartans may be allowed to think that 58.2 would not in itself cancel them. The King will have already indicated that he is prepared to restrict the operation of his will.

CHAPTER FIVE

After the conclusion of the third treaty, Thucydides' narrative still has some six months to go before it breaks off with a sentence in which Tissaphernes sacrifices to Artemis at Ephesos. Diana of the Ephesians is a decidedly peculiar goddess,[1] and one should not think that there is anything particularly symbolic about the Persian satrap sacrificing in a Greek city at the end of Thucydides. We need not, I think, follow in detail the deterioration of Spartan relations with Tissaphernes which he describes and the eventual decision to transfer their fleet to the north and cooperate with Pharnabazos, though we shall eventually have to consider some points.

Thucydides does not mention any further negotiations, and this will have contributed to the present universal conviction that his last treaty represents the final statement of Spartan-Persian relations during the Peloponnesian War. It is held that, although the Spartans ended the war still proclaiming liberation, that the day on which the Athenian walls were demolished was the beginning of freedom for Greece,[2] the claim was by then the purest hypocrisy. For De Ste Croix[3] it always had been, and he holds that the behaviour of Sparta in placing all the Asiatic Greeks under the Persian yoke is sufficient to show that the Spartan promise to liberate the allies of Athens was mere propaganda, except insofar as it happened to coincide with Sparta's own selfish interests. My own views used not to be very different, but I am now inclined to think that Sparta may have had a better case in 404 than we have been allowing and that we have been misled seriously by the ending of Thucydides' narrative in 411 and our inevitable subsequent reliance on Xenophon. As another colleague of mine has

---

[1] For Tissaphernes' interest in her, cf. X. *Hell.* I 2.6. In general, see Picard, *Ephèse et Claros* (1922) 610 ff. Her νεώκορος was called Megabyxos as early as 394 (X. *Anab.* V 3.6) and this may already have been as much a title as a name; it remained a title until at least the first century B.C. (Str. XIV 1.23, App. *B.C.* V 36); cf. Hicks, *Inscr. Brit. Mus.* III p. 84, to which add *I. Priene* 3, 231. For the correct form of the name, see Benveniste, *Titres et noms propres en iranien ancien* 109.

[2] See page 67.

[3] *OPW* 154-8.

remarked,[4] "The silences of Xenophon have ceased merely to amaze; they have become a scandal ..... the silences of Xenophon can never prove that what he does not recount did not happen."

The severe judgement of Spartan behaviour is of course not purely modern. We find it, without surprise, in fourth-century Athens. In the funeral speech in Plato's *Menexenos* [5] it is said that at the end of the war the Greeks were enslaved either by each other or by barbarians,[6] and, when we come on to the peace-negotiations of 392, there is a reference back to an earlier phase and to the Greeks on the mainland which the Spartans had previously handed over to the King.[7] Isocrates' *Panegyricus* of 380 is apparently equally explicit: "We should criticise the Spartans in that at the beginning they entered the war to free the Greeks, but at the end they thus handed over many of them; they made the Ionians revolt from our city but handed them over to the barbarians'.[8] But even the *Panegyricus* tells a slightly different story when it says [9] that Artaxerxes II achieved by the King's Peace what none of his ancestors ever had; the only possible difference between what is said there and what is presently believed of Darius II would lie in the assent of Athens as well as of Sparta to the subjugation of the Ionian cities. Forty years on, at the end of Isocrates' life, the *Panathenaicus* offers another version. There the Spartans secure the revolt of Athens' allies by promising them freedom, and negotiate friendship and alliance with the King by *offering* him all the inhabitants of Asia. When they have won the war, they break faith with both, enslaving the Greeks worse than helots and repaying the King (a different King, as is not noted) by setting his brother on him.[10] Their crimes are against both Greeks and barbarians.[11] It will not be disputed that in both the *Panegyricus* and the *Panathenaicus* the real Spartan crime lies in the King's Peace, and the *Panegyricus* does not conceal that between 404 and that Peace the Spartans fought Persia hard and with some success.[12]

---

[4] Cawkwell, *CQ* n.s. 23, 1973, 57-8.
[5] Whatever one thinks about this speech, it is not in this respect likely to depart from Athenian popular belief.
[6] 244 c.
[7] 245 b.
[8] IV 122.
[9] IV 137.
[10] XII 103-4.
[11] XII 105.
[12] IV 144.

Let us look closer. I start with the passage which has been thought conclusive proof that the Spartans in 411 abandoned the Ionians at least for the duration of the war. Later in the summer of 411, as Peloponnesian discontent with Tissaphernes is increasing, we find that Tissaphernes has built a fort in Miletos.[13] The Milesians seized it and expelled its garrison. In this they had the support of the other allies, particularly of the Syracusans.[14] But Lichas was displeased with them and told the Milesians that they and the rest of those in the King's territory should subject themselves to some extent to Tissaphernes (the Greek is sharper 'be his slaves to a moderate extent') and keep his favour, until the war was success-fully over. The Milesians were furious and, when he died shortly after, they interfered with his burial.[15]

We tend to regard Lichas' intervention as settling the matter, but it should be clear that it does not. Even in the fleet it does not. Later in the summer we find another of Tissaphernes' garrisons removed from Antandros.[16] Diodorus asserts Spartan complicity in this outright; Thucydides does not exclude it and makes it clear that Tissaphernes believed in it. But we should go beyond the fleet. In the next chapter [17] after Lichas' intervention, the Spartan admiral Astyochos, having reached the end of a stormy period of office, goes home. He is accompanied by a largish gathering. A Milesian embassy is going to denounce Tissaphernes, and so is the Syracusan Hermokrates, with the intention of ex-pounding his view that Tissaphernes is double-crossing the allies and in a plot with Alcibiades to ruin the allied cause. Tissaphernes sends an ambassador too, one Gaulites, a bilingual Carian,[18] to denounce the Milesians about the fort and to defend his own conduct in general. We are thus assured that Sparta is going to be faced, not only with the question of Tissaphernes' general behaviour,

---

[13] Thuc. VIII 84.4.

[14] Syracusan sailors are mostly free and more vocal in demanding their pay (ibid., VIII 84.1).

[15] The implication of Paus. VI 2.3 that Lichas survived until after 400 to set up his own statue at Olympia is clearly false. Westlake, *Essays on the Greek Historians and Greek History* (1969) 193 n. 38 seems to be wrong in reading Thuc. VIII 87.1 as conclusive evidence that Lichas went to Aspendos. He evidently never got there (VIII 99).

[16] Thuc. VIII 108.4-5, 109 (the troops come from Abydos and Tissaphernes thinks the Peloponnesians responsible); D.S. XIII 42.4.

[17] VIII 85.

[18] See page 14.

but also with the problem of the position of the Greeks of Asia, at least as it was manifested in the question of Persian garrisons in Greek cities. Miletos was not the last place where the problem would arise. Before the summer was out, Tissaphernes' garrisons had been ejected also from Antandros, as we have seen, and from the Spartan colony of Knidos.[19] Lichas has been coerced by the necessities of the situation in Asia Minor as he saw them. Can we be confident that the Spartan assembly would see matters in the same light?

At this crucial point Thucydides deserts us. It is as if were watching a complex play on television and reception is disrupted by an electric storm. We can make one fairly good guess. The discontent of the home government with Tissaphernes will already have increased greatly. The new admiral Mindaros waits only to receive further reports that the Phoenician fleet is not coming and that Tissaphernes is a swindler to transfer the entire fleet to the north.[20] Lichas' mission had not been given that option [21] and Mindaros is surely acting on instructions brought with him. Sparta will certainly be prepared to hear no good of Tissaphernes. But of the assembly itself we get only one glimpse. Hermokrates, Xenophon tells us incidentally,[22] spoke against Tissaphernes at Sparta, Astyochos bearing witness as well, and seemed to speak the truth. Was this only about Tissaphernes' double-dealing and not also about the position of the Greeks of Asia? Thucydides has after all told us that the Milesians had had the sympathy of the Syracusans about the fort.[23]

I will not pretend that it is easy to determine all the factors and arguments which may determine the decisions of a Spartan assembly. Even in our very sketchy evidence,[24] the reported arguments are very various. The assembly is likely to be hostile

---

[19] VIII 109.1.

[20] VIII 99. Not quite the entire fleet. D.S. XIII 38.5 is certainly right to say that he despatched 13 ships under Dorieus to Rhodes at the same time, but they too went to the north before long (D.S. XIII 45.1).

[21] Thuc. VIII 39.2.

[22] *Hell.* I 1.31. The only reason we are told at all is to explain Pharnabazos' goodwill to Hermokrates.

[23] It is to be conceded that Hermokrates' first priority is the defeat of Athens and that he had not ruled out Carthaginian help in achieving it. (Thuc. VI 34.2).

[24] I am essentially working from the list of Spartan assemblies compiled by Andrewes, *Studies . . . . Ehrenberg* 6.

to commanders who have got out of line,[25] and this could conceivably extend to ambassadors. It can be influenced by grudges
of long standing [26] and, of course, prejudice may enter into straightforward power-calculations,[27] which are always possible.[28] There
are traces of impatience with diplomatic manoeuvring in cases which
seem to be clear.[29] Straight arguments about the bolstering of
Spartan power are relatively rare.[30] Mythological arguments can
be used to the Spartans,[31] but are unlikely to have carried much
weight.[32] Sentiment however is a possibility, as when the Spartans
in 404 decline to destroy Athens, a Greek city which had done
great good to Greece in the greatest dangers.[33] They can be prevailed on to defend the independence of a city,[34] and they are
certainly likely to be swayed by an appeal to their duty to allies.[35]

In my second lecture, I was prepared to confine the importance
of the assembly to cases where the leadership was split. It would
in fact seem hard to believe that the leadership was much split on
this occasion. The balance of forces was, we have already seen,
prepared to jettison Tissaphernes. Support of him had never been
Agis' personal policy, and we have heard nothing of the other king,
Pleistoanax, for seven years.[36] Endios, once committed to Tissa-

---

[25] Thuc. V 63, X. *Hell.* V 2.32 (cf. Chapter Two, note 159).

[26] X. *Hell.* III 2.23. That Spartan demands on Elis are couched in the
form of a demand for autonomy for her subject cities is, I agree, likely to be
no more than a cloak.

[27] Thuc. I 86, X. *Hell.* VI 3.5, 4.3. Hostility to Athens is presupposed
throughout Thuc. VI 88.10-93.2.

[28] Thuc. V 77.1, X. *Hell.* V 2.11-20.

[29] Thuc. I 86, X. *Hell.* VI 4.2-3.

[30] For De Ste Croix's view of Thuc. I 86 see Chapter Three, note 127.

[31] X. *Hell.* VI 3.6.

[32] But see Thuc. I 107.2 and III 92.4 (as a partial reason).

[33] X. *Hell.* II 2.20. No motives are assigned at II 4.38 for what is essentially
a decision to abandon the Thirty; I would be fairly confident that the gap
can be filled by the discoveries about the conduct of the Thirty reported by
Lys. XVIII 10.

[34] X. *Hell.* V 2.14. Of course, Akanthos is only a special case of the
Olynthian threat, but has not Xenophon missed part of the point? If it
is the wish of the Akanthians τοῖς πατρίοις νόμοις χρῆσθαι καὶ αὐτοπολῖται
εἶναι, are they not likely to have reminded the Spartans of the assurances
that they had received from Brasidas, reinforced by oath, in 424 (Thuc. IV
86.1-4, 88.1)?

[35] This, I repeat, is what Sthenelaidas' speech at Thuc. I 86 is all about.
X. *Hell.* IV 6.3 is a more problematic case, since the Achaeans are threatening
secession a good deal more openly than the allies of 432 (Thuc. I 71.5-6).

[36] Thuc. V 75.1.

phernes, we shall shortly find arguing for a compromise peace.[37] The men on the spot, Astyochos and Hermokrates, still perhaps carrying the glamour of the Athenian defeat in Sicily, are reporting that Tissaphernes is a dead loss.

The Milesians are not likely to have pulled any punches. They will surely have reminded the Spartans of their obligations to Greek freedom and their special place in the Greek world.[38] If any prejudice came into play, it will surely have been anti-Persian prejudice. Someone might have put power-political arguments in the other scale, the impossibility of permanent support of Ionia [39] and the necessity of Persian help. But, as far as Tissaphernes is concerned, this last argument will never have seemed weaker, and it might well have been hoped that Pharnabazos could be prevailed on to avoid provocative behaviour. My strong inclination is to believe that, after this assembly, the third treaty at least lost a great deal of its importance, and that, for all practical purposes, it went the way of its predecessors.

For much of the treaty, this seems relatively clear. The detailed clauses of the treaty prescribed that Tissaphernes was to produce pay, that the King's fleet would come, and that Tissaphernes and the Spartans would collaborate in the conduct of the war. Tissaphernes did not provide pay, the fleet got no further than Aspendos,[40] and the return of Alcibiades to the Athenian fleet contributed to the impression of Tissaphernes' unreliability.[41] The Spartans could therefore consider themselves freed from obligations to collaborate with Tissaphernes, and, despite the fact that he chased after them to the Hellespont to explain,[42] he went permanently on to their

---

[37] D.S. XIII 52.2.

[38] Cf. X. *Hell.* III 1.3 the Ionians' request ἐπεὶ πάσης τῆς Ἑλλάδος προστά-ται εἰσίν, ἐπιμεληθῆναι καὶ σφῶν τῶν ἐν τῇ Ἀσίᾳ Ἑλλήνων, ὅπως ἥ τε χώρα μὴ δῃοῖτο αὐτῶν καὶ αὐτοὶ ἐλεύθεροι εἶεν, an appeal which works without any reference to power politics, though the power arguments would be all in the other direction. (Judeich, *Kleinasiatische Studien* 41 thought that the Spartans were adopting Lysander's plans for an Asiatic empire; I do not see on what grounds.) The assembly does not happen to be mentioned, but we cannot doubt that it was consulted.

[39] Cf. Hdt. IX 106.2.

[40] Thuc. VIII 87.3. That there may have been good reason for this does not affect the issue.

[41] Thuc. VIII 87.1.

[42] The end of the journey described by Thuc. VIII 109 is of course badly documented. There can be no reasonable doubt that the explanation about the Phoenician ships attributed by Diodorus to Pharnabazos at XIII 46.6

black list. Collaboration with Tissaphernes is henceforth a possible political charge at Sparta.[43] Furthermore, despite the fact that they got much better collaboration out of Pharnabazos, the Spartans evidently did not consider themselves bound by the provision, common to all three treaties, that they were not to make a separate peace without Persia. In the dark days of summer 410, when their fleet had been wiped out, a Spartan embassy led by Endios [44] came to Athens suggesting peace on the basis that each side should keep what it had.[45] The speech we have in Diodorus is not very likely to be authentic [46] and the King is only mentioned as the provider of Sparta's financial resources. It does not seem to me impossible that the difficulties of Sparta's relations with Persia will have contributed to her wish for peace, and this is not her last attempt at it.[47] It seems hard to think that Sparta is taking the third treaty seriously.

I pass to more general considerations which seem to me to cast doubt on the proposition that, after the third treaty, Sparta was

belongs to Tissaphernes; Diodorus conflates the two for the whole of Book XIII. We have no material at all for the Spartan reaction, which will have been unfavourable. Alcibiades' approach to Tissaphernes and consequent imprisonment for 30 days in Sardis (X. *Hell.* I 1.9) belongs here. One of Tissaphernes' motives for imprisoning Alcibiades is said by Plut. *Alc.* 27.7 to be his bad reputation with the Spartans, that is, it is part of his attempt at reconciliation. Alcibiades claimed, not necessarily falsely, that Tissaphernes had connived at his escape (Plut. *Alc.* 28.1), which will have nullified the operation altogether.

[43] X. *Hell.* I 1.32. For the problem about the text see Chapter Four note 43. It could of course happen that Tissaphernes and Spartans might find themselves on the same side; the new fragment of the Hellenica Oxyrhynchia seems to have Spartans at the Battle of Ephesos in 409 (Koenen, *Studia Papyrologica* 15, 1976, 58-9). We are very badly informed about the small Spartan detachments left behind when Mindaros went to the north. Iasos, if it is Iasos, and Ephesos will not be the only examples, and it should be clear that the south was not simply left to the Persians.

[44] Endios' own policy was now in ruins, but his position may have been improved by the lack of success of the 'northerners'. Is he now returning to sponsor the old policy of Athens-Sparta collaboration, or is he simply here as an Athens specialist (cf. Chapter Two, note 65)?

[45] D.S. XIII 52.2-53. There will be more to be said about the peace terms later.

[46] That the narrative rests ultimately on the Hellenica Oxyrhynchia is virtually certain; cf. the language of 53.1 with that of Hell. Oxy. VI 3. But there is still no evidence that that author gave speeches, and what we have here will be free composition (apart from the peace terms).

[47] Another attempt in 408/7 (Androtion *FGH* 324 F 44). The final attempt after Arginusae (Arist. 'Aθ. Πολ. 34.1) is not strictly in point here, since on my view, as will be seen, another Sparta-Persia treaty has intervened.

held to have abandoned the Greeks of Asia. As far as I can see, the problems about Persian garrisons in Greek cities do not arise again until after the end of the war, and there is no further trace of Ionian complaints. In fact, when Lysander arrives in 407, it is clear that one of his main strengths is the enthusiastic support which he receives from Greek cities in Ionia, notably in Ephesos,[48] and I see no sign of a Persian garrison or a direct Persian presence. The fleet which won Aegospotami and brought an end to the war was represented as an allied fleet. In the victory-dedication at Delphi which commemorated Aegospotami,[49] the statues of the commanders included, along with those from the mainland and the islands a Cnidian, an Ephesian, a Milesian and, probably,[50] an Erythraean. Is this enthusiasm for the prosecution of the war really compatible with the knowledge that the end of the war would see the cities handed over to full Persian control?[51]

This is a difficult question to answer, and attitudes of Ionians to Persia probably differed from city to city and from group to group. The devastation and enslavement which accompanied the Persian suppression of the Ionian revolt in 494 [52] were long in the past, and were not necessarily to be expected in a more peaceful transition of power. Individual cases of harsh behaviour by Persian officials to Greeks were known.[53] They would certainly be remembered and their repetition might be feared.[54] Nevertheless, Medising groups are visible throughout the fifth century [55] and it is certainly not to be excluded that some people will have preferred Persia to Athens if it meant that they could assert their own

[48] D.S. XIII 70.4, Plut. *Lys.* 3.3-4, X. *Hell.* I 8.6.

[49] Paus. X 9.9; cf. *ML* 95.

[50] No other state is likely to be described as ὑπὲρ τοῦ Μίμαντος and the collocation with the Chians adds some confirmation.

[51] The difficulty is felt by Lotze, *Lysander und der Peloponnesische Krieg* (1964) 19, who suggests that Lysander may have received some assurances from Cyrus, longer-sighted than his father, about the Greek cities. But these would hardly have sufficed, if they had not been made public.

[52] Hdt. VI 19.3-20, 31, 32, 33.2.

[53] The most conspicuous wrong to be avenged in 479 was Artayktes' behaviour at Elaious (Hdt. IX 116, cf. VII 33).

[54] Arsakes' treacherous behaviour to the Delians at Atramytteion in 422 was well-known to their near neighbours at Antandros eleven years later and, when he started giving orders which they could not bear, whatever is meant by that, they preferred not to risk a repetition (Thuc. VIII 108.4-5).

[55] For the mainland, the most obvious certain cases are Erythrai in the 450s (*ML* 40.27, but they have only fled to the Medes) and Kolophon in 430 (Thuc. III 34).

position over that of their political opponents. It is not in dispute
that Lysander owed much of his support to the political base which
he created in the cities,[56] but, though his supporters were certainly
anti-democratic, it is at least clear that they formed only a section
of the upper classes,[57] and their attitude to Persia is totally obscure.[58]
In general, there is perhaps some probability that land-owners will
have had more to gain from affiliation with Persia than those with
more maritime interests.[59] Culturally, it is certainly likely that some
places were more Asiatic than others. "The Cypriotes are barbarians",
I was told by a reluctant Athenian settler in Cyprus in 1953 when
the Greek press was telling a very different story, and, on Plutarch's
account, Ephesos was under very heavy Persian cultural influence
when Lysander made it his base in 407.[60] However, it is certainly
clear that the cities of Ionia were not enchanted with Persian rule
when they appealed to Sparta in 399, and already in 406 the
Spartan admiral Kallikratidas takes it for granted that at least

[56] D.S. XIII 70.4, Plut. *Lys.* 5.5-7, 8, 13.5-8, X. *Hell.* III 4.2, 5.13, Nep.
Lys. 1.5.

[57] Their victims at Miletos include 300 of the wealthiest democrats
(D.S. XIII 104.5), and Plut. *Lys.* 13.7 (cf. 5.5-6) (perhaps reflecting the
prejudices of Theopompus) is firm that Lysander chose his friends οὔτε
ἀριστίνδην οὔτε πλουτίνδην. Lotze, op. cit. (note 51) 17-9 struggles with the
difficulties of establishing the class-basis of the dekarchies. It might be
simpler to believe the sources and think that loyalty to Lysander was
their main qualification. Hegyi in Welskopf (ed.), *Hellenische Poleis* II
(1974) 1026-7 sees the difficulties of finding class lines much more clearly.

[58] I find it difficult to follow De Ste Croix *OPW* 39 in thinking that the
dekarchies were composed of men with large estates granted by the Persian
King. There are of course doubtful cases like the site near Kolophon discussed
by J. M. Cook, *Proc. Camb. Phil. Soc.* n.s. 7, 1961, 16.

[59] Cf. in general Cook, op. cit. 9-18 with the comments of De Ste Croix
OPW 313; De Ste Croix's 'propertied class' seems to me too simple (cf. note
57).

[60] Plut. *Lys.* 3.3. The passage is by no means free from difficulty. On any
orthodox view, the royal generals who have been spending time there can
only have been doing so since 413/2. It is certainly presented as a consequence (and possibly as an intention) of Lysander's activity there that it
became more prosperous and, by implication, more Hellenic. Lotze (15, 25)
argues against this (and against Schaefer, *Würzburger Jahrbücher* 4, 1949/50,
301-2) that Lysander positively preferred the Persian links of Ephesos to the
greater Greek national consciousness of Miletos.

There is of course much in Plutarch's characterisation of Ephesos; cf.
Dunbabin, *The Greeks and their Eastern Neighbours* (1957) 63 "the close
neighbourhood of the Lydian kingdom . . . . produced at Ephesos a more
thoroughly mixed culture, part Greek, part Asiatic, than we know anywhere
else in the Greek East." For Persians and Artemis, see note 1.

the Milesians had much to complain of in Persian behaviour and will be glad to assert their independence of the Persians.[61]

The attitude of Kallikratidas, in between Lysander's two terms of office, is in itself interesting. He was unable to establish any rapport with Cyrus, and is reported to have complained that the Greeks were fools to court the barbarians for money and to have intended, when he got home, to do his best to reconcile the Athenians and the Spartans.[62] There is no explicit reference to the Greeks of Asia having been betrayed, but perhaps we should not expect it.

There are more significant silences about the Spartan concessions of 411, if we turn to the period beginning in 400. Apart from Tissaphernes' initial demand that all the cities of Ionia should be subject to him,[63] there is no suggestion in any of the diplomatic negotiations which follow that it has been agreed that Ionia should be fully subject to Persia. In 397 Derkyllidas' terms for peace are that the King should let the Greek cities be autonomous, which Tissaphernes and Pharnabazos are prepared to report to the King, if Derkyllidas will report to Sparta their demand that the Greek army should evacuate the *chora* and the Spartan harmosts leave the cities.[64] There is evidently nothing manifestly unacceptable in Derkyllidas' demand, and when Agesilaos repeats it the next year. Tissaphernes asserts that it will be possible to sell it to the King. [65] In the next year, it turns out to be acceptable to the King as well, at least in the form that 'the cities in Asia shall be autonomous and pay him the ancient tribute'.[66] It is not until 392 that the autonomy of the cities ceases to be a Spartan claim.[67] It seems to me important that no Persian treats the point as a prima facie unreasonable claim which goes back on a position which Sparta has long since conceded.

To determine the status of the cities of Ionia between 411 and

---

[61] X. *Hell.* I 6.8. The passage essentially constitutes Lotze's evidence for greater Greek national consciousness at Miletos.

[62] X. *Hell.* I 6.7, cf. Plut. *Lys.* 6.8.

[63] X. *Hell.* III 1.3 ἑαυτῷ ὑπηκόους.

[64] X. *Hell.* III 2.20.

[65] X. *Hell.* III 4.5, *Ages.* I 10, Plut. *Ages.* 9.1, Polyaen. II 1.8. That Xenophon considers Tissaphernes to be insincere in making this truce does not affect the point I am making, I think. It is clear from what follows that the King knew what the Spartan demand was and has been kept in touch with the negotiations.

[66] X. *Hell.* III 4.25.

[67] X. *Hell.* IV 8.14.

400, we will need to turn to the direct evidence about the status of
Ionia in the Persian empire. The early fifth century evidence is
not necessarily relevant, but Yauna does appear in the lists of
peoples under Darius and Xerxes [68] and Ionia is part of a *nomos*
in Herodotus' account of Darius' financial arrangements.[69] This
does not mean that Ionia is necessarily a separate satrapy, and
in fact we find it under the satrap of Sardis in 493.[70] If the Persians
maintained claims to Ionia between 478 and 413, and we have
seen that it is likely that they did,[71] they will have certainly subordinated it to the satrap of Sardis. It is consistent with this that
in 412 we find a hyparch of Ionia [72] under Tissaphernes' orders;[73]
we have no clear statement on the name of Tissaphernes' satrapy.
Apart from two unconvincing passages of Diodorus [74] our next
explicit evidence, which is also our first documentary evidence,
comes in 391-388 when Strouses or Strouthas is described as satrap
of Ionia.[75]

[68] See most recently Cameron, *JNES* 32, 1973, 47-50, who argues con-
vincingly against the prevailing view that these are lists of provinces or
administrative satrapies.

[69] III 90.1. The νόμος also includes Magnesia, Aeolians, Carians, Lycians,
Milyeis and Pamphylians. Herodotus certainly considers his list to be a list
of satrapies (89.1), but I would doubt whether Cilicia was ever a satrapy
(there is surely something to be said for Krüger's emendation of Κιλικίης
to Λυκίης at Hdt. IX 107.3); it is absent from all the lists of peoples. Toynbee,
Study of History VII 582 ff., rightly speaks in terms of 'taxation-districts'.

[70] Hdt. VI 42.

[71] See page 87.

[72] Tamos, Thuc. VIII 31.2. Thucydides uses σατραπεία once (I 129.1)
and σατράπης never; he was certainly as capable as Herodotus (passim)
or Xenophon (rare, but cf. *Anab.* IV 4.4 against D.S. XIV 27.7) of using
ὕπαρχος to mean satrap, but this is the only place in his work where a hyparch
is hyparch of an area rather than of a person (always Tissaphernes, VIII
16.2, 87.1, 108.4), and I suspect he is indicating fact rather than trying to
translate a Persian title.

[73] Thuc. VIII 87.1.

[74] XIV 19.6, 35.3. Both again concern Tamos. The first says that at the
beginning of his *anabasis*, Cyrus put Persian kindred as ἐπιμεληταί of Lydia
and Phrygia and Tamos of Memphis of Ionia and Aeolis and the neighbouring τόποι (it may be worth noting that X. *Hell.* III 1.10 in attesting
an Aeolis of Pharnabazos implies another Aeolis as well). The second describes him as satrap of Ionia. For Xenophon (*Anab.* I 2.21, 4.2) Tamos is
merely a fleet commander. The fleet went back to Ephesos after the Syrian
gates were passed (D.S. XIV 21.5). Tamos may have been given a general
supervisory role by Cyrus, but I doubt if anything definite about the organisation of the empire is deducible from such an ad hoc arrangement.

[75] Tod, II 113.42. Only his position as satrap of Ionia is relevant to this
arbitration by the Ionian League, which is why it alone is mentioned;

When Cyrus arrived to replace Tissaphernes in 407, he was, besides being general of the forces in the plain of Kastolos,[76] satrap of Lydia, Great Phrygia and Cappadocia.[77] Tissaphernes seems to have been reduced to Caria.[78] Ionia is noticeably absent, but we are told in 405 that Cyrus is in a position to concede to Lysander the φόροι from the cities οἱ αὐτῷ ἴδιοι ἦσαν.[79] The gender of οἱ .... ἴδιοι is important. Cyrus is in private possession of φόροι from certain cities;[80] we are not even told that they are Ionian, though they probably are. These cities, and perhaps only the φόροι from them, are in Cyrus' personal control; they need have nothing to do with the satrapal system.

evidently the arrangements made by Artaphernes a hundred years earlier are being revived. Formally, we have no evidence for the rest of his position except that he is ἐπιμελησόμενος τῶν κατὰ θάλατταν (X. Hell. IV 8.17), but I have a reluctance, perhaps not more than instinctive, to believe the epitome of Theopompus (FGH 115 F 103.4) when it says that Autophradates was satrap of Lydia at this time and thus exclude Strouses from Sardis; Autophradates was satrap of Lydia much later (D.S.XV 90.3) and perhaps this was what Theopompus said.

It should be noted that, from the King's Peace to the end of the empire, no satrap of Ionia is named who does not have a more extended government: Ariobarzanes in Lydia-Ionia-Phrygia (Nep. Dat. 2.5, surely wrong); Rhosakes in Ionia-Lydia (D.S. XVI 47.2); Spithridates in Lydia-Ionia (Arr. I 12.8; Lydia alone named, Arr. I 16.3; Ionia alone named, D.S. XVII 19.1, 20.2). I suppose an alternative explanation of Thuc. VIII 31.2, 87.1 might be that Tamos was satrap of Ionia subordinated to Tissaphernes only as strategos, but if he was in this position either in 412 or 401, he would be unique.

76 See Chapter Three, note 26.
77 X. Anab. I 9.7.
78 So, tentatively ("if he retained any territory at this time"), Andrewes, Phoenix 25, 1971, 208. The main argument for supposing that he had a new, separate, satrapy of Caria (which certainly existed not long after his death; see e.g. Crampa, Labraunda III 2, 1972, p. 7) rather than that he simply retired to his οἶκος will lie in X. Hell. III 1.3 where he is sent down as satrap ὧν τε αὐτὸς πρόσθεν ἦρχε καὶ ὧν Κῦρος. It is a possible but less likely interpretation of this that he received not merely what he had had until 407 but what Cyrus had had in 407-1. The statement is not without its difficulties in any case, since there is reasonable evidence for Ariaios as satrap of Phrygia in 395 (D.S. XIV 80.8, Polyaen. VII 16.1).
Busolt (GG III 1567 with an unhelpful back-reference to 1418 n. 3) left Tissaphernes with Ionia-Caria-Lycia, apparently by simply deducting the areas given to Cyrus. Judeich, Kleinasiatische Studien 36, 40-41, also left him with Ionia-Caria. I do not see what cities they think this left for Cyrus.
79 X. Hell. II 1.14.
80 Rightly interpreted as personal revenues by Busolt, GG III 1613 n. 2, comparing Hell. I 5.3. I am not much impressed by the variation in D.S. XIII 104.4 where Cyrus gives Lysander τῶν ὑφ' αὐτὸν πόλεων ἐπίστασιν, still less by Plut. Lys. 9.2 τὴν αὐτοῦ διεπίστευσεν ἀρχήν. Nor was Busolt.

On the accession of his brother Artaxerxes II in 405 [81] Cyrus fell into temporary eclipse.[82] It must be at this point that Tissaphernes in some sense receives the Ionian cities, καὶ γὰρ ἦσαν αἱ ᾽Ιωνικαὶ πόλεις Τισσαφέρνους τὸ ἀρχαῖον ἐκ βασιλέως δεδομέναι.[83] There are a number of possibilities about this grant. Andrewes argued [84] that, on Artaxerxes' accession, Cyrus lost the satrapy of Sardis and never got it back officially. He recognised that there was strong counter-evidence,[85] but preferred to rely on a passage of Xenophon [86] where one Orontas has at one time held Sardis against Cyrus on the instructions of Artaxerxes. "This clearly shows that Kyros was not then the satrap of Lydia, which must have reverted to Tissaphernes." The conclusion about Tissaphernes was surely unsound; at the most we could say that Lydia was vacant in 404. And, in view of the evidence for the direct dependence of some phrourarchies on the King,[87] it might not even follow at all that Cyrus was not satrap of Lydia at the time.[88] In fact, Andrewes was surely wrong to think that Cyrus never recovered Lydia. If we consider his movements in 401, we can see that he is moving freely in the satrapy and assembling forces at Sardis. His excuse at this point is that he is preparing a campaign to drive the Pisidians out of the *chora*. [89] Tissaphernes takes some time longer to become convinced that this is untrue, and even then he has only suspicion to go on.[90] It is certain that Cyrus is in Sardis as of right, and we

---

[81] The precise date is deplorably uncertain. Essentially, all we can say is that, since the Babylonian year 404/3 was year 1 and not the accession year, his accession will fall between April 21, 405 and April 10, 404. If we could have any confidence in D.S. XIII 108.1, Darius' death was a little after the fall of Athens and right at the end of the year; see Andrewes *HCT* IV 12 for argument that Athens fell in March, not April. But I am not happy about Diodorus' ability to use his chronographic source in this rare instance of his trying to weld it into his narrative. Since Darius died in Babylon (Ktesias 57), the summer of 405 is perhaps unlikely (cf. X. *Cyr.* VIII 6.22).

[82] Most clearly in X. *Anab.* I 1.3, the only text to mention a period of imprisonment. Cf. Ktesias 57, Plut. *Art.* 3.

[83] X. *Anab.* I 1.6.

[84] *Phoenix* 25, 1971, 208-9.

[85] X. *Anab.* I 1.3, Ktesias 57, Plut. *Art.* 3.6.

[86] X. *Anab.* I 6.6.

[87] Chapter Three, note 21.

[88] Orontas was evidently induced not to complain to the King.

[89] X. *Anab.* I 2.1.

[90] X. *Anab.* I 2.4.

can eliminate Andrewes' view that Tissaphernes held the Ionian cities as an appanage of the satrapy of Sardis.[91]

In what other ways could Tissaphernes have been given the cities? If the normal view is correct and Ionia is a full part of the Persian empire, we can suggest two possibilities which would come to the same thing. An independent Ionia could have been created or recreated, so that Tissaphernes would have become satrap of both Caria and Ionia, which meets with the difficulty that Xenophon never speaks of Ionia, but only of the cities. Alternatively, Caria could have been extended to include the Ionian cities. Neither state of affairs is attested for any other period; when Ionia is a satrapy, it is always dependent on Sardis. And there is a further difficulty. In between 404 and 401 all the cities in question except Miletos [92] revolted from Tissaphernes to Cyrus. Artaxerxes is alleged not to have minded.[93] Would he really have been tolerant of an actual shift in provincial frontiers?

After the defeat of Cyrus, Tissaphernes was in a position to reassert his claim on the cities and did so, thus precipitating the Spartan invasions of Asia in the 390s. That his claim is in the form that they should be subject to him [94] can of course be equivalent to a claim that they should be subject to the King, but one passage suggests another possibility. In 397 ambassadors came from the Ionian cities to Sparta and said that it was in Tissaphernes' power to let the Greek cities be autonomous and that, if his own country of Caria was ravaged, they thought he would rapidly make that concession.[95] Nothing whatsoever is said about the King. Similarly

---

[91] Andrewes agrees with this conclusion. His argument about the dating of the end of the dekarchies is not affected.

[92] Miletos' preference for Tissaphernes over Cyrus might not be thought to fit very well with Lotze's view (see notes 60-61) that there was greater Greek national consciousness there, but Xenophon makes it clear (*Anab.* I 1.7, 2.2, 9.9) that each of them had their own faction of Milesians. I agree with Andrewes, *Phoenix* 25, 1971, 213-4 n. 15, that the Pharnabazos who is so kind to exiled Milesian democrats in D.S. XIII 104.6 is really Tissaphernes. If Tissaphernes put them back in Miletos when he had the opportunity, their fierce opposition to Lysander's partisans, now backed by Cyrus, would be intelligible.

[93] X. *Anab.* I 1.8. He is of course being surprisingly tolerant anyway, and the case might be held to fit rather well Bickermann's extreme view of the decentralisation of the Persian empire (*Four Strange Books of The Bible* 194-5) which in general I reject for the fifth and early fourth centuries.

[94] ἑαυτῷ ὑπηκόους X. *Hell.* III 1.3.

[95] X. *Hell.* III 2.12, mysteriously traced by Judeich, *Kleinasiatische Studien* 32 n. 1 to a hypothetical renunciation by Cyrus.

when the King's envoy had executed Tissaphernes, he put the view to Agesilaos that Tissaphernes had caused all the trouble and that no obstacle now remained to a settlement.[96]

The solution to these difficulties which I would prefer cannot be more than tentative. It is that, from 407, the cities of Ionia were not part of the Persian empire in the sense that they were part of administrative satrapies and that their relationship, first to Cyrus and then to Tissaphernes, was to them as persons and not as satraps. They could therefore be described as autonomous in relation to the King. The King will still have maintained a claim to revenue from them,[97] but he makes a grant of the revenues [98] to individuals; in fact, I am suggesting that the grant is a larger-scale version of the grants made to Themistocles and others.[99] If the individuals assert further rights beyond a claim to revenue, that will to some extent be a matter of what they think they can get away with,[100] but their claims may also be limited by agreements with the cities themselves or by undertakings to a third party, in this case, Sparta.

---

[96] X. *Hell.* III 4.25.

[97] As he does in 395 (ibid.).

[98] Or the bulk of them? In X. *Anab.* I 1.8 Cyrus keeps the King satisfied, even after the cities have revolted from Tissaphernes to him, by sending τοὺς γιγνομένους δασμοὺς βασιλεῖ ἀπὸ τῶν πόλεων. Murray, *Historia* 15, 1966, 154, holds that δασμός is the basic correct word for the royal tribute and (ibid., n. 66) implies that the King was getting the tribute from the cities throughout the period. He reduces the φόροι of X. *Hell.* II 1.14, 3.8 to private revenues accruing to Cyrus from the cities. I find this implausible. Presumably he would think that these private revenues were on a substantially smaller scale than the royal tribute, yet the surplus from them over the period when Lysander was in control of them (rather less than two years) appears to be a considerable part of 470 talents (X. *Hell.* II 3.8). X. *Hell.* I 5.3 shows that what the King has given Cyrus personally is large enough to be relevant to the expenses of the war. Either Cyrus is sending the whole of the tribute, in order to exhibit that it is not money which is his primary concern, or, in this case, the δασμός for the King is some smaller obligation which the King gets even though he has made the bulk grant. I admit that I have not yet found a case where the King still has a right to something even when he has made a grant to an individual (see Chapter Three note 32 for some very doubtful cases); on a larger scale, the analogy of Cilicia, which is independent but tributary, is conceivably relevant.

[99] See pages 53-55.

[100] Cyrus and Tissaphernes can be said to ἄρχειν the cities (X. *Anab.* I 1.8) as if they were like Themistocles at Magnesia (Thuc. I 138.5). I am not clear whether this simply refers to physical control or to the way the King phrases his grant. We must always consider it likely that the Persian attitude to a situation may differ from what it is convenient to put into a treaty with Greeks (cf. Murray's observations on the non-mention of tribute in the Peace of Kallias, op. cit., 155-6).

The details must remain obscure, but it does seem to me a strong possibility that in the last phase of the war a position had been arrived at by which the bluntness of the third treaty had been softened and in which it was possible to maintain that the cities were, after a fashion, autonomous, though they were going to have financial obligations on the Persian side. It seems possible that either individual cities or the cities in general also received more specific assurances about how their autonomy was to be interpreted. We have seen that one very substantial element in Greek worries had been the question of Persian garrisons. There does seem to me to be a certain amount of evidence to suggest that this is something that the Persians were prepared to be conciliatory about,[101] and, as I have said, it does seem to have ceased to be an issue in the later stages of the war.[102]

I have in effect argued that there is good ground for believing that the third treaty ceased to control Spartan-Persian relations soon after it was made and that, in the last phase of the war from the arrival of Cyrus in command of the west in spring 407, the basis of their relations was somewhat different. If this is so, there can be very little doubt to my mind when the whole problem was

---

[101] Two general statements, one of them fictional, seem to be relevant. In 394, after the battle of Knidos, Pharnabazos and Konon sail round the islands and the ἐπιθαλαττίδιαι πόλεις driving out Spartan harmosts (X. Hell. IV. 8.1-2). They encourage the cities by the announcement that they will not fortify acropoleis and will leave the cities autonomous. The policy is attributed to Konon who convinces Pharnabazos that this will secure the friendship of the cities, which would resent enslavement and would revolt. Even more interesting is X. Cyr. VII 4.9 where the Greeks who live by the sea (sc. the Hellespont) by giving substantial gifts secure from a general of Cyrus the Great the terms, εἰς μὲν τὰ τείχη βαρβάρους μὴ δέχεσθαι, δασμὸν δὲ ἀποφέρειν καὶ στρατεύειν ὅποι Κῦρος ἐπαγγέλλοι; this was held by Meyer GdA IV 1.53-54 n. 1 to represent the fourth-century position of Greek cities in the empire. We can thus distinguish two possible situations, one where there would be no garrisons at all and another where, if there were garrison-troops, they would not be barbarians.

[102] It is of course obvious that Cyrus did have garrisons in Greek cities in 402/1, X. Anab. I. 1.6. They are clearly composed of Greeks and could doubtless have been defended on the ground of the necessity to protect the cities against Tissaphernes. During the war, it might have been hard to distinguish whether a Persian presence in a city was a garrison or a necessary part of cooperation in the war against Athens. In the clearest cases where there was Persian encroachment on the independence of Greek cities, Mania's acquisitions in the Troad on behalf of Pharnabazos, it is clear that only Greek troops were used both for their acquisition and for the garrisons (X. Hell. III 1.13, 16).

renegotiated. We do after all know something about one Spartan embassy which dealt with the King in person. Cyrus' appointment was immediately preceded by an embassy under an unknown Boiotios which came back from the King in spring 407 proclaiming that the Spartans had secured all they wanted from the King.[103] There is at least no doubt that the whole Persian policy changes at this point.

Since Xenophon gives us no other detail on this embassy, we are accustomed to think that there was no formal treaty and that the 'all' was only assurances of Cyrus' support. The Treaty of Boiotios does not have a place in the books alongside the Peace of Kallias. In fact, there is no entry for it in Professor Bengtson's collection of ancient treaties. But you will see that there is reason to suppose that the various treaties of 412/1 were in need of replacement by an arrangement more satisfactory to both sides, and it would seem unlikely that the first Spartan embassy to deal directly with the King since before 424 came back in such a state of satisfaction if some fairly explicit arrangement had not been reached. In fact, there is evidence that there was a treaty and we have a clause from it. Cyrus is shortly afterwards found maintaining, in response to a request from Lysander for more pay, that the treaty says that 3000 drachmai a month shall be given for each ship, for as many ships as the Spartans wish to maintain.[104] This is a new clause. None of the treaties of 412/1 has a figure, though one of them implies the existence of one.[105] Certainly none of them makes an open-ended commitment to pay the Spartans for as many ships as they like.

Does the assurance of Persian help, unlimited as to the number of ships, but limited and unsatisfactory[106] as to the amount of pay, quite justify the statement that the Spartans had got all they wanted from the King? I think not. A new treaty must have involved negotiation of the territorial clause. I suggest that, on the evidence, this clause is likely to have been more explicit than that of the third treaty and that it provided for the autonomy of the

---

[103] X. *Hell.* I 4.2-3.

[104] X. *Hell.* I 5.5 εἶναι δὲ καὶ τὰς συνθήκας οὕτως ἐχούσας, τριάκοντα μνᾶς ἑκάστῃ νηὶ τοῦ μηνὸς διδόναι, ὁπόσας ἂν βούλωνται τρέφειν Λακεδαιμόνιοι.

[105] Thuc. VIII 58.5 κατὰ τὰ ξυγκείμενα. If this is a reference back to VIII 29.2, as seems most likely (but see Chapter Four, note 84), that figure was not a simple 3000 drachmae.

[106] X. *Hell.* I 5.4-7.

Greek cities of Asia Minor, possibly with more explicit assurances as well, on condition that they paid the ancient tribute to the King. We do not indeed need to go far back in Spartan diplomatic history to find a model which would do. Perhaps there was a clause like that of the Thracian cities in the Peace of Nikias,[107] that the cities should be autonomous, providing they paid the tribute, and that they will be secure from Persian armed action if they do; that would in fact neatly explain the wording of a Spartan ultimatum to Tissaphernes in 399.[108] At a further guess, there may have been a provision for the withdrawal of Spartan forces at the end of the war. Whatever precisely was in the Treaty, it will have been enough to relieve the worst fears of the Ionian cities and to calm the Spartan conscience. As we have seen, that honourable man Kallikratidas is not credited with complaining that the Ionians had been sold out.

I have had to use material from a great deal later in the story in order to argue that Spartan-Persian relations were once again regulated in the winter of 408/7, and I must now return to the end of Thucydides' narrative in order to see what the factors may have been which produced an agreement along the lines I have been contemplating. The most obvious point for us is the steady improvement in Athens' position, particularly as it was expressed in the performance of the Hellespont fleet under Alcibiades. It is true that the major loss of Euboea in 411 had not been repaired and that most of mainland Ionia was still outside Athens' control, but, apart from Chios, the greater part of the islands still remained firm and in 408 the recovery of Byzantion and Chalkedon had once again opened the route to the Black Sea. King Agis in Decelea could still see the cornships coming through to the Piraeus.[109] Pharnabazos had been a much better ally to the Spartans than Tissaphernes, but, after the Spartan fleet was destroyed at Kyzikos in spring 410, its reestablishment was desperately slow. Sparta's allies in Sicily and Italy, on whom high hopes had been placed,[110] never produced as large a force as might have been expected and, after the Carthaginian invasion of Sicily in 409, what had come went home and no more was to be expected.

---

[107] Thuc. V 18.5; see page 69.
[108] πρὸς Τισσαφέρνην ἔπεμψαν πρέσβεις τοὺς ἐροῦντας μὴ ὅπλα πολέμια ἐπιφέρειν ταῖς Ἑλληνίσι πόλεσιν (D.S. XIV 35.6).
[109] Cf. X. Hell. I 1.35.
[110] Thuc. VIII 2.3.

Other constraints on Sparta are to be inferred, some of which will have touched her at her most sensitive points. Slight though our knowledge of the Spartan peace-missions to Athens in 410 and 408/7 is, one point is common to our information about both of them, a request for an exchange of prisoners.[111] On both occasions, the initiative comes from the Spartan side and it looks as if the number of Spartiates in Athenian hands may once again have risen to the point where there was strong internal political pressure for an arrangement which would bring the boys home. As in the period from 425 to 421, this can have been a factor which dwarfed all more general considerations. In 410 Diodorus adds, not only a proposal that each side should keep the cities which it had, but a suggestion that each side should remove the forts which it had in the other's territory. The meaning is not doubtful. Sparta will evacuate Decelea if Athens evacuates Pylos. Pylos and the threat of Messenian revolt which it continually posed will have been one of the strongest cards still in Athens' hands after the disaster in Sicily, and it is clear that great importance was attached to holding on to it right to the time when it actually fell, some time after the peace-mission of 410, but before that of 408/7.[112] Given the possibility that there is substantial unease in Sparta about the prospects of collaboration with Persia, we can see every reason why Sparta should have tried for a negotiated peace in 410.

---

[111] D.S. XIII 52.3; Androtion *FGH* 324 F 44.

[112] D.S. XIII 64.4, Arist. 'Aθ. Πολ. 27.5. I am in general so strong a supporter of the low chronology for these years, by which Alcibiades returned to Athens in 407, that I see no reason to refer to alternatives, but I should record a worry at this point. Xenophon *Hell.* I 2.18 puts his (oddly-phrased) reference to the fall of Pylos in the winter that Alcibiades and Thrasyllos spent at Lampsakos, i.e 409/8 on the low chronology, 410/09 on the high chronology. The high chronology is supported by Diodorus' text, which says that the Athenians had held it for 15 years; this should mean it fell in 410. There has been no disposition to believe this since Ferguson, *Treasurers of Athena* (1932) 42-4. In the course of a demonstration that *IG* I² 301 was the Athenian expense-account for 409/8, Ferguson pointed to the references in it to an Athenian expedition round the Peloponnese, said that it could not have gone after the fall of Pylos and that it must in fact be the expedition of Anytos which failed to relieve Pylos; the low chronology seemed thereby proved. I have lost faith in Ferguson's arguments for dating *IG* I² 301 (for reasons akin to, but wider than, those of De Sanctis, *Riv. Fil.* 63, 1935, 211-3) and now wonder whether one should not prefer Diodorus' source to Xenophon for dating this event. (That Diodorus' headings put the seizure under 425/4 and the fall under 409/8, which is not fifteen years on any method of counting, is simply a fact about Diodorus.)

In 408 her position will have been improved by the recovery of Pylos, but worsened by the loss of her Sicilian allies. The year which had seen the destruction of Selinus and Himera will not have been particularly conducive to a policy of cooperation with the barbarian, and it is not surprising, as I see Sparta, that it was decided to make a further attempt at peace with Athens [113] before embarking once more on negotiations with Persia.[114] The Athenians did agree to an exchange of prisoners, but no more. Boiotios and his colleagues were sent off on the long road to Babylon to seek better Persian help, if that could be obtained on terms which were not too discreditable.[115]

I turn now to the experiences of the Persian satraps in this period. Until well into 408, Pharnabazos was unwavering in his support of the Spartans. There were no complaints about pay, he provided them with shipbuilding facilities in 410 after the destruction of their fleet,[116] he was repeatedly to be found actually in battle in their support. He seems to have had a largish mercenary force of his own,[117] and all in all he must have got through a great deal of money.[118] However, the progress he made in his main aim, to recover the Greek towns in his ἀρχή,[119] was eventually negligible. Kyzikos, the nearest substantial Greek town to the heart of his satrapy, had been briefly in his hands or those of the Spartans on

---

[113] A request for peace is not relevant to the purposes of the Aristotle scholiast and is not mentioned. That it is likely to have been implicit in the mission was held e.g. by Busolt *GG* III 2.1565 and wrongly doubted by Ehrenberg, *RE* XV 329 (cf. Jacoby, *FGH* III b suppl. II p. 139). (Busolt used the high chronology and therefore makes Alcibiades present in Athens and against peace.)

[114] I have no doubts about the date, mid-summer 408 or a little later. It is staggering to find Jacoby (loc. cit.) agnostic on the point, despite his conviction in other places (e.g. on Philochoros, *FGH* 328 F 157) that Atthidographic items introduced by ἐπὶ τούτου are the first items recorded in their year.

[115] It is a gap in our knowledge that we simply cannot say what Sparta's normal allies thought about her Persian policy at any stage later than Thuc. VIII 8.2. The successes of Boiotios and Lysander eventually meant that Sparta had no need to care, but it is unlikely to have looked quite like that in 408.

[116] X. *Hell*. I 1.25.

[117] Most obviously at D.S. XIII 51.

[118] Not only on the war against Athens; his generosity to Hermokrates, X. *Hell*. I 1.31, D.S. XIII 63.2.

[119] Thuc. VIII 6.1, 99. In the latter passage τὰς λοιπὰς ἔτι πόλεις is a trifle obscure, since all we have been told of on the Asiatic side so far is Abydos (VIII 62.1). But Kyzikos may already have been taken.

two occasions, Lampsakos once.[120] Nearest the Black Sea, Kalchedon remained in revolt from Athens rather longer.[121] Only further south, where Abydos remained the main Spartan base from 411 to the end of the war,[122] and in the Troad, is there any suggestion of more permanent gains.[123] There is some ground for thinking that he acquired Antandros, which had rejected Tissaphernes forcibly.[124]

In 408 Kalchedon was on the point of being recaptured by Athens, and we find Pharnabazos is now prepared to talk to the Athenian commanders.[125] The episode has recently been carefully studied by Amit,[126] who has shown that we are dealing with a

---

[120] Kyzikos in revolt from Athens (Thuc. VIII 107.1), a revolt caused by Pharnabazos and Klearchos (D.S. XIII 40.6), recovered by Athens (Thuc., loc. cit.), captured by Mindaros (D.S. XIII 49.4), recovered by Athens (X. Hell. I 1.19). Lampsakos, Thuc. VIII 62.1-2.

[121] The date of the revolt of Kalchedon is obscure. Nothing is said of it in summer 410 when Alcibiades fortifies Chrysopolis in its territory (X. Hell. I 1.22) and the other references to it in 410 (X. Hell. I 1.26, 35) are ambiguous. But my suspicion is that its revolt will have followed that of Byzantion fairly closely. In 408 it has a Spartan harmost (X. Hell. I 3.2); there is clearly no arrangement by which Pharnabazos takes over sole responsibility for cities in Asia.

[122] Pharnabazos was involved in the revolt of Abydos (Thuc. VIII 62.1), but the Spartan presence will have been dominant.

[123] As early as Thuc. VIII 102.1 the land opposite Sestos is πολεμία to the Athenians. Mindaros in Ilion (X. Hell. I 1.4); a Peloponnesian (?) garrison at Dardanos (D.S. XIII 45.4).

The chronology of the expansion of the hyparchy ('Pharnabazos' Aeolis') controlled by the Dardanians Zenis and Mania remains doubtful. Gergis, one of its two centres (X. Hell. III 1.15), never paid Athenian tribute, a fact less surprising now that its site has been found well inland (J. M. Cook, The Troad, 1973, 347-51). The other, Skepsis, paid until 440 at least; that it appears in the latest assessment-list, ATL II A 13, proves nothing. Other inland cities disappear early, Βηρύσιοι after 445, Κεβρήνιοι after 446. Nearer the coast, Dardanos is still paying in 428, and there is no trace of early encroachment on the Actaean cities, the Mytilenaean peraia taken over by Athens in 427; Ophryneion (IG I² 328.11) and Kolonai (Hesperia 35, 1966, 84) are still in Athenian hands in 413. After succeeding her husband Zenis, Mania, before 398, had captured Larisa, Hamaxitos and Kolonai, using Greek mercenaries (X. Hell. III 1.13); I take it that Ilion (ibid., 16) had already been acquired by Zenis, perhaps in 410, when Mindaros is attested there. No evidence is likely to give us certainty as to when these now autonomous cities were incorporated into Pharnabazos' satrapy and garrisoned. I admit that they are a prima facie breach of the Treaty of Boiotios as I envisage it, even though Pharnabazos' intermediaries are Greek and the garrisons Greek (ibid., 16).

[124] He appears to be in control of Antandros at X. Hell. I 1.25. For Antandros and Tissaphernes see page 110 with note 16.

[125] X. Hell. I 3.8-12, D.S. XIII 66.3, Plut. Alc. 31.1-2.

[126] L'antiquité classique 42, 1973, 436-57.

situation of greater complexity than has been thought. He has shown that it is at least possible that the negotiators were feeling their way to a position by which Athens would admit the King's rights in Asia in return for some financial support. It is certainly clear that Pharnabazos was at any rate wavering in his support for Sparta and was prepared to conduct an Athenian embassy to the King.

At the end of Thucydides [127] we saw Tissaphernes considerably discomfited by the Spartan transfer of their forces to the north and their attitude to his garrisons. He was certainly not thinking in terms of general benefit to the King. He was, Thucydides says, aggrieved at the prospect that Pharnabazos would now succeed against the Athenians with less time and expense. We may surely add that he will be worried about what the King will say about his failure to hold the Spartans in line. As we have seen, although he pursued the Spartans to the Hellespont, they declined to accept his explanations. At this time, he was also being pressed by Alcibiades, now in command of the Athenian fleet and boasting of his influence with him. On the face of it, the road of collaboration with Athens is closed to him; the King's instructions are still to make war on the Athenians.[128] So he put Alcibiades in jail, but was unable or unwilling to keep him there.[129] We then hear very little of him for some time, apart from his stout resistance to the Athenian attack on Ephesos in spring 409.[130]

However, there are strong reasons for believing that at some time between 411 and 407 he moved a good deal closer to Athens. Tantalising fragments of an Athenian decree of the period in honour of Evagoras of Salamis [131] almost certainly mention him. What is more, they seem to show the Athenian assembly under the belief that the King is an ally of theirs.[132] We can hardly offer

---

[127] VIII 109.

[128] X. *Hell.* I 1.9.

[129] See note 42.

[130] X. *Hell.* I 2.6 ff.

[131] *IG* I² 113 (*SEG* X 127). Recent adjustments to the text by Osborne, *BSA* 67, 1972, 129-56, *ZPE* 9, 1972, 55-6, *Hermes* 102, 1974, 87-90, are not relevant here.

[132] I incline to prefer a 42-letter line to the 43-letter line still supported by Osborne. The following seems to me to be a conservative text of the beginning of the amendment of Kleophon (?):

Κλεο[. .]
[. εἶπε· τὰ μὲν ἄλλα καθάπερ τῆι βολῆ]ι, ἐπειδὲ δέ ἐστ[ιν]
[. . . . . . . .20. . . . . . . .Εὐαγόρα]ς ho Σαλα[μ]ίνιο[ς . .]
[. . . . . . . .24. . . . . hό τ]ι δύναται ἀγαθὸ[ν τ]-

a precise date,[133] but obviously the Athenians are taking a very optimistic view of some negotiations. That they felt themselves relatively close to Tissaphernes in 407 seems to be proved by the fact that, even after Cyrus' arrival in the west, they chose Tissa-

---

[ὸν δῆμον τὸν Ἀθεναίον καὶ βασι]λέα καὶ τὸς ἄλλ[ος χ]-
[συμμάχος . . . . . .14. . . . . . hόπος] ἂν πλεῖστοι φ[. . . .]
[. .5. . τõι δέμοι τõι Ἀθεναίον κ]αὶ βασιλεῖ κα[ὶ τοῖ]-
[ς ἄλλοις χσυμμάχοις . . .7. . . Τισ]σαφρένεν hο[. .5. .]
etc.

I see no way of twisting these lines to support the view of Meyer *GdA* IV² 2.322 that Athens is hoping for Evagoras' support against Tissaphernes and the King. Beloch *GG* II 1.425 n. 2, who dated the text 407-5, must have overlooked them altogether. Meyer's implication that the text referred to corn-shipments is not true of the preserved portions.

[133] The text would be irrelevant at this point if we followed Grégoire and Goossens, *CRAI* 1940, 224-7, in dating it to the first visit of Peisander to Athens in January 411 and seeing it as relevant to the negotiations with Tissaphernes which were going on then. That Thucydides should not have picked up information about the participation of Evagoras, I would not find particularly surprising, but it is hard to believe that he was wrong about what Peisander said about relations with the King; VIII 53 would not allow the Athenians to believe that an alliance had been concluded already. Despite Grégoire's arguments from Euripides *Helen*, I still incline to think that January 411 is too early for Evagoras to be on the scene at all, let alone to have rendered services to Athens sufficient to justify this long decree. Even if, as has sometimes been thought, the corn brought by Andocides to the fleet at Samos (Andoc. II 11) came from Evagoras, for which there is no evidence (Costa, *Historia* 23, 1974, 45-6), this will be later, in the summer, and irrelevant to Athens herself. Corn from Cyprus is first attested in 407 (Andoc. II 20-21); that it came from Evagoras is a reasonable deduction from Lys. VI 28 (Lys. VI 7 is a virtual admission that Andocides was once on good terms with Evagoras, and cf. Andoc. I 4, 132).

Meyer evidently thought that the text belonged to 410, mysteriously adding that the date was fixed by the mention of Tissaphernes; Tissaphernes is certainly unlikely after the arrival of Cyrus in 407 (408 for Meyer). Spyridakis, *Evagoras I von Salamis* (1935) 49-50 suggested that Evagoras participated in Alcibiades' negotiations with Tissaphernes in late 411 (Thuc. VIII 88, 108.1) and considered a whole range of implausible indications, including one for 409, without coming to a conclusion (Costa, op. cit., n. 30 is confused and inaccurate). Followers of Andrewes, *JHS* 73, 1953, 2-9, will not be much inclined to believe that participation in negotiations with Alcibiades in 411 would have resulted in a decree of the Athenian state.

I myself have a very slight inclination to bring the text as late as possible in 408/7 before Athens finds out about the arrival of Cyrus, possibly in connexion with the news of or arrival of a corn-shipment. So, essentially, Hatzfeld, *Alcibiade* 307 n. 5, who sees the importance of X. *Hell.* I 5.8.

The importance of Costa's article in general (*Historia* 23, 1974, 40-56) is to show that there is no reason to believe that Evagoras made any attempt to get out of line with Persia in the early part of his reign. It should follow that he had no reason to believe that shipping corn to Athens in 407 was out of line with Persian policy as he saw it at that time.

phernes as their intermediary to Cyrus in the hope of weakening his support for Sparta. Tissaphernes is prepared to argue to Cyrus for the continuation of his old policy of wearing both sides down, but Cyrus is deaf to his advice.[134]

It is in fact too late for any such suggestion. Despite Tissaphernes' failure to maintain good relations with the Spartans and his preference for a more even-handed policy, despite Pharnabazos' evidently growing conviction that the Athenians were a force which had to be reckoned with permanently and that there might be a case for exploring their attitude further, the King himself has come down for a clear policy of supporting Sparta. Western Asia Minor will be put in the hands of one man with a larger satrapy than Tissaphernes had had [135] and apparently with wider supervisory powers.[136] That he is coming with the King's backing is made further clear by the fact that he is the King's son. His instructions are to collaborate with the Spartans [137] and he is provided with money to make the policy work.[138] There can be no doubt now that

---

[134] X. *Hell.* I 5.8-9. Xenophon simply says οἱ Ἀθηναῖοι leaving their identity (assembly or fleet?) and the chronology hopelessly obscure. If this is Alcibiades, relying on his old association with Tissaphernes (so, without hesitation, Amit, *Grazer Beiträge* 3, 1975, 7), no one has told us.

[135] Cf. note 77.

[136] Whatever precisely is meant by κάρανος τῶν εἰς Καστωλὸν ἀθροιζομένων (X. *Hell.* I 4.4, *Anab.* I 9.7), it becomes immediately clear (X. *Hell.* I 5.5-7) ·hat Pharnabazos is subordinated to Cyrus in a way in which he had not ›een subordinated to Tissaphernes.

[137] X. *Hell.* I 4.3, 5.2-3.

[138] 500 talents are mentioned at X. *Hell.* I 5.3 as the King's contribution. They had of course run out by 405 (X. *Hell.* II 1.11). These will pay e.g. 100 ships for 10 months at the 3 obol rate envisaged originally, for $7\frac{1}{2}$ months at the rate agreed with Lysander (X. *Hell.* I 5.5-7) but Lysander only has 70 ships at the moment (X. *Hell.* I 5.1, D.S. XIII 70.2). I would suppose that Cyrus was empowered to use the tribute of his extended satrapy as well, even before he got on to the private resources he envisages using. I decline to take the total expenditure of 5000 talents (Andoc. III 29; even more, Isoc. VIII 97) at all seriously, and D.S. XIII 70.3 is surely not to be believed in saying that Cyrus said that his father had instructed him to provide the Spartans with all they needed; X. *Hell.* II 1.14 is, however, nearly as optimistic.
    It is not easy to make sense of the 10,000 darics allegedly handed over by Cyrus on the spot (D.S. XIII 70.3, Plut. *Lys.* 4.6). It certainly is less than the arrears plus a month's pay which appear in X. *Hell.* I 5.7. Busolt *GG* III 2 1372 n. 1 thought it was Ephorus' attempt at a month's pay, taking a month's pay for 70 ships at 4 obols a day correctly at 280,000 drachmae and equating 10,000 darics with 250,000 drachmae on the evidence of X. *Anab.* I 5.6 that a siglos (of which there were 20 to a daric) was worth $7\frac{1}{2}$ Attic obols. This is fair enough for a silver siglos of $\pm$ 5.50 grams, but other

Darius himself is putting his full weight behind the Spartans.[139]

We have seen no reason to doubt that, for Darius, Athens has been throughout the enemy and not merely an impediment to his control of Asia. Though his satraps had seen an alliance with Sparta as the obvious way to recover the control of their satrapies which his request for tribute in 413 had enforced on them, it is not clear that he himself has been committed to operating through Sparta, and in the case where we saw most reason to suspect his intervention, that of the third treaty, the stress placed on the arrival of his own fleet may suggest that he was thinking of a way of securing his ends which gave Sparta a relatively minor role.[140] There is no evidence that he ever greeted with any sympathy any inclination by his satraps to come to terms with Athens and, on the one occasion on which his own instructions are quoted, they are in the form that Tissaphernes is to make war on the Athenians.[141] He will doubtless have heard of the Athenian willingness to make concessions in 411 and of Alcibiades' assurances that the Athenians were not naturally interested in land power, but he may be a good deal more impressed by Athenian actions, which have in the last

---

passages (e.g. X. *Anab.* I 7.18) show that the conventional equivalent of a daric is only 20 drachmae. The explanation is that, although Persia continued to coin on weights which presupposed a 13.3 : 1 gold-silver ratio (cf. Robinson, *Num. Chron.* 1958, 191), the market-rate at the end of the century was nearer 10.5 : 1 (see the evidence for Athens, *Essays in Greek Coinage Presented to Stanley Robinson*, 105-10). It may have been a little higher in 407 before Cyrus started putting gold into the monetary system, but Busolt's calculations must be well off the mark.

[139] Scholarly enthusiasm for defending or emending the three years of Thuc. II 65.12 has been such that it is frequently overlooked that, for Thucydides looking back at the end of the war, the contributions made to the war against Athens by Tissaphernes and Pharnabazos could be simply ignored and that he found Cyrus alone worth mentioning. Consider the proportions of Gomme's note.

[140] If the 147 ships which actually arrived at Aspendos (Thuc. VIII 87.3) were really fewer than the King had ordered (VIII 87.5), the role contemplated for the Spartans would not be large. Had the King really ordered 300 ships (D.S. XIII 36.5, 37.4) ? The last Persian fleet to go into action before this is also said to have had 300 ships (D.S. XII 3.2), and the same number is planned in 397 (X. *Hell.* III 4.1). Despite Thucydides, I find it a little hard to believe that the fleet was intended to be purely Phoenician.

I do not put much faith in Plut. *Lys.* 4.1 which asserts that Tissaphernes had an order from the King to *help the Spartans* and drive the Athenians off the sea. This is a simple expansion of Lysander's complaints against Tissaphernes in X. *Hell.* I 5.2.

[141] X. *Hell.* I 1.9.

two years carried destruction into Lydia, Pharnabazos' satrapy and Bithynia, areas where Athenian forces are unlikely to have been even in his father's lifetime.[142] He will be no less inclined than he has been since 414 to settle his account with Athens.

The question will be why he is now prepared to use Sparta as his main instrument for doing this, and why he is now prepared to make concessions to Sparta about the Greeks of Asia (if I am right about this) which make a distinct change from the bleak assertion of his rights which he seems to have insisted on in 411. It seems to me likely that the answer should be found in a consideration of the whole empire and of the demands which it makes on his resources. Nearly twenty years ago I argued [143] that it was natural for Greek historians to take too narrow a view, to assume that the King had nothing on his mind but Aegean affairs. I than produced evidence to show that Thucydides may have been mistaken in thinking that the failure to use the Phoenician fleet in 411 was purely due to Tissaphernes' preference for a balancing policy [144] and that there was some substance in a suggestion in Diodorus [145] that the fleet had had to be withdrawn to Phoenicia [146] because of trouble in Egypt. I admit that the trouble in Egypt seems to have been over by early summer 410 and that no evidence at present exists to show why the fleet was not available in 408/7 and not used for the rest of the war,[147] but some may yet appear. I also pointed out that there was clear evidence for serious trouble near the centre of the empire in this period with a Median

---

[142] In 409 Thrasyllos had raided Lydia, burnt many villages, and taken substantial booty (X. *Hell.* I 2.4). In the following winter Lampsakos had been the base for raids into the βασιλέως χώρα (ibid., I 2.16). In 408 Alcibiades sailed into the Black Sea to apply pressure to the Bithynian Thracians (ibid., I 3.3; they are evidently in a mood at this moment which Calchedon can trust, and that Pharnabazos later found them tiresome and expendable, ibid., III 2.2, is hardly relevant). An Athenian force had marched through their territory in 424, but with no hostile intent (Thuc. IV 75.2).

[143] *Historia* 7, 1958, 392-7.

[144] Thuc. VIII 87.4.

[145] XIII 46.6.

[146] D.S. XIII 42.4 suggests that the fleet had already gone back to Phoenicia before the end of Thucydides' narrative.

[147] If we can trust Plut. *Lys.* 9.2, Cyrus saw no reason in 405 why ships should not be brought up from Phoenicia and Cilicia. There is no trace of this in the parallel narrative of X. *Hell.* II 1.13-14. Genuine non-Xenophontic material, akin to but by no means identical with that of D.S. XIII 104.7-8, certainly appears in Plut. *Lys.* 9.3-5, and Cyrus' promise, even if fiction, is not likely to be Plutarch's fiction.

revolt which did not end until 408/7 and which had to be followed by a campaign against the Kadousioi.[148] What I did not then see was that, even if Darius was only thinking of Asia Minor, there were strong reasons for creating a unified command there and that the new commander-in-chief would have a great deal on his mind besides the war with Athens. In my third lecture,[149] I drew attention to the substantial evidence for trouble in Asia Minor in this period, principally, but not only, with the Mysians and Pisidians. This, I take it, is why Greater Phrygia is included in Cyrus' command and why all his own campaigning, from the time he arrives,[150] is in the interior. It would be sensible and rational to use oriental troops on this campaigning and to leave the fighting against Athens to the Spartans, using Greek manpower hired with Persian money. If the Spartans wanted a modification of the terms in which the King's control of Asia was expressed, the price was not too high to pay. What the realities of the situation would be after the war when the Spartans went home, either under the new treaty or because their financial backing could be removed, was a question which could be left to the future.

Cyrus was only 16.[151] Richard III of England also held substantial positions in his teens, and there is no visible trace of Cyrus having been given any form of governor.[152] We should not, I think, too hastily assume that the new plan for the west was solely constructed on strategic grounds. The sources are too emphatic about the influence of the Queen, Parysatis, and her preference for her younger son Cyrus over the older Arsikas, later Artaxerxes II,[153]

---

[148] X. *Hell.* I 2.19, II 1.13.

[149] See page 56.

[150] X. *Anab.* I 9.14.

[151] This follows from Plut. *Art.* 2.4, since he was born after Darius' accession, and is consistent with his description as νεανίσκος (D.S. XIII 70.3) and μειράκιον (Plut. *Lys.* 4.3). The view that he was born much earlier (Bunger, *Fleckeisens Jahrb.* 151, 1895, 375 ff., which I have not read) has been revived in ever more fantastic forms by Hüsing *Porysatis* 45-6 (as a possibility) and König, *Die Persika des Ktesias von Knidos* 88-92, 98; I do not propose to discuss it.

[152] Tissaphernes is of course available, but his advice is rejected (X. *Hell.* I 5.9). According to X. *Anab.* I 1.2 Tissaphernes was still φίλος to Cyrus in 405; Plut. *Lys.* 4.2 will be embroidery in the light of later events.

[153] Olmstead *HPE* 369 traces this to Arsikas' standing against his mother's intended vengeance on his wife Stateira. This is simple misreading of the sources (Plut. *Art* 2.2-3, Ktesias 56) which, on the contrary, taken together, clearly imply that Arsikas used his mother to protect his wife from a much more determined Darius.

for us entirely to neglect the possibility that this large command for Cyrus was in part created at her suggestion as a move in the forthcoming succession-struggle.[154] There has been modern speculation on the point. We find Parysatis considering the possibility of reviving Lydian national consciousness by in effect restoring their king and, more practically, thinking that Sardis would be a good place to pick up Greek mercenaries.[155] Alternatively, she is simply getting Cyrus the possibility of winning the gratitude and support of the Spartans, the best professional soldiers in the world, thus unpatriotically abandoning the policy of "divide and conquer" so wisely followed by Tissaphernes and Pharnabazos.[156] We can surely at least reflect that Cyrus is being given a chance to win glory and satisfy some of his ambitions. That he is being given something of a power-base as well may not seem important to Darius. Pissouthnes had got nowhere after all.

---

[154] How imminent the succession-struggle seemed in 408/7 will depend on Darius' age, for which there is no direct evidence. His son, Artaxerxes II, is a notorious μαχρόβιος, dying in 359/8, at 94 (Plut. *Art*. 30.9 from Deinon) or 86 (Lucian *Macr*. 15). If the lower of these two ages is correct, Darius would have been approaching 60 in 408/7, but even this is doubtful, since it involves a 21-year gap in Parysatis' childbearing career between Artaxerxes and Cyrus, with two sons to come according to Plut. *Art*. 1.2 and ten children to come according to Ktesias 49, who said he got his information from Parysatis. There are even more complications if we consider Artaxerxes' rivalry with his son for Cyrus' mistress Aspasia (Plut. *Art*. 26-27). My inclination is to suppose that Darius was not particularly old in 408/7, but we do not know the state of his health or how far Parysatis could be thinking ahead.

There is no indication in the texts that Parysatis had anything to do with Cyrus' original appointment, but this does not appear in Photius' epitome at all, though Ktesias can hardly have omitted it. The implication of Plut. *Art*. 2.4-5 might be that Cyrus' appointment followed a decision about the succession, but it would be unsafe to press it.

[155] Hüsing *Porysatis* 46.
[156] Olmstead *HPE* 369.

CHAPTER SIX

It was not for twenty years after Boiotios' mission, as far as we know, that another Spartan ambassador dealt directly with a different King. There is much less in current accounts of Spartan-Persian relations during these years which I feel disposed to question, and I think I can confine myself to a much more summary account.

The young Cyrus, on his arrival in the west in 407, was instantly charmed by the new Spartan admiral Lysander, and they established an excellent relationship. In fact, they established too good a relationship for Cyrus to carry out his father's orders with quite the speed which had been contemplated. There is no reason to suppose that his failure to give as enthusiastic support [1] to Lysander's successor Kallikratidas is due to anything but pique at being robbed of a congenial collaborator by the archaic Spartan rules which recalled Lysander. [2] After Kallikratidas' death, he reinforced with his own messengers the allied delegation which went to Sparta to urge Lysander's reappointment [3] and, before he had to go to his father's deathbed, he was able to renew his relations with Lysander, remind him of his goodwill to Sparta in general and Lysander in particular, and lay the foundations of the campaign which ended with the final victory of Aegospotami. [4]

We can hardly expect to know whether Cyrus in fact made a serious attempt at the throne on his brother's accession. One court source clearly thought that he did, [5] but the rest [6] go no further than saying that Tissaphernes accused him of a plot and that the King was prepared to be convinced, but that Parysatis not only got him off but sent back to the west. On the argument of my last lecture, he did not quite regain all that his father had given him, since

---

[1] He does give Kallikratidas some support (X. *Hell.* I 6.18).

[2] Tissaphernes' continued φιλία with Cyrus (X. *Anab.* I 1.2) would allow the possibility that Cyrus was temporarily more impressed than he had been at first with the merits of an even-handed policy, but it hardly suits either his short-term or his long-term aims.

[3] X. *Hell.* II 1.6-7.

[4] X. *Hell.* II 1.11-14.

[5] Plut. *Art.* 3.5-6.

[6] Ibid., 3.3-5, presumably the same line as Ktesias 57. Cf. X. *Anab.* I 1.3.

Tissaphernes acquired some rights in the Greek cities, an advantage fairly soon nullified by the active preference shown by the cities for him over Tissaphernes.[7]

It certainly appears that after the end of the war[8] Sparta evacuated Asia Minor. On a conventional view, this is not surprising. She is doing it in conformity with treaty obligations, and I would agree that, even on my view of the Treaty of Boiotios, it is likely that Sparta promised to withdraw troops from Asia after the end of the war. There are however difficulties in a view which holds that Sparta now gave up any claims to any kind of interest in the Greek cities. Well-known passages refer to a time when the ephors proclaimed the abolition of Lysander's dekarchies, and they clearly refer to Asia Minor as well.[9] The precise dating of this proclamation must be doubtful, but it surely lies between the end of the war and Sparta's military return to Asia in 399. I must admit that I do not see much[10] to stand in the way of a view that, in this period, the cities have a financial obligation to Tissaphernes, but that they are in theory autonomous. That they are autonomous does not mean that they are not subject to the political strife of parties dependent on Tissaphernes or on Cyrus, insofar as his partisans are distinct from those of Lysander, and does not even rule out physical intervention on behalf of a group, like that of Tissaphernes in Miletos.[11] I would admit that the garrisons which Cyrus introduced, doubtless on the ground that the cities needed protection against Tissaphernes,[12] might have been thought to be overstepping the mark a little, had they not been Greeks, not employed by so philhellene a master. That the proclamation of the ephors that there should be

---

[7] For an argument that Tissaphernes was in effective control of the cities until possibly well into 403, see Andrewes, *Phoenix* 25, 1971, 213-5. That I am holding against Andrewes (see page 120) that Cyrus recovered all his satrapal position at this point does not affect the arguments he uses for the length of Tissaphernes' control.

[8] Which does not mean after Aegospotami; cf. X. *Hell.* II 2.2 where Lysander appoints a harmost of Byzantion *and Kalchedon*. But there may be something out of the way about Kalchedon in any case; cf. the Spartan garrison there in 400 (X. *Anab.* VII 1.20).

[9] For the whole question, see Andrewes, op. cit., 206-16, who settles for late 403 or early 402.

[10] Were it not for X. *Anab.* I 1.8, on which see Chapter Five, note 100, I would say I saw nothing.

[11] X. *Anab.* I 1.7.

[12] X. *Anab.* I 1.6.

ancestral constitutions, that Lysander's friends were no longer
necessarily Sparta's friends, should be heard in Asia and was
relevant to party strife, does not seem to me surprising.[13]

In 401 Cyrus went into open revolt, failing only when he had
practically reached Babylon. There was no doubt that his attempt
had had the active backing and sympathy of the Spartan state.[14]
The knowledge of that had multiple consequences. It surely explains
why Artaxerxes II hated the Spartans, thinking them the most
shameless of all men,[15] a view which certainly has its effect on
Persian policy. It must also be the case that Sparta was so deeply
compromised that she had little to hope for from Persia for some
time, and this will have made her more inclined to follow anti-
Persian policies.[16]

Tissaphernes had taken the right side at the accession and in
401. His services in the battle of Cunaxa were at the least less bad
than those of the rest of the King's generals[17] and his success in
capturing and killing the generals of the undefeated Ten Thousand
and shepherding the rest away from sensitive areas of the empire
was undoubted. He returned in 400 to Cyrus' position.[18] His first
reported move was to demand that the Ionian cities should be
subject to him and he seems actually to have started military

---

[13] Andrewes, op. cit., 216, suggests that Cyrus, anxious for Spartan help,
would not be unwilling to jettison the dekarchies, which might not be
popular in the cities he was engaged in winning over.

[14] The point is muted in the *Anabasis* (I 4.2-3), but amply made in the
Hellenica (III 1.1), where it stands as an essential preliminary to the Spartan
interventions in Asia which follow; that only the ephors are referred to is of
no consequence. D.S. XIV 19.4-5 adds explicitly that Cheirisophos' contingent was sponsored by Sparta, a fact clear enough from their method of
arrival (X. *Anab.* I 4.3), but systematically obscured by Xenophon; it is e.g.
obviously relevant to Cheirisophos' mission to Byzantion (*Anab.* V 1.4) and
is implicit in the episode of a choice of a single commander at *Anab.* VI
1.25 ff. Cf. Isoc. XII 103-4. Judeich, *Kleinasiatische Studien* 37 n. 1, goes
too far in arguing dissension at Sparta from D.S. XIV 21.2 and confusion (his
own as well as the sources') about the naval squadrons.

[15] Deinon, *FGH* 690 F 19 ap. Plut. *Art.* 22.1.

[16] The new situation will take some time to sink in, which is why Anaxibios and then Aristarchos are still anxious in 400 to conciliate Pharnabazos
by getting the Ten Thousand into Europe and keeping them there (X.
Anab. VII 1.2-3, 2.12-15), perhaps remembering his past services.

[17] Xenophon (*Anab.* I 10.7) admits that he did not flee, but says he did
not kill anyone either; D.S. XIV 23.6 reports heroic behaviour; he does not
appear in Plutarch's battle at all.

[18] For doubts about Phrygia see Chapter Five, note 78.

operations on the coast.[19] As I have said, there is elsewhere a suggestion that he was exercising his own discretion,[20] and he may well have thought that any existing guarantees given to the cities were invalidated by Cyrus' revolt and the support Cyrus had had from Sparta and the cities.[21] The cities, wishing to be free and afraid of Tissaphernes because of their preference for Cyrus over him, refused to admit him and sent ambassadors to Sparta asking the Spartans, as leaders of Greece, to take care of the Greeks in Asia too, so that their land should not be ravaged and they might be free.[22] No hesitation is reported in Sparta and an embassy to Tissaphernes warning him to keep his hands off the cities[23] was followed by a substantial force under Thibron. It is true that the exploits of the Ten Thousand will have encouraged a belief in Persian weakness, but I do not find it easy to write this Spartan expedition off as, for example, a selfish determination to extend the new Spartan empire.[24]

In this first phase the war is described as a war against Tissaphernes,[25] and Thibron seems to have begun with a substantial thrust inland against his main bases, Magnesia and Tralles,[26] a penetration greater than the Athenians had ever made. Lack of cavalry,[27] however, reduced his effectiveness, and he was not approved of by the Ionian allies. His successor Derkyllidas who arrived in 398, knowing that Tissaphernes and Pharnabazos were

---

[19] X. Hell. III 1.3. An attack on Kyme, D.S. XIV 35.7. It is unfortunate that Ephoros' testimony about Kyme is always suspect (Str. XIII 3.6), but this does happen to be an area where some Persian penetration may be inferable from the later resistance of Phokaia to Agesilaos (Polyaen. II 1.16, Front. Strat. III 11.2).

[20] X. Hell. III 2.12.

[21] If we take the three preserved treaties of 412/1, the Spartans were clearly in breach of Thuc. VIII 18.3, 37.2, 58.3-4, and there will surely have been some corresponding provision in the Treaty of Boiotios.

[22] X. Hell. III 1.3.

[23] D.S. XIV 35.6; cf. page 125.

[24] Despite Judeich, *Kleinasiatische Studien* 41-2, who himself speaks of the honour of the Spartan name, a return to Asia does not in itself connote the adoption of Lysander's plans or policies. Dekarchies had not been restored in 396 (X. Hell. III 4.2, 7).

[25] X. Anab. VII 6.1, 7.

[26] D.S. XIV 36.2-3, not in Xenophon, who had not yet arrived on the scene, and exaggerated by Isoc. IV 144; for Magnesia cf. Thuc. VIII 50.3, for Tralles X. Anab. I 4.8. I do not share Meyer's preference (*Theopomps Hellenika* 108-12) for Xenophon's silence over Diodorus.

[27] X. Hell. III 1.5, D.S. XIV 36.4.

on bad terms, came to terms with Tissaphernes and proceeded
against Pharnabazos. If Tissaphernes bribed him, Xenophon does
not say so; he evidently thinks his own motive, that Derkyllidas
had an old grudge against Pharnabazos,[28] a perfectly credible one.
It is fair to say that Tissaphernes is not known to have controlled
any Greek coastal cities at this point[29] and that the nine Aeolic
cities which Derkyllidas captured in eight days [30] certainly included
some which had not been under Persian rule for very long.[31]
Pharnabazos preferred repeated truces to retaliation,[32] Derkyllidas
had time to move across the Hellespont and settle the Chersonese,[33]
and then came back and subdued a nest of Chian exiles at Atarneus
which had been making themselves a general nuisance in Ionia.[34]
All seemed impressively peaceful.[35] It might be thought that
Sparta had demonstrated her power to protect Ionia.

The Ionians were not however satisfied with a merely inactive
Tissaphernes, and applied to Sparta again to have pressure brought
on him to concede their autonomy formally. The ephors evidently
thought this reasonable and told Derkyllidas to collaborate with
the Spartan fleet against Caria.[36] However, before this operation
gets going, we discover that the King has taken a hand. Tissaphernes has now been made general in the west and Pharnabazos
subordinated to him.[37] They have got a largish force in the field,
particularly impressive in cavalry.[38] A truce reveals what their instructions are; the Greek army is to leave the *chora*; the Spartan
harmosts are to leave the cities.[39] Derkyllidas stands on his instructions, that the Greek cities are to be autonomous, and a longer
truce is arranged for both sides to report back.[40]

The King's determination evidently goes further than this. It is

---

[28] X. *Hell.* III 1.8-10.
[29] For the possibility about Phokaia see note 19.
[30] X. *Hell.* III 2.1.
[31] See Chapter Five, note 123.
[32] X. *Hell.* III 2.1, 9.
[33] X. *Hell.* III 2.8-10.
[34] X. *Hell.* III 2.11, cf. D.S. XIII 65.3-4.
[35] X. *Hell.* III 2.9, 11-12.
[36] X. *Hell.* III 2.12.
[37] X. *Hell.* III 2.13.
[38] X. *Hell.* III 2.15-16.
[39] X. *Hell.* III 2.20.
[40] I think it must be here, if anywhere, that we should fit in a Spartan
mission to the King, which was imprisoned (Ktesias 63).

in this summer of 397 [41] that he begins a programme of naval
rearmament which eventually led to the defeat of the Spartan fleet
at Knidos in 394 and essentially reestablished Persian power in
Ionia.[42] It should not be too easily assumed that he has only Sparta
in mind. An independent Egypt now constitutes a substantial
preoccupation as well.[43]

Artaxerxes' disquiet is easily intelligible. All Alcibiades' predictions to Tissaphernes [44] were now coming true. The Spartans did
see themselves as liberators and they were more of a land-power
than Athens had been. His father and brother had given them
control of the Aegean as well. They had used their power to back
Cyrus against him. They were now using it not only to protect the
Greeks of Asia, who will now not be paying tribute to him or to
Tissaphernes, but to maintain an army on the mainland which might
at any moment, as Thibron had already done, carve deep into his
chora, reduce his revenues and upset the structure of Persian
settlement in Asia Minor which had lasted for over a hundred years
and which Athens had done nothing to disturb. It will not be
surprising that he sees Sparta as the enemy.

That Sparta was taking the war seriously became clearer in 396
when king Agesilaos arrived still demanding that the cities in Asia
should be as autonomous as those in Greece.[45] Tissaphernes offered

---

[41] In X. *Hell*. III 4.1-2 the news of activity in Phoenicia is the preliminary
to Agesilaos' arrival in 396. The archon-year 397/6 is clearly relevant to the
start of Konon's operations in Philochorus 328 F 144-145. Cf. the three
years of Isoc. IV 142.

[42] The prehistory of the naval rearmament is so intolerably complex that
I omit it altogether, despite its interest for the way things were done in Persia.

[43] Looked at from an Aegean point of view, the Persian naval revival
seemed mean, inept and slow (Isoc. IV 142, Hell. Oxy. 19.2); the author of the
Hellenica Oxyrhynchia thought that this was merely a matter of the King's
parsimony. We should, I think, not forget that one of the consequences of
Cyrus' failure was that the King of Egypt acquired his fleet of 50 triremes
(D.S. XIV 35.4-5; their number in 19.5), a useful windfall. Egypt is never
short of cordage (cf. D.S. XIV 79.4), but, from the New Kingdom onwards,
it is clear that ship-timbers depend on a friendly or subject Phoenicia. For
a partial appreciation of the situation, cf. Kienitz, *Die politische Geschichte
Ägyptens* 79-80. Herodas the Syracusan may have been wise to be agnostic
about the destination of the Phoenician ships (X. *Hell*. III 4.1). There is
however no evidence that Persia did do anything to take advantage of what
was apparently a troubled change of Pharoah at this time.

[44] Thuc. VIII 46.3.

[45] X. *Hell*. III 4.5. I would not dispute that anti-Spartan Greeks might
find a meaning in this which Agesilaos did not intend and might reflect
that the kind of autonomy which Sparta generally preferred was one which

to refer this demand to the King, and a further truce was arranged,
which gained Tissaphernes time. When he became more confident
that he was to be reinforced, he simply told Agesilaos to get out of
Asia.[46] The consequences were disastrous, particularly after
Agesilaos improved his cavalry. The war was taken deep into the
King's *chora* and a battle won outside Sardis. The King was enraged
at Tissaphernes' failure and sent Tithraustes down on a mission to
execute Tissaphernes and with powers to rectify the situation.[47]
Both strands of the Greek evidence hold that the King held Tissaphernes responsible for the war,[48] and it could certainly be reflected
that, had he not tried to enforce his claims on the Greek cities
physically, there would have been no Spartan force in Asia.
Tithraustes enunciated the King's terms: Agesilaos should sail
home and the cities in Asia should be autonomous but tribute-
paying.[49] On my view, this is a proposal to revert to the Treaty
of Boiotios.[50] Agesilaos said that the authorities at home would
have to be consulted, arranged a truce with Tithraustes and moved
to the north against Pharnabazos.[51] A message came from home

was good for Sparta (cf. Thuc. I 19, 144.2 and De Ste Croix *OPW* 98-9), but
Agesilaos does not seem to have taken any very clear line on internal politics
in Ionia, said by X. *Hell.* III 4.7 to be disturbed at that time. The impression
left by that passage and Plut. *Ages.* 7 is that there was a pattern of moderate
oligarchies already of the type that Sparta was generally at home with and
that Agesilaos had no general principle except to be rude to friends of
Lysander.

[46] X. *Hell.* III 4.11.

[47] D.S. XIV 80.7. For Tithraustes as chiliarch see Chapter One note 96.
Despite Diodorus' use of ἡγεμὼν to describe his position, it is pretty clear
(cf. Hell. Oxy. 19.3) that there was no intention that he should remain
long. The letters he carries to cities and satraps are to make it easier for him
to carry out a reorganisation. Beloch *GG* III 1.46 n. 1 rightly observes that
the timing makes it unlikely that the battle of Sardis was the determining
factor in Tissaphernes' disgrace, though Anderson, *Cal. Stud. Class. Ant. 7*,
1974, 52, presupposing the need for a gap between the battle and Tithraustes'
arrival, attempts to fill it with Hell. Oxy. 12, D.S. XIV 80.5, which will
not stretch very far.

[48] X. *Hell.* III 4.25; D.S. XIV 80.6 adds the motif of Parysatis' vengeance,
cf. Plut. *Art.* 23.1; there is a faint chance that this was in the Hellenica
Oxyrhynchia where she has been found in the]απαρ[of Col. VII 15.

[49] X. *Hell.* III 4.25.

[50] Note that for Wade-Gery (in 1940), *Essays* 225, it also had the ring of a
restatement, though for him it was the Peace of Kallias which was being
restated. I am not as confident as Wade-Gery that the offer was insincere.

[51] X. *Hell.* III 4.26. The truce is in D.S. XIV 80.8 and referred to by
Hell. Oxy. 21.1 from which it results that it only covered Lydia. For Xenophon, Tithraustes positively and specifically encouraged Agesilaos to move

instructing him to take charge of the fleet as well.[52] His power and success, the greatest ever achieved by a Spartan king, were at their height, and he spent part of the winter of 395/4 in Pharnabazos' palace at Daskyleion, though it may be doubted whether he took full advantage of it, since he preferred to sit on the grass.[53]

Eighteen months later Pharnabazos in command of a Persian fleet was taking his revenge by ravaging the coast-line of Laconia.[54] The Spartan fleet had been destroyed. Every large state in Greece was in arms against Sparta. Agesilaos had been called home with his troops. In Ionia, the Hellespont and the islands, very little remained under Spartan control. It will not be profitable to investigate how far it was Spartan unpopularity and how far Persian gold and diplomacy which had produced this result. There was much talk of Persian bribery of political leaders, which may or may not have had a significant effect. It is certain that the fleet which won the battle of Knidos was paid, however erratically, with Persian money and built in Persian-controlled harbours. It is likely that the rapidity of the Spartan collapse was due, not only to their own past behaviour, but to the assurances given by Konon and Pharnabazos that the cities would be free and ungarrisoned.[55]

against Pharnabazos, and it is evident that he did not succeed, even if he tried, in creating a general armistice. The parallel between this and the arrangement between Derkyllidas and Tissaphernes in 398 (X. *Hell*. III 1.9) is not as close as it seems, since Tithraustes seems to have superior powers in the west of a type which Tissaphernes did not have in 398 and Tithraustes and Pharnabazos seem to be cooperating in Hell. Oxy. 19.1. It was clearly uncomfortable to have Agesilaos sitting near Lydia, but I still find Tithraustes' behaviour surprising. Grote treated it as a specimen of the way in which satraps (which Tithraustes was not) acted more like independent or even hostile princes than cooperating colleagues; Meyer (*Theopomps Hellenika* 21) thought his motive was to draw Agesilaos away from Caria and the developing naval offensive at all costs; Judeich (*Kleinasiatische Studien* 68) evidently took Tithraustes' words (Xenophon wavers in this passage between ambassadors and Tithraustes himself) μεταχώρησον εἰς τὴν Φαρναβάζου, ἐπειδὴ καὶ ἐγὼ τὸν σὸν ἐχθρὸν τετιμώρημαι as an allusion to unknown hostility between himself and Pharnabazos, and I have felt the same inclination.

[52] X. *Hell*. III 4.27-29. As we saw (page 35), he nominated his brother-in-law.

[53] X. *Hell*. IV 1.15-16, 30.

[54] X. *Hell*. IV 8.7.

[55] X. *Hell*. IV 8.1-2. That the cities freed by the fleet were not pushed too hard is suggested by Diodorus' distinction between those who expelled their Spartan garrisons and kept their freedom and those who attached themselves to Konon's fleet (XIV 84.4).

The problem of the status of the Ionian cities between 393 and 387 is one of the most intractable which we have. It is clear from Tod II 113 that a

Spartan foreign policy now made the most rapid of all its switches. I have been arguing that Spartan panhellenism was substantially genuine. I would not argue that it took precedence in Spartan policy over her need to retain supremacy in the Peloponnese and internal stability in Laconia and Messenia. That the Peloponnesian League had been reduced to a torso and the position of the old enemy Argos sharply enhanced by the secessions of 395 and 394 has always been clear enough. What I do not find in the books is a realisation that a threat has developed to Sparta even nearer home. In spring 393 Pharnabazos captured and garrisoned the Spartan island of Kythera off the south coast of Laconia.[56] I do not know whether the move is prompted by simple good sense or by a reading of Herodotus. We, however, should read Herodotus [57] and recall that in 480 the exiled Spartan king Demaratos is said to have told Xerxes that the one sure way of beating Sparta was to occupy Kythera, raid the mainland from it and terrify the Spartans; if they had such a local war on their hands, they would be incapable of thinking of anything else.[58] Six years after the conspiracy of Kinadon [59] Spartan reaction is likely to have been violent.[60]

satrapy of Ionia existed in this period and also that the Persians were pre-pared to devolve a good deal of responsibility for settling disputes between the cities on the Ionian League (cf. Chapter Five, note 75). For further guidance, we can only look at the operations of Thrasyboulos in 390/89. It is clear from X. *Hell.* IV 8.27 that the cities of Asia are thought of as being within the King's sphere. That Thrasyboulos intervenes in Kalchedon (ibid., 28) is evidently a function of Pharnabazos' friendliness for Athens (ibid., 31). That he was applying pressure to Aspendos when he dies (ibid., 30) is on the face of it tactless behaviour. It is the major fault of Badian's admirable paper on Alexander's administration of Asia Minor (*Studies....* *Ehrenberg* 37-61) that he assumes Aspendos to be a Greek city; the slightest glance at its coins would have shown this to be false. Tod II 114 of 387, which shows Athenian interference in Klazomenai, is not relevant, since Athens and Persia are by now hostile. New evidence, which I cannot refer to explicitly, may suggest that in one Ionian city it was the King's Peace which constituted being handed over to the barbarians. (Tod, II 110, which shows Knidos in the Athenian alliance, is certainly a fifth-century text, as Jameson will show. The ΣΥΝ-coinage (see Cawkwell, *JHS* 83, 1963, 152-4) has nothing to say on a juridical level.)

[56] X. *Hell.* IV 8.8, D.S. XIV 84.5.

[57] VII 235.

[58] That Herodotus' emphasis on this reflects the events of 424 was of course said (and resisted) before Fornara, *JHS* 91, 1971, 33-4. It has its attractions.

[59] See page 28.

[60] A secondary consideration in the occupation of Kythera is at least possible. If one of the Athenian motives for taking it in 424 was that it was

The political background to the Spartan change of policy is obscure, but I see no good reason to suppose that even Agesilaos was opposed to it.[61] Antalkidas [62] was sent to the new Persian commander in the west, Tiribazos.[63] He was equipped with a seductive diplomatic argument, that the Athenian Konon was using the Persian fleet in the interests of Athens rather than of Persia, and with even more attractive terms, which he could rightly think would constitute a peace which the King would welcome.[64] The Spartans would give up their fight [65] against the King for the Greek cities in Asia; it would be sufficient if all the islands and the other cities were autonomous. The latter formula, as later events showed, was capable of unlimited manipulation to Spartan advantage in mainland Greece. What it offered to the King is clear from Antalkidas' strategic gloss. Not only would there be no Spartan force on the mainland, but there would be no naval power in the Aegean either to sustain the Greeks of Asia by sea. If we are to speak of Spartan betrayal of panhellenism, this is the moment to see it. The only excuse we can offer is that the Spartans were very hard pressed.

---

the point of arrival for merchant-ships from Egypt and Libya (Thuc. IV 54.3), the motive will be yet stronger in 393 when the Spartans had been in touch with the King of Egypt and he has been sending them supplies (D.S. XIV 79.4).

[61] Since the only passage (Plut. *Ages.* 23.2-4) which asserts Antalkidas' hostility to Agesilaos also attests Agesilaos' acceptance of Antalkidas' policy, there is really nothing to discuss. (Plutarch makes a rapid transition from 392 to 387, as Ziegler, to judge from his marginal date, does not recognise.) See Smith, *Historia* 2, 1953/4, 277 n. 6. Smith goes on to see Agesilaos behind Antalkidas' first mission, but against the Sparta conference which followed, but he has a totally wrong view of the Sparta conference.

[62] For an attempt to place Antalkidas in a Spartan context see Chapter Two, note 65.

[63] His career as an adviser and friend of Artaxerxes goes back to at least 401 (Plut. *Art.* 7.3, X. *Anab.* IV 4.4). It is not clear whether his satrapy of western Armenia, attested by the latter passage, is earlier or a reward for his services at Cunaxa (Plut. *Art.* 10.1). It is clear from X. *Hell.* IV 8.12, D.S. XIV 85.4 that in 392 he held a military command and was not simply satrap of Sardis.

[64] X. *Hell.* IV 8.12.

[65] Ibid., 14. My avoidance of 'claim' for ἀντιποιεῖσθαι is not merely due to a wish to avoid the suggestion that the Spartans had been ruling the cities, but also to the fact that the presence of the dative brings the passage under *LSJ* ἀντιποιέω II 2 rather than II 1. The distinction to be drawn is not very sharp.

Tiribazos was delighted,[66] but such a change went far beyond his instructions. Xenophon[67] says he did not think it safe to switch to the Spartans without the consent of the King. He put Konon in jail and assured Antalkidas of his sympathy. A Greek conference was held at Sparta to hammer out the details of the autonomy-clause. Except for Argos, they reached an agreement, which broke down when it went to the Athenian assembly, which declined to accept the abandonment of the Greeks of Asia.[68] It would not have made much difference if they had accepted. When Tiribazos went to the King to report the Spartan offer and ask for instructions, he seems to have been turned down flat. He is replaced by Strouthas, friendly to the Athenians and hostile to the Spartans, remembering all the damage Agesilaos had done to the King's *chora*.[69] He is certainly acting on the King's instructions. We may well think that Tiribazos' judgement of the King's interests was correct, but the King himself will not have been prepared to forgive or forget the consistency of Spartan hostility to him since his accession.[70] If he took any other advice, we may reflect that Pharnabazos seems to have maintained a consistently pro-Athenian attitude throughout this period.[71]

Hostility between Sparta and Persia thus dragged on for three more years. It was not until Athens had justified all Antalkidas' arguments, by supporting Evagoras of Salamis, now in revolt

---

[66] Ibid., 15.

[67] ·Ibid., 16.

[68] I regard the relationship of the Sardis and Sparta conferences as too obvious to argue; I am in substantial agreement with e.g. Jacoby's commentary on Philochoros 328 F 149, with qualifications only about his treatment of Xenophon. Andocides' entirely understandable silence about Asia Minor will not stand against Philochoros. Philochoros' phrase διότι ἐγέγραπτο ἐν αὐτῇ τοὺ[ς τὴν ᾿Α]σίαν οἰκοῦντ[ας] Ἕλληνας ἐν βασιλέως οἴκ[ωι π]άντας εἶναι συννενεμημένους is tantalising in the extreme. It is alien to Greek diplomatic language, but I cannot translate it into Aramaic. Prolonged contemplation of Greek and Persian passages about 'the King's house' leaves me still in doubt about the full implications.

The ambiguities of Athenian attitudes to Persia in this period are very beautiful. I defer discussion until Stroud and I publish new fragments of Tod, II 109.

[69] X. *Hell.* IV 8.17.

[70] This will be one of the many occasions on which Tiribazos was rejected for κουφότης (Plut. *Art.* 24.4). See also Chapter Three, note 59.

[71] Still in X. *Hell.* IV 8.32.

against the King,[72] and by allying herself with Egypt,[73] that another attempt was made. This time Antalkidas reached the King himself.[74] Artaxerxes, actually at last faced with a real Spartan, was charmed and paid him a famous compliment by sending him his own wreath, drenched in the finest scent.[75] They rapidly came to terms. Antalkidas received financial support, and Tiribazos, at last justified, returned to his command with instructions to support him. Pharnabazos, who might have taken a different view,[76] was called above to be married to the King's daughter.[77] After a brief campaign, Tiribazos was in a position to summon the Greeks, exhibit the King's seal and read the King's edict: "Artaxerxes the King thinks it just that the cities of Asia shall be his and of the islands Klazomenai and Cyprus, and that the other cities, small and great, shall be autonomous except Lemnos, Imbros and Skyros; these shall be Athenian as formerly. Whichever side does not accept this peace, I shall make war on them along with whoever wishes, by land and by sea, with ships and with money".[78] Formally, he was settling a bilateral war,[79] but no one could be in any doubt whose side he was on.[80] Sparta and Persia have at last settled their diplomatic differences.

---

[72] The absurdity of Athens' position is best brought out by X. *Hell.* IV 8.24.

[73] Ar. *Plutus* 178, which seems good enough, but the wild guessing of the scholia, of which even the best substitutes Amasis for Akoris, suggests that there was not much to be found in the Atthidographers.

[74] It seems unlikely that εἰς Πέρσας in Plut. *Art.* 22.1 means Persepolis this time; contrast Chapter Three, note 159.

[75] Plut. *Art.* 22.1 with four other passages quoted by Ziegler, ad loc. According to Ael. *V.H.* XIV 39, Antalkidas was capable of behaving like a Spartan even in what Plutarch regards as his hour of disgrace and observed that the natural scent was better.

[76] The Spartans are causing him trouble to the last, X. *Hell.* IV 8.33; he will have recovered these Aeolic cities after 393.

[77] X. *Hell.* V 1.28.

[78] X. *Hell.* V 1.31. Other passages are collected by Bengtson, *Die Staatsverträge des Altertums* no. 242.

[79] I have searched without success for someone else who attaches importance to the indubitable fact that ὁπότεροι means 'which of two'.

[80] I am wholly resistent to the revival by Cawkwell, *CQ* n.s. 23, 1973, 53 of the old view that the Spartans were actually named in a document as the προστάται of the Peace. If I had to give a single reason, it would be the periphrastic way in which the King in 367 indicated his switch to the Thebans (Plut. *Pel.* 30.7), but my objections go a good deal wider; in 377 the Athenians did not denounce the Peace, as Cawkwell thinks, but were proclaiming that Sparta had broken it.

Before I bring these lectures to an end, there are two themes which seem to me to call for more extended comment, the affinities between Persia and Sparta which have sometimes emerged from the narrative and the historical problem posed by the Greek settlement of Asia Minor.

For different reasons, Herodotus and Xenophon both have a good deal to say about both Persia and Sparta. We should not, I think, be in any doubt that, despite Herodotus' praises of Athens, it is Sparta which for him was Persia's principal antagonist.[81] It is consistent with this that he makes comparisons and contrasts between Sparta and Persia which it would not occur to him to make between Athens and Persia. I am not thinking of his detection of interesting parallels between the occurrences on the deaths of Spartan and Persian kings.[82] It is rather that it seems to me to be a theme of the History that the Persians gradually discover what the Spartans are like. To start with Cyrus the Great, he shows himself totally mistaken in dismissing the Spartans, as if, like the other Greeks he knows about, they were in the habit of bargaining and telling lies in the marketplace.[83] Xerxes has every reason to be better informed, since he has the exiled Spartan king Demaratos to tell him, but, told at Doriskos that a thousand is a reasonable number for an effective Spartan army, he merely thinks the talk funny,[84] and, even before Thermopylae, he cannot believe that these men combing their hair before battle are the kernel of Greek resistance.[85] After Thermopylae he knows better,[86] and at Plataea Mardonios takes it for granted that the Spartans are the best Greek warriors.[87] Courage is the quality which the Persians find it easiest to appreciate[88] and, on the one occasion in Herodotus when a Persian and Spartans talk on reasonably equal terms,[89] it is Spartan

---

[81] See e.g. Fornara, *Herodotus* 50.

[82] Hdt. VI 58.2-59.

[83] Hdt. I 153.1-2. He does not need to underline the grotesque inappropriateness of describing the Spartans in this way. The exact responsion to this passage comes in VIII 26 where it is learnt that Greeks do after all pursue ἀρετή rather than money.

[84] Hdt. VII 101-105.

[85] Hdt. VII 209.

[86] Hdt. VII 234.

[87] Hdt. IX 48.

[88] Hdt. I 136.1, VII 238.2 (where he finds Xerxes' behaviour to Leonidas' corpse surprising), VIII 90.4.

[89] Hdt. VII 135.

courage which brings them the offer of the King's friendship. On that occasion, it is their love of freedom which explains their continued hostility to the King, a freedom dependent, as Demaratos has explained not long before,[90] on their obedience to *nomos*. Herodotus leaves us in no doubt that there are many admirable features about the Persians.[91] If they failed in 480, it was in part a question of the Greek passion for freedom, in part because of Xerxes' hybris. As the History nears its end, we also begin to see more clearly that luxury has weakened the resolve of an originally simple warrior people. The Spartans are still uncorrupted and Pausanias has his Spartan meal prepared among the splendours of Mardonios' captured tent.[92]

That luxury destroys empires is for us a commonplace over-simplification, a historical explanation which is more useful for dealing with societies of relatively simple organisation, though powerful enough there, as can be seen in the hands of its leading exponent, Ibn Khaldun.[93] Tied to moral explanations about perjury which provokes the wrath of the gods, it formed a considerable part of the thinking of Xenophon about both Persia and Sparta. For him, both of these had at one time been model societies which had solved the problem of leadership which preoccupies him in most of his writing. Both of them in his own time had become manifestly nothing of the kind, and both the *Cyropaedia*[94] and the *Constitution of the Lacedaemonians*[95] contain sections which attribute a good deal of the blame to greed and luxury. That their institutions

---

[90] Hdt. VII 104.4.

[91] The strongest expressions of approval run through I 136-138, but there are other nuances to be observed. I take it that the implication of the μὲν ... δὲ at IX 116.1 is that Artayktes' villainy is untypical, and he takes trouble to say that even some of the major Persian atrocities were occasioned by provocation; cf. III 147.1 where Otanes is going against Darius' orders, V 102.1.

[92] Hdt. IX 82 (Pausanias' later career is of course glanced at, as implied by Fornara, *Herodotus* 62-6). That luxury had been the Persian ruin is the implicit message of the last chapter of all, IX 122, on which nothing need be added to Bischoff, *Der Warner bei Herodot*, Diss. Marburg 1932, 78-83 (reprinted in Marg (ed.), *Herodot* 670-6).

[93] His actual doctrine on the Achaemenids is distressingly vague. They are included among those ruling houses whose ruling ability is destroyed by luxury, and replaced by the Sassanids (I 297-8), which leaves a good deal out. Elsewhere (III 113-4) he knows perfectly well that Alexander killed Darius and took over the empire. (I quote by volume and page of Rosenthal's translation of the Muqadimmah.)

[94] VIII 8.

[95] 14.

were in themselves at fault he does not contemplate, though others had a good deal to criticise in those of the Persians at least.[96]

Xenophon never draws direct comparisons between Spartan and Persian education and society, though occasionally he describes their educational practices in very similar language.[97] We have sometimes had occasion to observe that quite different political institutions were capable of producing very similar effects, notably in 412 where rivalry between Agis and Endios was neatly matched by rivalry between Pharnabazos and Tissaphernes. The desire to shine, φιλονιχία, which Finley[98] has recommended us to see as a leading motive in Spartan affairs, is just as visible in Persia, where the King is the sole fount of honour.[99] It would not be greatly exaggerating to say that status with the King takes precedence over nearly all other motives for a Persian nobleman.

The point is made most clearly when Agesilaos suggests to Pharnabazos that he will be better off as a ruler free from the King. Tissaphernes has just been executed and Pharnabazos indicates that his attitude will depend on whether he is put under another commander-in-chief or is given the command himself. If he is once again subordinated,[100] he will, he says, accede to Agesilaos' suggestion and join the Spartans.[101] If he is given the command, his φιλοτιμία will dictate that he prosecutes the war against Sparta to the limit of his abilities. This is a concept of honour which Agesilaos

---

[96] Isoc. IV 150-153, Plato *Laws* 697 c-d. Momigliano, *Alien Wisdom* 135 is over-critical.

[97] There are clear affinities e.g. between *Anab.* I 9.3-4 and *Lac. Pol.* 5.5-6.

[98] *Sparta* 151.

[99] Cf. Hdt. VIII 69.2, 86, where Xerxes, rightly in Herodotus' opinion, thinks that his presence will produce a substantial improvement in military performance.

[100] His jealousy at Tissaphernes' original appointment asserted at X. *Hell.* III 2.13.

[101] Xenophon always takes a favourable view of Pharnabazos' character, but, with Meyer, *Theopomps Hellenika* 31, I find it hard to see much sincerity in this offer, in view of his general bitterness about the Spartans. The situation about the command at this point is hard to probe. The landforces seem already to have been given to Ariaios and Pasiphernes (Hell. Oxy. XIX 3; I think 'Herbst 394' must be a slip for 'Herbst 395' in Meyer, op. cit., 30); if ἐπὶ τῶν πραγμάτων meant that they had succeeded to Tissaphernes' full powers, Pharnabazos would already have been subordinated in the way he fears. One would have thought that he had had a great deal to do with the fleet already, as is asserted by D.S. XIV 39.2 and implied by Hell. Oxy. XIX 1, but he may be uncertain as to whether he will get the formal command and a free hand to use it.

understands and applauds,[102] and the scene ends with the sealing of *xenia* between him and Pharnabazos' son.[103]

This is only the most explicit illustration that we have of the fact that in our period it was repeatedly found perfectly possible for Greeks, and, I think, particularly Spartans, to get on the same wavelength as the Persians with whom they came into contact. I am not suggesting that it was only Spartans who felt this. Alcibiades was evidently capable of talking to Tissaphernes, Hermokrates and Konon to Pharnabazos. Nor did all Spartans have the ability to get on with all Persians, as Derkyllidas' brushes with Pharnabazos and Kallikratidas' troubles with Cyrus showed. But the rapport so rapidly reached between Cyrus and Lysander was clearly remarkable, and Cyrus was on nearly as good terms with Klearchos, the commander of the Ten Thousand.[104] Years of absence from Asia did not destroy Lysander's ability to get on with Persians, and virtually his only achievement on Agesilaos' staff was to secure the defection of Spithridates from Pharnabazos.[105] Agesilaos, to put it generously,[106] got on well with Spithridates and his family and used them in an attempt to win over the King of Paphlagonia.[107] The Persian villain is nearly always Tissaphernes. Many years later Xenophon, in drawing a contrast between the antique honesty and reliability of the Persians and their present faithlessness and dishonesty, saw the turning-point in the Persian breach of oath in killing the

---

[102] X. *Hell.* IV 1.35-38. Alexander the Great's attitude would be precisely the same (Q.C. VI 5.2).

[103] X. *Hell.* IV 1.39-40. Similarly Agesilaos at some stage became a xenos of Mausollos (X. *Ages.* 2.27) and Antalkidas of Ariobarzanes (X. *Hell.* V 1.28).

[104] X. *Anab.* I 1.9 is unduly brief and the reference of II 6.4 is uncertain. But their relation was one of confidence, III 1.10 (Klearchos is being very disingenuous at I 3.5). That Cyrus should give such a position to a Spartan exile at a time when his plans depended on Spartan cooperation suggests to me that he saw in Klearchos not merely a useful general, but a replacement for Lysander.

[105] X. *Hell.* III 4.10. For Spithridates see Chapter Three note 200.

[106] In the *Hellenica* Xenophon is silent about Agesilaos' affection for Spithridates' son Megabates, but cf. *Ages.* V 4-6, Hell. Oxy. XXI 4, Plut. *Ages.* 11. It is not clear to me how Herodotus (I 135) could know that pederasty was a trait that the Persians learnt from the Greeks.

[107] X. *Hell.* IV 1.1-15, Hell. Oxy. XXII 1. That the whole episode ended in disaster was not the fault of Agesilaos, but of his subordinate Herippidas who, either out of greed (X. *Hell.* IV 1.26) or out of untimely rectitude (Plut. *Ages.* 11.4), took an ungenerous view of his barbarian allies' claims to booty.

generals of the Ten Thousand after Cunaxa;[108] everyone knew who
had sworn that oath.[109] It was Lysander who said that dice were for
cheating boys, oaths for cheating men,[110] and Xenophon certainly
saw a parallel decline in Spartan honesty which brought divine
vengeance on them.[111] Neither Spartans nor Persians are likely to
have been much affected by the rise of the sophistic movement, but
they seem to have had more positive similarities as well, which
they could see. One of the claims made by Tarn for Alexander the
Great was that Alexander was quite remarkable in transcending
the normal Greek attitude to barbarians and in seeing merit in and
the possibility of collaboration with the upper classes of Iran.[112]
Tarn's evidence was drawn entirely from Plato and Aristotle and
gave a very partial account even of their thinking.[113] For readers
of Xenophon the claim must seem simply absurd.[114]

Lastly, it may be helpful if I try to clarify some of the cultural
and strategic issues which underlie the negotiations we have been
discussing. The Greek cities of Asia Minor were undeniable facts.
The Greeks had come there by sea and remained largely maritime
in their orientation. They were nevertheless physically part of the
mainland and a natural attraction to whatever land power ruled
the interior. The Persians had no objections to ruling Greeks any
more than to ruling Egyptians or Babylonians. All three had
strong national traditions, however, and were liable from time to

---

[108] X. *Cyr.* VIII 8.3.

[109] X. *Anab.* II 3.26-28. The details of oath-taking between Greeks and
Persians are obscure. No significant differences in attitude are referred to,
but I know of no evidence for the gods used by the Persians (there are
serious problems about *Tituli Asiae Minoris* II 3.1183). If Hdt. I 74.6
covers Persians as well as Medes and Lydians, it must have rapidly been
recognised that it would be difficult to get Greeks to go in for bloodlicking.
Doubtless it was only necessary for alliances, cf. Tac. *Ann.* XII 47.

[110] Plut. *Lys.* 8.5.

[111] X. *Hell.* V 4.1. One of the most powerful passages about the sanctity
of oaths is put by Herodotus (VI 86) in the mouth of a Spartan and ignored
by the Athenians.

[112] *Alexander the Great* I 9, 54-5. It is not in dispute that Eratosthenes had
said something of the kind.

[113] See Andreotti, *Historia* 5, 1956, 257-66, probably too extreme about
Aristotle, cf. Badian, *Historia* 7, 1958, 440. Stern, *Aristotle on the World-
State* 30-1, is worth consideration.

[114] Alexander is hardly likely ever to have thought that Pharnabazos'
son Artabazos, who had strong Greek connections and spent some time at
Philip's court (Berve, *Alexanderreich* no. 152), was a natural slave. See note
102.

time to object to being ruled by the Persians. This national resistance was complicated in the case of the Greeks by the fact that they were tied by culture and sentiment to the rest of the Greek world, and other Greeks sometimes felt an obligation to help them. Darius I may have considered the possibility of solving the problem by transporting the Greeks elsewhere.[115] The Spartans, who also thought in land terms, certainly did.[116] Under Darius at least the Persians solved their problem by acquiring naval strength and controlling a large part of the Aegean islands as well; the Asiatic Greeks tried and failed to shake off this naval grip. Xerxes, quite unnecessarily, attempted to push still further forward into the Greek world. His naval disasters produced the revolt of that part of the Greek world which he had held before and also the creation of a Greek naval power with the strength and the will to preserve the independence of the Asiatic Greeks. After another thirty years of fighting had produced a naval deadlock which defined the limits of Athenian seapower, Artaxerxes I acquiesced in the unfamiliar concept of a sea-league or sea-empire abutting on a land-empire. He could do this with greater security because Athens did not have the ambition and certainly did not have the land power to make itself a nuisance to the Persian possessions of the interior.[117] The position was symbolised by the fact that the cities were to be unwalled [118] and made more precise by reciprocal undertakings about military movements.[119]

---

[115] Hdt. VI 3. In view of the long history of deportations in the Near East, including Persia (cf. page 7), there is no reason to assume that Histiaios simply made this up.

[116] Hdt. IX 106.2.

[117] Toynbee, *The Western Question in Greece and Turkey* (2nd edition 1923) 221, seems to me totally mistaken in saying that Agesilaos was carrying on the Anatolian policy of Pericles. Pericles had no Anatolian policy.

[118] First seen by Toynbee, loc. cit., and more firmly grounded by Wade-Gery, *Essays* 219-20, though dissent persists around me (Meiggs, *The Athenian Empire* 149-51, Brunt, *Studies. . . . Ehrenberg* 92 n. 54). See also Cawkwell, *CQ* n.s. 23, 1973, 54 n. 3, whose citation of Isaiah XLV 1-2 on normal conditions under the Persians would have been more convincing if he had also attempted to grapple with the problems posed by Nehemiah's wall-building at Jerusalem four years after the Peace of Kallias. For neighbours this is a sign of rebellion (Neh. II 19, cf. the earlier complaints Ezra IV 12-16). The story I declined to spin in Chapter Three, note 5 would involve Jerusalem's being a royal, not a local, fortress.

[119] See Wade-Gery *Essays* 215-9, with the modifications of Andrewes, *Historia* 10, 1961, 16-8. I do not at the moment see how the investigation can be taken further.

With the disappearance of the Peace of Kallias and the weakening
of the Athenian navy, the situation became a good deal more fluid.
The Persians could now hope for greater control of the Greek cities,
but they were now exposed to the threat of raids by land into the
chora. We have from time to time seen them moved by these threats
or by actual raids. In effect, I have been arguing that, both before
and after the rupture of Spartan-Persian relations in 401, they
were always in the last analysis prepared to make concessions about
the status of the Greek cities if they could be secured from the
presence of a hostile landpower on the mainland.

From 399 on, their position became steadily worse. The cities
were now protected by a power which had strength by both sea
and land. The only immediate Persian asset was that, although
they were inferior to the Spartan infantry,[120] they were much
superior in cavalry and this restricted Greek movements.[121] When
Agesilaos managed to remedy that, there were virtually no limits
on his freedom of movement. Doubts have been expressed about
the realities of his success and the chances of its having any permanent result. More than fifty years ago, Toynbee[122] conducted
a masterly demolition-exercise on all attempts to conquer Anatolia
from the west, on the ground that it was impossible to hold any
very small area, since all natural boundaries were far to the east.
Agesilaos had had no effect on his enemies' will to continue the war.
Alexander had managed to destroy the Persian empire, but not to
rule Asia. Rome had had terrible trouble, was led a dance all the
way to the Caucasus and the Euphrates until she was confronted
with the new power of Parthia and established a frontier which
lasted for seven hundred years, but drained her in the end. If I had
to hazard a guess at the way in which Agesilaos might have been
thinking of solving his problem, I would point to his negotiations
with the Paphlagonians and with Pharnabazos and suggest that
he might have envisaged an Asia Minor of small buffer-states.[123]

---

[120] They did of course have some Greek infantry of their own (X. *Hell.*
III 2.15), but these were a shade unreliable for use against Greeks (cf. e.g.
X. *Hell.* III 1.18).

[121] X. *Hell.* III 1.5 and, more notably, III 4.13-15. Xenophon's own
attempt to belittle the importance of Persian cavalry (*Anab.* III 2.18-19)
is surely a mere pretence to encourage his men; so, Anderson, *Xenophon*
(1974) 124.

[122] Op. cit. (n. 117) 213-4, 219-24.

[123] There seem to me to be clear traces of thinking of this kind in Isoc.
IV 161-166 of 380. If Hell. Oxy. XXII 4 fin. represents Agesilaos' geographic

As I have said repeatedly, Persian Asia Minor was by no means monolithic.

All this was however dependent on the command of the sea. When Sparta lost this in 394, the position was transformed. All that could be hoped for was that Persia would not push her new naval power to Sparta's destruction. All rights on the mainland would be foresworn. Sparta would guarantee that neither she nor Athens would maintain the naval empire necessary to support that part of the Greek world in independence. The King eventually saw sense and agreed, adding only that the formula about the autonomy of the islands should not include Klazomenai and Cyprus.[124] The frontier has been defined as a land frontier, denying cultural and geographic facts which go across it.[125]

It will by now be clear to you that the diplomatic and military manoeuvres which I have been discussing are only an episode in one of the longest-running problems in world history. It was a long time before the situation caused by the Greek occupation of the Aegean basin recurred in anything like the same form. The conquests of Alexander and of Rome provided the conditions under which Greek culture and institutions were carried to the Euphrates and in some forms far beyond it, and even after the Arab conquests the frontiers of the Greek world still stood on the Taurus. The Turks pushed their conquests far to the west of the territories which have been concerning us. Succeeding where the Persians had failed, they reduced virtually the whole Greek world to the status Ionia had had under the King's Peace, though we should not overlook the fact that some Greeks under the Ottoman empire enjoyed a status and opportunities in the imperial administration not unlike

---

beliefs, as is likely, this supposed 'waist' of Asia Minor will represent the limit of what he hoped to detach from the King (X. *Hell*. IV 1.41), but neither his resources nor existing military techniques would have sufficed to produce a frontier defensible militarily.

[124] The mention of these is specifically directed against Athens, cf. Ryder, *Koine Eirene* (1965) 34. Athens is in return allowed to break the uniformity of the Peace by getting Lemnos, Imbros and Skyros.

[125] Toynbee, op. cit., 333-4, prefigures, sometimes verbally, the more extended discussion of the Europe-Asia distinction which appears in *Study of History*, VIII 708-29. Everything he has to say about the unity of both sides of the Aegean and the Hellespont is of course true, but landpowers will surely have a natural wish to hold whatever lies within their physical geographic boundaries. I need only mention Goa and Gibraltar. For the Persian attitude I recall again Hdt. IX 116.3.

those we have dimly seen for Greeks in the Persian empire.[126]

In the nineteenth century the Great Powers established a Greek kingdom, and there was once again a political focus for Greeks beyond its borders. The Greeks of Asia had been pushed back almost to their classical areas of habitation by the centuries of Turkish rule. As they once again expanded economically and culturally into their hinterland, they were watched with increasing sympathy and interest from Athens, where the μεγάλη ἰδέα, the dream of a restored Byzantine Empire, steadily gained ground.[127] The defeat of Turkey in 1918 and the apparent sympathy of the Great Powers encouraged Greece to accept the offer of substantial territory in Asia Minor enshrined in the abortive Treaty of Sèvres. For nearly three years there was a large Greek military and political presence in western Anatolia, occupying, as Toynbee pointed out at the time,[128] much the same area as Agesilaos had done in 396-394 and, in his view, with as little prospect of success. As he wrote, Turkey transformed itself from the rump of a universal empire into a national state and the Greek army collapsed. As Smyrna burned, the Greeks of Asia fled to the mainland in their hundreds of thousands. The problem of the Greeks of Asia seemed to be solved, since they had ceased to exist. A new Greek regime was given plenty to occupy it.

However, it remained true that the Aegean was a unity, and the rulers of Anatolia were not indifferent to what went on beyond their coastline. When the Peace Conference met at Lausanne, the problem of the Aegean islands seemed one of the easiest to be dealt with.[129] Tenedos and Imbros, close to the Dardanelles, would go to

---

[126] "Turkish scorn of languages and their artlessness as negotiators led Phanariot Greeks, as Dragomans of the Sublime Porte, to play a considerable part in the foreign policy of the Empire. Greek Phanariot princes reigned vice-regally from the vassal thrones of Moldavia and Wallachia. Greek bankers handled finance; Greek mountaineers—the Armatoles—'guarded' the mountain passes; Greek seamen manned the warships of the Turkish fleet." (Leigh Fermor, *Roumeli* (1966) 110).

[127] A useful and clear statement will be found in Llewellyn Smith, *Ionian Vision* (1973) 1-34. The whole book is an essential guide to the Greco-Turkish War of 1919-22, but does not cover the peace making adequately.

[128] See note 117 (the first edition, with identical main text, is of March 1922).

[129] Nicolson, *Curzon: the Last Phase* (1934) 300-1. It was taken early because it was straightforward and because it might bolster Greek self-confidence, since it dealt with areas still under their control. The latter hope

Turkey with some provision for the rights of their Greek population.[130] Lemnos, Mytilene, Chios, Samos and Nikaria would go to Greece. Ismet Pasha,[131] without knowledge of Antalkidas and Tiribazos, suggested that they be put under some form of autonomous regime, which he made no attempt to describe. Lord Curzon described this as a 'try-on', and it is clear that what Ismet really had at heart was their demilitarisation. He eventually secured not only that there would be no naval base or fortification in these islands, but, in a farsighted innovation which no one seems to have thought much of at the time, that there should be an air frontier as well as a sea frontier.[132] The demilitarisation held and, when the

---

was ruined by the unfortunate fact that the day when the relevant sub-commission reported (November 29, 1922) was also the day when the Greeks shot the politicians responsible for the disaster, an action which nearly lost them all diplomatic support.

The First Commission took up the question on 26 November; for the proceedings on that day I have used the *Times* of 27 November p. 12, supplemented by Curzon to Henderson of 26 November (*Documents on British Foreign Policy 1919-39*, First Series XVIII no. 226). The sub-commission reported back on 29 November; see the *Times* of 30 November p. 12, supplemented by Curzon to Crowe of 30 November (1.15 a.m.) (ibid., no. 241). The same volume of *Documents* contains (p. 994) a draft text of the relevant articles (12-14) of the Treaty of Lausanne which is virtually identical with that of the final Treaty (for which see *British and Foreign State Papers* 117, 543-639); the only substantial change was a sentence added to article 12 placing islands within three miles of the Asiatic coast and not otherwise named under Turkish sovereignty.

[130] Article 14. I have heard it said that virtually nothing was done to implement this, but do not know the facts. On November 26 Ismet had asked for Samothrace as well, but he can hardly have expected to get it.

[131] Not yet Inonu, after the battle which marked the turning-point of the campaign.

[132] Article 13 represents the final form, which provides for the local training of local troops doing their military service and for gendarmerie and police on the same scale as for Greece as a whole. The Turks had wanted complete demilitarisation and still had reserves on this point after the sub-commission reported. I see no evidence that the sub-commission considered aviation, which seems to have been a new point raised on the 29th, in the form that aviation should be forbidden in the islands. Late at night, Curzon reporting home did not bother to mention it specifically: "two points of minor importance". The final form was that Greek military aviation was forbidden to fly over the territory of the coast of Anatolia, Turkish to fly over the islands.

Llewellyn Smith, op. cit., 334, is mistaken in excluding Lemnos from the demilitarised islands. It does not appear in the sub-commission's report of 29 November, but at that stage it was reserved for treatment with the northern islands and the Dardanelles, and it is certainly in the Treaty.

Dodecanese were handed over by Italy to Greece in 1947, it was extended to them as well.[133]

When the Cyprus question erupted in the 1950s, one of the arguments used against the claim for union with Greece was that Turkey, on strategic grounds alone, could not and at any rate would not remain indifferent to Greek possession of an island so near to and athwart her coastline. The argument was dismissed as an ingenious fabrication of British imperialism,[134] but, when in 1974 that union seemed imminent, it was justified by the violence of the Turkish reaction, which nearly brought Greece and Turkey back to the state of war ended in 1923 and once again broke a Greek regime. By this time new complications had arisen about the boundary of Europe and Asia, undreamed of in 387 B.C. and 1923 A.D. and, even, which is more surprising, in 1947, this time as it affected the bed of the sea. It is easy for outsiders to say that a negotiated solution is the only rational one, but the study of history does not always encourage a belief in human reason. It is not in dispute that the islands are no longer demilitarised, and in August the Prime Minister of Turkey noticeably changed his description of them from 'the Greek islands' to 'the Aegean islands'. After a few days, he explained: "These islands were in Ottoman hands for more than 600 years. As a Turkish boy and the Prime Minister of the Turkish Republic, nobody can want me to call the Aegean islands Greek islands."[135] We should not think that our story is yet at an end.

---

[133] The relevant article (14.2) of the Italian Peace Treaty (*British and Foreign State Papers* 148, 402) is much simpler in form: "These islands shall be and shall remain demilitarised." Turkey was not a party to this treaty, but her interests were apparently being watched.

[134] And was still thought totally irrational by even intelligent Greeks in August 1975.

[135] *The Financial Times*, August 24, 1976 p. 4, reporting a speech by M. Demirel at Luleburgaz the previous day.

INDICES

I. General

II. Passages discussed

III. Words discussed